21世纪经济管理新形态教材·国际经济与贸易系列

跨境电商专业英语

谢桂梅 ◎ 编著

U0360661

清华大学出版社
北京

图书在版编目（CIP）数据

跨境电商专业英语 / 谢桂梅编著. —北京：清华大学出版社，2024.1

21世纪经济管理新形态教材. 国际经济与贸易系列

ISBN 978-7-302-65200-7

Ⅰ.①跨⋯　Ⅱ.①谢⋯　Ⅲ.①电子商务－英语－高等学校－教材　Ⅳ.①F713.36

中国国家版本馆CIP数据核字(2024)第034021号

责任编辑：梁云慈
封面设计：汉风唐韵
责任校对：王荣静
责任印制：杨　艳

出版发行：清华大学出版社
　　　网　　　址：https://www.tup.com.cn，https://www.wqxuetang.com
　　　地　　　址：北京清华大学学研大厦A座　　　　　邮　　编：100084
　　　社 总 机：010-83470000　　　　　　　　　　邮　　购：010-62786544
　　　投稿与读者服务：010-62776969，c-service@tup.tsinghua.edu.cn
　　　质 量 反 馈：010-62772015，zhiliang@tup.tsinghua.edu.cn
印 装 者：大厂回族自治县彩虹印刷有限公司
经　　销：全国新华书店
开　　本：185mm×260mm　　　**印　　张**：14.25　　　**字　　数**：268千字
版　　次：2024年3月第1版　　　**印　　次**：2024年3月第1次印刷
定　　价：49.00元

产品编号：100495-01

前 言 **Preface**

在传统外贸向跨境电商贸易转型升级的过程中，中国探索出了自己独特的跨境电商之路。得益于过去几十年全球化的发展和中国改革开放的经济环境，跨境电商作为一种新业态、新模式，在促进中国经济发展的过程中成为一道亮丽的风景线，成为外贸的新引擎和中国经济的增长点。中国把握住了这个千载难逢的机会，这也是中国制造业的一次机会，更是跨境服务业的美好机遇。作为《国际贸易实务（英文版）》（清华大学出版社）的姊妹篇，《跨境电商专业英语》这本书既是对国际贸易的深化，更反映了我国在对外贸易领域取得的举世瞩目的成就。跨境电商蓬勃发展的背后，有政策红利的引导，更有各大跨境电商平台和服务企业中商界精英的努力和智慧。中国智慧铸就了跨境电商的现在，中国智慧也一定会塑造跨境电商的美好未来。

2020 年以来，外部环境面临全球经济增长乏力、贸易保护主义抬头、地缘政治紧张等复杂国际局势，产业环境更加区域化，外贸企业转型升级的压力不断加大。互联网技术的发展，大数据、物联网、云计算、人工智能、绿色低碳经济的深入将促使跨境电商走进一个新时代。2015 年被称为跨境电商元年，随着我国跨境电商的不断发展和经验的积累，未来跨境电商的运营将更加精细化、更加规范化，也会以更加用心的态度为世界人民带来福祉，贡献中国的产品、服务、智慧和方案。未来的跨境贸易，不仅会有优秀的中国企业家、优秀的跨国公司、优质的现代供应链，也一定有中国特有的质量和品牌，尤其是一定有跨境电商造就的 DTC（direct-to-consumer，直面消费者）品牌。

本书内容从跨境电商的定义和发展历史入手，包含了跨境电商的模式分类，世界范围内的知名跨境电商平台，跨境电商营销，跨境电商物流，跨境电商支付，中国跨境电商的发展状况、知名跨境电商平台、成就、政策和实践、监管和运营，以及跨境电商的未来机会和挑战。本书既有全球视野，又有中国角度，非常适合电子商务专业人士和本科、专科生作为入门级知识研读，进而进入跨境电商的研究和实践。

　　本书受"北京物资学院教材建设基金项目"（2022）资助，感谢北京物资学院外语学院王淑花院长的支持及同事的真诚鼓励，以及教务处给予的各项便利和支持，感谢清华大学出版社梁云慈编辑的审阅及沟通等各项工作。

北京物资学院 外语学院

谢桂梅

目 录 **Contents**

Chapter 1

Ecommerce and Cross-border Ecommerce
电商和跨境电商

Objectives

1. Master the definition of ecommerce and cross-border ecommerce

2. Understand the ecosystem of cross-border ecommerce

3. Understand the developmental phases and trends of ecommerce

4. Understand the advantages and challenges of cross-border ecommerce

Open Case: Watch the movie and answer the questions

Movie: Amazon Empire: The Rise and Reign of Jeff Bezos (1:53:16)

Questions:

1. How did Amazon establish its business empire?

2. What are the issues that Amazon is facing?

视频资源链接

Cross-border ecommerce (CBEC) starts from ecommerce. The "e" in ecommerce has been an overwhelming success around the world. Ecommerce is **ubiquitous** and we are doing ecommerce anywhere and anytime. It is also one of the most rapidly changing industries and it quickly adopts the latest technologies and becomes one of the trendsetters for other industries as well. When commerce is electronically empowered, it becomes a very influential commerce which is taking place around every corner of the world especially in developed places like the United States, EU, as well as in South and East Asian countries like India, Indonesia, China, Japan, Korea, etc. There are about 2.56 billion people in 2022 around the world involved in ecommerce daily or even hourly, whether in their work or in personal life. In 2022, worldwide ecommerce sales exceeded \$5 trillion for the first time, accounting for more than a fifth of overall retail sales. The total spending of ecommerce will surge past \$7 trillion by 2025.[①]

---

① eMarketer,《2022 年全球电商市场预测报告》。

1. 1　Definition of Ecommerce 电商的定义

Ecommerce, to put it simply, is commerce conducted electronically via the Internet by companies or individuals. It is also known as electronic commerce or Internet commerce, refers to the buying and selling of goods or services using the Internet, and the transfer of money and data to execute these transactions. Ecommerce is often used to refer to the sale of physical products online, but it can also describe any kind of commercial transaction that is facilitated through the Internet.

Ecommerce operates in different types of market segments and can be conducted over computers, tablets, smartphones, and other smart devices. Nearly every imaginable product and service is available through ecommerce transactions, including books, music, plane tickets, and financial services such as stock investing and online banking. As such, it is considered a very **disruptive technology**.

Web sites (or websites) such as aliexpress.com, amazon.com and ebay.com are internationally known ecommerce platforms. While in China, tmall. com, taobao.com, jd.com are popular platforms and growing exponentially during the period of 2015–2019, especially during the pandemic 2020, when the world stopped manufacturing and China performed prosperously in producing and manufacturing.

Almost anything can be purchased through ecommerce today. For this reason, ecommerce is highly competitive and enjoys a bright future. Some experts contended that it was likely to be a substitute for **brick-and-mortar stores**, though some businesses choose to maintain both. It involves more than one party along with the exchange of data or currency to process a transaction. Ecommerce is often mentioned in broad and narrow senses. In practice, ecommerce bears a narrow sense, a broad sense and a pan-commerce sense, where it covers different scopes of businesses.

1. 1. 1　Narrow Sense of Ecommerce 狭义的电商

The narrow sense of ecommerce, just as we mentioned above, is the commodity trading activities, known as electronic transactions or online transactions through an ecommerce platform, especially **a third-party platform**, which offers services like electronic information release, online ordering etc. Amazon, Alibaba, AliExpress, Taobao, Tmall, Pinduoduo, Jd, TikTok, Douyin, Xiaohongshu etc. are typical representatives of ecommerce, see Figure 1-1.

A lot of participants make an ecosystem of ecommerce. In the ecosystem of ecommerce, all parties are working in a coordinative way following a fixed procedure shown in Figure 1-2. In importing ecommerce, foreign products are sold on some platforms like Amazon, JDWorldwide, Tmall Global, etc. With the help of the third-party comprehensive service platforms, payment platforms, logistics service providers, after the clearance of customs, foreign goods would reach customers.

While in the process of exporting, domestic producers export their products through ecommerce enterprises or export by themselves on cross-border ecommerce platforms like amazon.com, aliexpress.com, dhgate.com, ebay.com, shopee.com, lazada.com etc. With the help of payment enterprise and logistics services, after agreement of customs, the goods would finally reach foreign customers (see the right column in Figure 1-2).

Figure 1-1　Ecommerce platforms

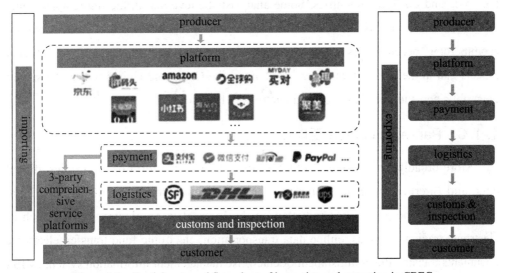

Figure 1-2　Participants and flow chart of importing and exporting in CBEC

1. 1. 2　Broad Sense of Ecommerce 广义的电商

In a broad sense, services and goods can be done through the Internet, from planning to social media communication, including email correspondence, social media advertisement, **search engine optimization (SEO)**, search engine management, etc. They are critical parts of ecommerce. Search engine companies like Baidu and Google, new tech companies like Apple and Xiaomi, social media companies like Facebook, Twitter, Pinterest, Instagram, Snapchat, YouTube, Tiktok, WeChat, Xiaohongshu, and many **on-demand service** companies (which form an on-demand service economy) like Uber, Didi, Airbnb, Meituan, Deliveroo, covering services from transportation to hotels, real estate, house cleaning, maintenance, grocery shopping. etc. Today, mobile, social and local media are the driving forces in ecommerce. In this sense, ecommerce can be defined as digitally enabled commercial transactions between and among organizations and individuals not only through platforms but also through apps. It is also known as digital commerce.

Apps have grown into a disruptive force ever since Apple company launched its App Store in 2008 and they have become a dominant force in ecommerce ecosystem. Apps have disrupted a long and prosperous list of industries covering every aspect of our life: communications, media, entertainment, logistics, education, healthcare, transportation (like taxi services) and hotel industries. Today, with the widespread of mobile devices like smartphones and tablets, **the app economy** is showing robust growth and consumers have gradually gravitated toward apps in China and other developed areas like North America, East Asia and European countries. Some analysists believe that in the future apps would replace web browser as the most common way to access service and content and do ecommercing, because apps are so much more convenient than the web browser in many aspects that in the most internet developed areas like China and United States, the size of the mobile app audience has exceeded that of web browser.

1. 1. 3　Pan-ecommerce 泛电商

More broadly, any business activities done through the form of electronics, digital data, and Internet could be ecommerce or **pan-ecommerce**. Most of the traditional businesses can be presently conducted on the Internet in an electronic way, such as electronic trading of goods, online data transportation, electronic fund transfer, electronic documents transfer, the establishment of enterprise management information system (MIS), electronic market investigation and analysis, planning, deployment of resources, etc.

Ecommerce is ubiquitous in our life and **ubiquity** is one of the characters of ecommerce. There are a handful of wording variations commonly seen for ecommerce on websites, news media (newspapers, journals, or industrial reports alike) or **feeds**, like e-commerce, E-commerce, Ecommerce, e-business, e-retailing, etc. They are often used interchangeably and share almost the same meaning. We use ecommerce in this book.

1.2　Cross-border Ecommerce 跨境电商

When ecommerce is done crossing over the border of a country, it is called cross-border ecommerce. Cross-border ecommerce refers to an international business activity in which participants of different customs areas conduct business transactions, make payment and settlement through ecommerce platforms, and deliver goods and complete transactions through cross-border logistics. As a new form of international trade with the help of modern information and telecommunication technology, cross-border ecommerce is much more complex than domestic ecommerce. There are more participants involved in cross-border ecommerce and the logistics &supply chain are systematically more complicated than domestic ecommerce.

1.2.1　Participants in Cross-border Ecommerce 跨境电商参与主体

More participants are involved in the smooth conduct of cross-border ecommerce than in domestic ecommerce. In a general sense, the upstream of the cross-border ecommerce industry chain is suppliers (**vendors** in Amazon), which could be either producers (manufacturers) or brands. The midstream is usually a cross-border ecommerce platform (**online retailers** or **e-retailers** in many research paper), which could be B2B or B2C mode or any other modes. Downstream of the supply chain are end consumers. Connected with each stream, there are numerous supportive service providers, mainly including logistics, payment, customs & inspection, financing, marketing, etc. forming an ecosystem, see figure 1-3.

1.2.2　Ecosystem of Cross-border Ecommerce 跨境电商生态系统

According to the theory of ecosystem, different species work together to support the smooth conduct of cross-border ecommerce, as shown in Figure 1-3. The core species is cross-border ecommerce platform, which offers a market space for both sellers (suppliers and producers) and buyers (customers). Both the suppliers and buyers make up critical components and they form an internal setting for ecommerce ecosystem. Supportive components embody business of payment, logistics, customs clearance, information and technology support, etc. International marketing and advertisement, promotion, translation task belong to peripheral segment. External setting means the political, economic, social, technological, environmental, legal (PESTEL) part of the macro-level setting which offers cross-border ecommerce a macro environment. Some researchers also study the macro setting from the perspective of **institutional distance** and **cultural distance**. The content of this book is arranged on the basis of this ecosystem.

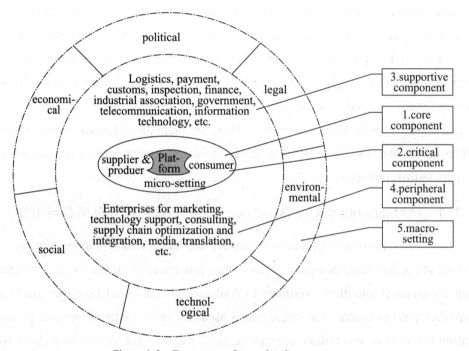

Figure 1-3　Ecosystem of cross-border ecommerce

1. 3　Difference with Traditional Commerce 与传统商务的区别

As to the differences between cross-border ecommerce and traditional commerce, it is easy to find that traditional commerce is often conducted more locally while cross-border ecommerce is done in a wider, national or even international level. Ecommerce has helped businesses (especially those with a narrow reach like small businesses) gain access to and establish a wider **market presence** by providing cheaper and more efficient distribution channels for their products or services.

Cross-border ecommerce has changed the way people shop and consume products and services. An increasing number of people are turning to their computers and smart devices to order goods, which can easily be delivered to their doorsteps. As such, it has disrupted the retail landscape. Amazon, Alibaba, and Jingdong (jd.com) have gained considerable market share among Internet users, forcing traditional retailers to make changes to the way they do business.

But that's not all. Individual sellers have increasingly engaged in ecommerce transactions via their own personal websites. And digital **marketplaces** such as Xianyu, eBay or Etsy serve as intermediaries where multitudes of buyers and sellers come together to conduct business like **a market fair**.

1.4　Trends of Cross-border Ecommerce 跨境电商的趋势

The 2020 pandemic brought a surprisingly great opportunity to the development of ecommerce, especially cross-border ecommerce. For cross-border ecommerce, trends may go like the following:

1. **Social, mobile and local ecommerce** are going to experience a global growth especially in new markets like Middle East, South East Asia and Africa, etc. Most social ecommerce business would be done locally by mobile apps. Social ecommerce, based on social networks and supported by advertising, emerges and continues to grow, generating billions of dollars worldwide.

2. The mobile app ecosystem continues to grow, with almost 2.8 billion people worldwide using mobile apps in 2020. Mobile marketing and advertising continues growing at astronomical rates.

3. **Data safety** and privacy are highly considered to be part of national security and individual rights. Data generated in cross-border ecommerce may be a huge fortune where a lot of valuable information is explored. Consumers in EU and North America think highly of individual privacy and may not trust platforms once personal profile is leaked.

4. **ESG** (Environment, Social Responsibility, Corporate Governance) issues are gaining more concern as fast fashion industry is producing more clothes and polluting the environment. Enterprises should shoulder more responsibilities to contribute more to a green and low-carbon economy. Labor protection and local market protection are attracting more concern as people begin to take employment into consideration.

1.5　Development of Ecommerce 电商的发展

It is difficult to pinpoint when ecommerce exactly began. The first known use of ecommerce is in 1993, according to Merriam-Webster dictionary. But the history of ecommerce usually begins with the first ever online sale on August 11, 1994 when a man sold a CD by the band Sting to his friend through his website NetMarket, an American retail platform. This is the first example of a consumer purchasing a product from a business through the World Wide Web—or "ecommerce" as we commonly know it today. The biggest cross-border ecommerce platform Amazon started its business in 1994. Since then, ecommerce has evolved to make products easier to discover and purchase through online retailers and marketplaces. Independent freelancers, small businesses, and large corporations have all benefited from ecommerce, which enables them to sell their goods and services at a scale that was not possible with traditional offline retail.

Ecommerce industry has gone through so many changes since then, resulting in a great deal of evolution. Traditional brick-and-mortar retailers were forced to embrace new technology in order to stay afloat as companies like Alibaba, Amazon, eBay, Etsy, and Jingdong became household names. These companies created a virtual marketplace for goods and services that consumers can easily access. New technology continues to make it easier for people to do their online shopping. People can connect with businesses through smart phones and other devices and by downloading apps to make purchases. The introduction of free shipping, which reduces costs for consumers, has also helped increase the popularity of the ecommerce industry.

Ecommerce is inextricably linked to Internet. From this sense, it is often accepted that ecommerce began in 1995 from America, prospers in China which produces and sells China-made products to the world. It came with the first **banner advertisements** placed by AT&T, Volvo, Sprint, and others on Hotwired in late October 1994, and the first sales of banner ad space by Netscape and Infoseek in early 1995.

In spite of its short history, ecommerce can be divided into three periods: 1995–2000, the period of invention; 2001–2006, the period of consolidation; and 2007–present, a period of reinvention with social, mobile, and local expansion, see Figure 1-4.

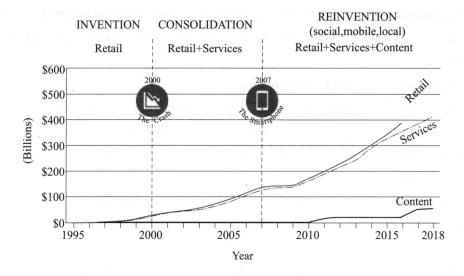

Figure 1-4   Stages of ecommerce development (Laudon &Traver, 2022: 64)

Ecommerce 1995–2000: invention

The first few years of ecommerce were a period of explosive growth and extraordinary innovation. Amazon was the one founded in 1994 at Seattle. During this period, ecommerce is mostly about goods retailing, usually goods of small-in-size and simple function, on the Internet. There simply was not enough bandwidth for more complex products. Marketing was limited to unsophisticated static display ads and not very powerful search engines. The web policy of most large firms, if they had one at all, was to have a basic static website depicting their brands. **Venture capital** played a vital role in supporting the rapid growth of ecommerce which was fueled by over $125 billion. This period of ecommerce came to an end in 2000 when stock market valuations plunged, with thousands of companies disappearing (the "dot-com crash" in the west).

The early development of ecommerce was driven largely by visions of profiting from new technology, with the emphasis on quickly achieving high **market visibility**. The source of **financing** was venture capital funds. The ideology of the period emphasized the ungoverned "Wild West" character of the Web and the feeling that governments and courts could not limit or regulate the Internet. People believed that traditional corporations were too slow and bureaucratic, too stuck in the old ways of doing business. Young entrepreneurs were the driving force behind ecommerce, backed by huge amounts of money invested by venture capitalists. The emphasis was on disrupting (destroying) traditional distribution channels and disintermediating existing channels, using new pure online companies who aimed to achieve impregnable **first-mover advantages**. Overall, this period of ecommerce was characterized by experimentation, capitalization, and hyper-competition.

Ecommerce 2001–2006: consolidation

In the second period of ecommerce, from 2001 to 2006, a sobering period of reassessment of ecommerce occurred, with many critics doubting its long-term prospects. Emphasis shifted to a more "business-driven" approach rather than being technology driven; large traditional firms learned how to use the Web to strengthen their market positions; brand extension and strengthening became more important than creating new brands; financing shrunk as capital markets shunned startup firms; and traditional bank financing based on profitability returned.

During this period of consolidation, ecommerce changed to include not just retail products but also more complex services such as travel and financial services. This period was enabled by widespread adoption of broadband networks in homes and workplaces, coupled with the growing power and lower prices of personal computers that were the primary means of accessing the Internet, usually from work or home.

Marketing on the Internet increasingly meant using search engine advertising targeted to user **queries**, **rich media** and video ads, and behavioral targeting of marketing messages based on ad networks and auction markets. The web policy of both large and small firms expanded to include a broader "web presence" that included not only websites, but also e-mail, display, and search engine campaigns; multiple websites for each product; and the building of some limited community feedback facilities. Ecommerce in this period was growing again by more than 10% a year.

Ecommerce 2007–present: reinvention

Beginning in 2007 with the introduction of iPhone, to the present day, ecommerce has been transformed yet again by the rapid growth of **Web 2.0**[①]and achieved quite a success around the world especially in China and developed countries, see Figure 1-5. China and the United States are the two biggest ecommerce economies in 2021.

---

① It means a set of applications and technologies that enable user-generated content, such as that posted on online social networks, blogs, wikis, and video- and photo-sharing websites and apps; widespread adoption of mobile devices such as smart phones and tablet computers; the expansion of ecommerce to include local goods and services; and the emergence of an on-demand service economy enabled by millions of apps on mobile devices and cloud computing.

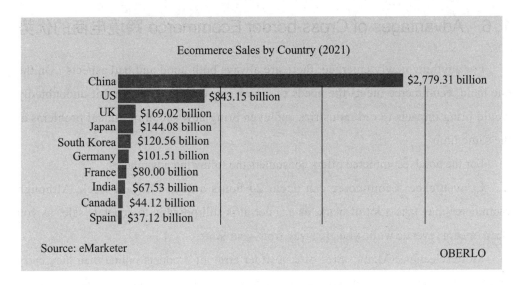

Figure 1-5　Ecommerce sales by country in 2021

This period can be seen as both a sociological, as well as a technological and business phenomenon. The defining characteristics of this period are often referred to as the "social, mobile, local" online world. Entertainment content has developed as a major source of ecommerce revenues and mobile devices have become entertainment centers, as well as **on-the-go shopping devices** for retail goods and services. Marketing has been transformed by the increasing use of social networks and much more powerful **data repositories and analytic tools** for truly personalized and targeted marketing. Firms have greatly expanded their online presence by moving beyond static web pages to social networks such as Facebook, Twitter, Pinterest, and Instagram in an attempt to surround the online consumer with coordinated marketing messages.

These social networks share many common characteristics. First, they rely on **user-generated content (UGC)**. "Regular" people (not just experts or professionals) are creating, sharing, and broadcasting content to huge audiences. They are inherently highly interactive, creating new opportunities for people to socially connect to others. They attract extremely large audiences (about 2.7 billion **monthly active users** worldwide as of June 2020 in the case of Facebook). These audiences present marketers with extraordinary opportunities for targeted marketing and advertising.

1. 6　Advantages of Cross-border Ecommerce 跨境电商的优势

For anything newly emerged, there are always both good and bad aspects . On the one hand, ecommerce meets the needs of a new era; On the other hand it undoubtedly would bring impacts to old industries and even bring new social or ethical problems at the same time.

For the good, ecommerce offers consumers the following advantages:

Convenience: Ecommerce can occur 24 hours a day, 7 days a week. Although ecommerce may take a lot of work, as a seller, it is still possible to generate sales as you sleep or earn revenue while you are away from your store.

More selections: Many stores offer a wider array of products online than they carry in their brick-and-mortar counterparts. And many stores that exist purely online may offer consumers exclusive inventory that is unavailable elsewhere.

Low start-up cost: Ecommerce companies may require a warehouse or manufacturing site, but they usually don't need **a physical storefront**. The cost to operate digitally is often less expensive than running a physical store, which needs to pay rent, insurance, building maintenance, and property taxes.

International sales:As long as an ecommerce store can ship to the customer by international logistics or **overseas warehouses** or **FBA (Fulfillment by Amazon)**, an ecommerce company can sell to anyone in the world and isn't limited by physical geography.

Easier to retarget customers: as customers browse a digital storefront, it is easier to entice their attention towards placed advertisements, directed marketing campaigns, or **pop-ups** specifically aimed at a purpose.

1. 7　Challenges of Cross-border Ecommerce 跨境电商的挑战

But there are certain drawbacks that come with cross-border ecommerce, too.

Limited customer service: If you shop online for a computer, you cannot simply ask an employee to demonstrate a particular model's features in person. Even though some websites let you chat online with a staff member.

Lack of **instant gratification**: When you buy an item online, you must wait a certain period for it to be delivered to your home or office. For international transaction, a few months waiting time is torturing the buyer's patience. However, ecommerce platforms and sellers and logistics companies are endeavoring to offer better logistic services and after-sale services. Some big companies or e-tailers like Amazon is making the waiting game a little bit less painful by offering **the same-day delivery** as a premium option for selected products.

Inability to touch products: Online images do not necessarily convey the whole story about an item, and so ecommerce purchases can be unsatisfying when the products received do not match consumer's expectations. Quite often an item of clothing may be made from shoddier fabric than its online image indicates, which is quite frustrating to buyers. And **return logistics** is a big challenge in cross-border ecommerce for international logistics is expensive and time-consuming.

Fierce competition and strict rules: Although the low barrier to entry regarding low cost is an advantage, ecommerce may involve fierce competition as more competitors can join the market easily. Ecommerce companies must have mindful marketing strategies and remain diligent on **SEO** and public relations to ensure they maintain a digital presence. With the increase of marketing cost, companies face more fierce competition. In cross-border ecommerce, government often set various rules and reinforce strict supervision for international business.

Moral and social problems: with the emergence of ecommerce, local buyers would buy goods from stores online, which would impact the local physical store. When there are not enough customers coming to local stores, local stores would close and this would bring unemployment and other social problems. Government concerns the issue the most when unemployment rate is rising. When huge amount of foreign products flow into a country, there is no opportunity for certain local industries to develop. What's more, big data emerging from ecommerce often give rise to the problem of personal privacy protection and information safety, especially in some developed countries.

High **traffic cost**: Marketing is becoming so difficult and traffic cost is increasingly high. For either Google search engine marketing or Facebook social media advertising, the expense is going up and fierce competition makes the cost on advertising a major part and the most difficult part for product selling, see figure 1-6.

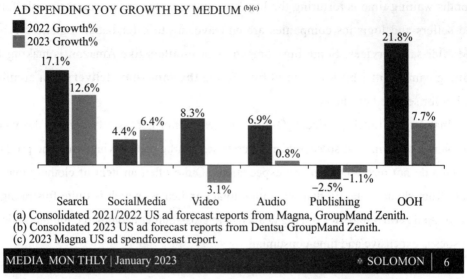

AD SPENDING YOY GROWTH BY MEDIUM (b)(c)

■ 2022 Growth%
■ 2023 Growth%

(a) Consolidated 2021/2022 US ad forecast reports from Magna, GroupMand Zenith.
(b) Consolidated 2023 US ad forecast reports from Dentsu GroupMand Zenith.
(c) 2023 Magna US ad spendforecast report.

MEDIA MON THLY | January 2023　　　　　　　　　　❖ SOLOMON | 6

Figure 1-6　Ad spending year-on-year growth by medium in USA[1]
Note: search: search engine or queryin platforms; YoY: year-on-year; **ooh: out-of-home media**

Layoff pressure: Big cross-border ecommerce like Amazon (laid off 18,000 workers) and big search engine company like Google made a layoff plan during the end of 2022 to reduce the pressure of global downturn economy and high inflation. It is a time of readjustment for cross-border ecommerce, see Figure 1-7. Chinese big tech companies also did their layoffs during the last half year of 2022.

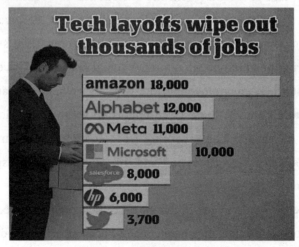

Figure 1-7　Big tech layoffs

---

① https://www. tmtpost. com/6401244. html, 7-2-2023.

1. 8   Ecommerce, Ebusiness and Digital Commerce
电子商务、电商（企业）和数字商务

While the three nouns could mean the same thing and be used interchangeably, they are also used in different scenarios. Ecommerce conventionally involves the online purchase and sale of goods and services via the Internet. Ebusiness involves more about the entire process of running a company via the Internet and Intranet. Ecommerce could be one part of running an ebusiness. For example, big ecommerce companies like Amazon, Alibaba and eBay set the way the retail industry works and forced many traditional retailers to shift their conventional business to ebusiness. Still, people sometimes equal ecommerce to ebusiness.

When ebusiness and ecommerce are done on the Internet and generate a flow of big data, it is digitally conducted and thus called digital trade or digital ecommerce. The perspective of digital commerce is on the information elements. Still some people don't equal digital commerce with cross-border ecommerce since digital commerce cover a much broader scope including ecommerce from other businesses like game playing.

📖 Words and Phrases 词汇和短语

ubiquitous 无处不在的

disruptive technology 颠覆性技术

brick-and-mortar stores 实体店

a third-party platform 第三方平台

search engine optimization (SEO) 搜索引擎优化

on-demand service 应需服务；随选服务

the app economy 应用经济；app 经济

pan-ecommerce 泛电子商务

ubiquity 无所不在

feeds 信息流广告；推送

vendors（亚马逊）供应商；卖家；商家

online retailers 网络平台

e-retailers（零售）电商平台

institutional distance 制度距离

cultural distance 文化距离

market presence 市场占有率

marketplace 市场；完全竞争市场

a market fair 集市

social ecommerce 社交电商

mobile ecommerce (m-commerce) 移动电商

local ecommerce 本地电商

data safety 数据安全

ESG 环境、社会责任和公司治理

banner advertisements 横幅广告

venture capital 风险投资；风投

market visibility 市场可见度；市场占有率

financing 融资

first-mover advantages 先发优势

queries（网上）查询

rich media 富媒体

Web 2.0 第二代互联网

on-the-go shopping devices 随时购物设备

data repositories and analytic tools 数据存储和分析工具

user-generated content (UGC) 用户原创内容

monthly active users (MAU) 月活用户

a physical storefront 实体门店

overseas warehouses 海外仓

FBA (Fulfillment by Amazon) 亚马逊配送

pop-ups 弹窗

instant gratification 即时满足

the same-day delivery 当日达

return logistics 退货物流

traffic cost 引流成本

ooh (out of home ad) 户外广告

 Exercise 练习

I. Reflections and Critical Thinking Questions.

1. How would you assess ecommerce including its success, surprises, and failures in a

comprehensive way?

2. Do you agree with the listed advantages and disadvantages of ecommerce in this chapter? Why or why not?

3. How do you think the future of cross-border ecommerce in the world?

4. What is the relationship of ecommerce and offline commerce?

II. True or False

1. Ecommerce involves both the selling and buying of both goods and services online. (   )

2. Alibaba.com and amazon.com are third-party platforms. (   )

3. On-demand service is a kind of ecommerce which offers service for foreign customers. (   )

4. In a narrow sense, any business that is done through internet could be ecommerce. (   )

5. In the ecosystem of cross-border ecommerce, the core element is the cross-border ecommerce platform. (   )

6. Cross-border ecommerce is not only subjected to micro setting, but also subjected to macro setting such as cultural distance and social distance. (   )

7. Mobile commerce is more popular than social ecommerce at present. (   )

8. Ecommerce started from the United States and prospered in China. (   )

9. At the beginning, it is with the help of venture capital that ecommerce got a chance to develop. (   )

10. The cost of opening an online store is usually lower than physical stores and people around the world all support the development of ecommerce. (   )

11. In ecommerce, it is easier for a company to conduct business and competition is thus less serious than traditional business. (   )

12. There are more participants involved in cross-border ecommerce than traditional commerce. (   )

III. Noun Explanation

1. Ecommerce &Cross-border ecommerce

2. Mobile ecommerce, social ecommerce, retail ecommerce

IV. Reading and Critical Thinking

The future of global ecommerce

Retailers everywhere should look to China[①]

Yet as we explain this week (see Business section) it is in China, not the West, where the future of ecommerce is being staked out (被明确界定). Its market is far bigger and more creative, with tech firms blending ecommerce, social media and razzmatazz (令人眼花缭乱的活动) to become online-shopping emporia (大型商业中心) for 850m digital consumers. And China is also at the frontier of regulation, with the news on December 24th that trustbusters (反垄断机构) were investigating Alibaba, co-founded by Jack Ma, and until a few weeks ago it's the most valuable listed firm. For a century the world's consumer businesses have looked to America to spot new trends, from scannable barcodes (条形码) on Wrigley's gum in the 1970s to keeping up with the Kardashians'(卡戴珊姐妹们) consumption habits in the 2010s. Now they should be looking to the East.

China's lead in ecommerce is not entirely new. By size, its market overtook America's in 2013—with little physical store space, its consumers and retailers leapfrogged ahead to the digital world. When Alibaba was listed in 2014 it was the world's largest-ever initial public offering(首次公开募股 , 上市).

Today the country's e-retailing market is worth $2trn, more than America's and Europe's combined. But beyond its sheer size it now stands out from the past, and from the industry in the West, in several crucial ways.

For a start it is more dynamic. In the past few years, new competitors, including Meituan and Pinduoduo, have come of age with effervescent (兴奋的) business models.

---

① *The Economist* (02 Jan, 2021), https://zhuanlan. zhihu. com/p/345015869, 13-7-2022.

One sign of fierce competition is that Alibaba's share of the market capitalisation of the Chinese ecommerce industry has dropped from 81% when it listed to 55% today. Competition has also led ecommerce and other tech firms to demolish (拆除) the boundaries between different types of services that are still common in the West. Point and click are passé: online-shopping platforms in China now blend digital payments, group deals, social media, gaming, instant messaging, short-form videos and live-streaming celebrities.

The obvious, multi-trillion-dollar question is whether the Chinese model of ecommerce will go global. As has been the case for decades, Silicon Valley's giants still tend to underestimate China. There are few direct links between the American and Chinese ecommerce industries, partly owing to protectionism on both sides (Yahoo sold much of its stake in Alibaba, far too early, in 2012). And Western firms have long been organised in cosy, predictable silos (发射井 , 各自的领域). So Visa specialises in payments, Amazon in ecommerce, Facebook in social media, Google in search, and so on. The main source of uncertainty in ecommerce has been just how many big traditional retailers will go bust (破产) —over 30 folded in America in 2020—and whether a few might manage the shift online, as Walmart and Target have.

Yet however safe and siloed Western e-retailing may appear to be, it is now unlikely that it will become the world's dominant mode of shopping. Already, outside rich countries, the Chinese approach is gaining steam. Many leading ecommerce firms in South-East Asia (Grab and Sea), India (Jio), and Latin America (Mercado Libre) are influenced by the Chinese strategy of offering a "super-app" with a cornucopia (全面、综合) of services from noodle delivery to financial services. The giant consumer-goods firms that straddle the Western and Chinese markets may transmit Chinese ideas and business tactics, too. Multinationals such as Unilever, L'Oréal and Adidas make more revenue in Asia than in America and their bosses turn to there, not to California or Paris, to see the latest in digital marketing, branding and logistics.

Already, Chinese characteristics are emerging in the retail heartlands of the West, partly as a result of the pandemic. The silos are breaking down as firms diversify. Facebook is now promoting shopping services on its social networks, and engaging in "social commerce", including in live-streaming and the use of WhatsApp, for messaging between merchants and shoppers. In December Walmart hosted its first live shopping event within TikTok, a Chinese-owned video app in which it hopes to buy a stake (股份). In France in the past quarter the sixth-most-downloaded ecommerce app was Vova, linked to Pinduoduo's founder. And new entrants may finally make progress in America—the share price of Shopify, a platform for Amazon exiles and small firms, has soared so that it is now valued at more than $140bn.

This shift to a more Chinese-style global industry promises to be excellent news for consumers. Prices would be lower, as China has seen fierce discounting by competing firms. Choice and innovation would probably grow. Even so, Chinese ecommerce has flaws. In a Wild West climate, fraud is more common. And there are those antitrust concerns. It may partly be that, but China's antitrust regulators are also keen to boost competition. That means enforcing interoperability（互用性）, so that, for example, payments services on one ecommerce platform can be used seamlessly on a rival one. And it means preventing ecommerce firms from penalising merchants who sell goods in more than one place online. So far American and European trustbusters have been ineffectual at controlling big tech, despite a flurry of lawsuits and draft laws at the end of 2020. They, too, should study China, for a sense of where the industry is heading and how to respond.

There is a pattern to how the West thinks about Chinese innovation. From electronics to solar panels（太阳能板）, Chinese manufacturing advances were either ignored or dismissed as copying, then downplayed and then grudgingly acknowledged around the world. Now it is the Chinese consumer's tastes and habits that are going global. Watch and learn.

Critical Thinking and Questions:

1. Why does Chinese ecommerce now stand out from the past, and from the industry in the West according to the author?

2. What are the differences between Chinse ecommerce and Western ecommerce according to the article?

3. What is a more Chinese-style global ecommerce?

4. Do you agree on the comments of Chinese innovations in the last paragraph? Please illustrate your reasons by your daily examples.

More Resource:

1. The Future of Ecommerce in 2021: 5 Trends[1]

Keys-1

---

[1]   https://www. bilibili. com/video/BV1xU4y177XY/, 7-03-2023.

Chapter 2

Business Models of Cross-border Ecommerce
跨境电商商业模式

Objectives

1. Master the classifications of business model in CBEC

2. Know the features of B2C, B2B, C2C

3. Understand the differences between models

4. Master the typical B2C, B2B, C2C companies

5. Master new variations of CBEC like mobile ecommerce, social ecommerce

Open Case: Watch the video and answer the questions

An interview with Jeff Bezos, founder of Amazon in 1999(7'25")

1. What are the factors that a company should focus on in order to be successful according to Jeff ? (1'45")

视频资源链接

2. What is the point that Jeff repeatedly mentioned for Amazon? Why?

3. What are the products that Amazon sell online?

Ecommerce can take on a variety of forms involving different transactional relationships between businesses and consumers, as well as different objects being exchanged as part of these transactions. It can be performed by the form of retailing or wholesaling. Retailing happens when the sale of product is finished by a business directly to a customer without any **intermediary**, while wholesaling takes place when the sale of products is done in bulk, often to a retailer or a **channel partner** or a **distributor** who then sells them directly to his consumers.

In ecommerce, **objects** being transacted could be physical or digital products, or even services. Physical products refer to any tangible goods that require **inventory** to be **replenish**ed and orders to be physically shipped to customers as sales are made.

Intangible goods could be digital products and services. Digital products go like downloadable digital goods, **templates**, and courses, or media that must be purchased for consumption or licensed for use. Services are mainly a skill or set of skills provided in exchange for compensation. The service provider's time and energy can be purchased.

2. 1　Classifications of Cross-border Ecommerce 跨境电商分类

Ways of classifying ecommerce could be very different in different countries. From the perspective of goods destination in transaction, cross-border ecommerce could be exporting ecommerce and importing ecommerce. Let's take Alibaba as an example. As one of the biggest ecommerce companies, Alibaba's businesses can be seen in Figure 2-1 and Figure 2-2. Among the whole system of Ali's ecommerce, alibaba.com is an exporting B2B platform, aliexpress.com is an exporting B2C platform, Tmall Global (www. tmall.hk) and kaola.com① are two importing B2C platforms.

Figure 2-1　Alibaba's ecommerce business

According to the ownership of goods sold on platforms, 3 models of ecommerce are popular: **platform model** (like Amazon, Taobao, Tmall, etc. who only offer platforms for sellers to sell goods of all **categories**), **platform+direct**

---

① Kaola. com was acquired by Alibaba in 2019 at a price of $2 billion. It goes into the origin of foreign products to directly purchase overseas goods suitable for Chinese market.

operating model (like Jingdong who itself sells goods on its own platform and at the same time invites other sellers to sell goods on its jd.com or jd.hk), **direct operating model** (like Walmart, SheIn, Lightinthebox etc. who purchase from producers and suppliers, have the ownership of all the online goods and sell them by themselves to make profit).

Based on the range of product categories sold online, ecommerce could be divided into **comprehensive platform model** (also called horizontal platform which sells **general products/categories**) or **vertical platform model** (focus on **niché markets** such as 3C[①] products, fashion, mother and baby products, wedding dress etc.). For example, SheIn was one of the most successful vertical fashion platforms. Some people are pessimistic about the future of this model. And it was reported that SheIn began to expand beyond its fashion categories since the end of 2022[②].

From the perspective of participants, the following 3 dominant ecommerce models can be used to describe almost every transaction that takes place between consumers and businesses. The three are B2C, B2B and C2C models. Simply speaking, 1). When a business sells goods or service to an individual consumer (e. g. You buy a pair of shoes from an online store), it is Business to Consumer (B2C) model.2). When a business sells a good or service to another business (e. g. A business sells software-as-a-service for other businesses to use, or a platform sells its goods to a wholesaler or a small wholesaler), it is Business to Business (B2B) model.3). When a consumer sells a good or service to another consumer (e. g. You sell your old furniture on eBay to another consumer), it is a Consumer to Consumer (C2C) model. Besides these 3 fundamental models, there are a few derivatives like D2C (or DTC: direct to customer) model, B2B2C model, C2B model suiting different situations. This is the most popular classification in cross-border ecommerce. China has established a whole map of cross border importing and exporting ecommerce, see Figure 2-2.

---

① Computer, Communication (including mobile devices) and Consumer Electronics.

② https://baijiahao. baidu. com/s?id=1746352716691415488&wfr=spider&for=pc, 8-2-2023.

Figure 2-2　Map of China's cross-border ecommerce in 2022

2.2　Business to Consumer (B2C) Model　B2C 模式

2.2.1　Definition 定义

Before the advent of the Internet, however, business-to-consumer was a term used to describe take-out restaurants, or companies in a mall. B2C became immensely popular during the **dotcom boom** of the late 1990s when it was mainly used to refer to online retailers who sold products and services to consumers through the internet.

In ecommerce, the term business-to-consumer (B2C) refers to the process of selling products and services directly between a business and consumers who are the end-users of its products or services. Because of **the end-user-as-customers**, it is also known as retail ecommerce in many studies and reports. Most companies that sell directly to consumers can be referred to as B2C retailers.

B2C ecommerce companies sell product directly to the end-user. Instead of distributing goods to an intermediary, a B2C company performs transactions with the consumer that will ultimately use the goods. This type of business model may be used to sell products (e.g. through your local sporting goods store's website) or services (e.g. through a lawn care mobile app to reserve landscaping services). This is the most common business model and is likely the concept most people think about when they hear ecommerce.

2. 2. 2   Global Situation of B2C Ecommerce   B2C 电商全球现状

One thing needs to be borne in mind is that though B2C ecommerce has drawn our eyeball a lot, it is still in the process of developing in terms of **Gross Merchandise Volume** (GMV). Compared to the whole retail industry, B2C ecommerce was only about 18% of the global retail industry in 2022, see Figure 2-3. Compared to the overall global retail market, B2C is still a small tree which has a great potential to grow.

The second thing worth mentioning is that in the global B2C market, China ranks the first. In the report released by the United Nations Conference on Trade and Development (UNCTAD), China's B2C online retail scale displays a large advantage, reaching US $1414.3 billion (more than 1.4 trillion) in 2020, which is the only country in the world with an online retail scale of more than US $1trillion, see Table 2-1.

overall global retail market $23.8 trillion

worldwide retail e-commerce $4.3 trillion

The retail e-commerce market is still just a small part of the overall global retail market, but with much room to grow in the future.

Figure 2-3   B2C business (retail ecommerce) is still to grow (Laudon & Traver, 2022)

Table 2-1   China ranks first in the global B2C market in 2020[1].

Economy	Online retail sales ($ billions)			Retail salles ($ billions)			Online share (% of retail sales)		
	2018	2019	2020	2018	2019	2020	2018	2019	2020
Australia	13.5	14.4	22.9	239	229	242	5.6	6.3	9.4
Canada	13.9	16.5	28.1	467	462	452	3.0	3.6	6.2
China	1,060.4	1,233.6	1,414.3	5,755	5,957	5,681	18.4	20.7	24.9
Korea(Rep.)	76.8	84.3	104,4	423	406	403	18.2	20.8	25.9
Singapore	1.6	1.9	3.2	34	32	27	4.7	5.9	11.7
United kingdom	84.0	89.0	130.6	565	564	560	14.9	15.8	23.3
United States	519.6	598.0	791.7	5,269	5,452	5,638	9.9	11.0	14.0
Economies above	1,770	2,038	2,495	12,752	13,102	13,003	14	16	19

Among the global top 10 B2C e-commerce enterprises in the world from 2018–2020 mentioned by the United Nations Conference on Trade and Development, Alibaba ranked

---

[1]   https://www. sohu. com/a/464910794_100110525, 8-2-2023.

the first, with commodity sales of more than US $1 trillion. In addition, jd.com ranked third, Pinduoduo ranked fourth, and Meituan ranked seventh. Amazon of the United States ranks second in the world, eBay ranks sixth, Walmart online retail ranks eighth, Uber[①] ranks ninth. Among the top ten, enterprises from China and the United States occupy eight seats. The remaining two are Shopify[②] (the fifth) and Rakuten[③] (the 10th).

2.2.3　Global Marketers of B2C　B2C 全球性大公司

Amazon. com

As the world's largest online retailer, Amazon is a **behemoth** in ecommerce marketplace, providing consumer products and subscriptions through its website. It was founded by Jeff Bezos in 1994 in Seattle, Washington State as an online bookstore company but has since expanded to include everything from toys, **apparel** to housewares, consumer electronics and music, etc. In fact, it is the world's largest online retailer and continues to grow, see Figure 2-4. As such. It is a huge **disrupter** in the retail industry, forcing some major retailers to rethink their strategies and shift their focus.

Its sales increased by 38% in 2020 from the previous year, totaling $386.1 billion compared to $280.5 billion in 2019. Amazon's **operating income** also jumped to $22.9 billion for the 2020 fiscal year from $14.5 billion in 2019. **Net income** rose from $11.6 billion in 2019 to $21.3 billion by the end of 2020.

---

① Uber is originally a taxi application software company and transformed to ecommerce.

② Shopify is the largest Canadian e-commerce software developer started in 2006, and headquartered in Ottawa, the capital of Canada. It is a one-stop SaaS e-commerce service platform, providing e-commerce sellers with the technology and template to build online stores, and managing omni-channel marketing, sales, payment, logistics etc. In 2015, Shopify was listed in New York and Toronto. More than one million enterprises have created online stores using the Shopify platform. In January 2022, JD and Shopify reached a strategic cooperation to open the commodity pool to Shopify's global merchants.

③ Rakuten is a Japanese enterprise founded on February 7, 1997. Its internet service covers ecommerce, finance, communications, tourism, real estate, sports and other fields. Its fashion ecommerce business is popular in east Asia.

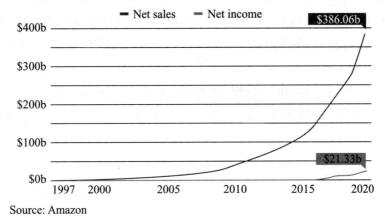

Figure 2-4　Amazon's growth in 2020[1]

As the world adapted to the constraints of COVID-19, ecommerce capitalized on the opportunity to further distance itself from in-store shopping. In 2021, Amazon's net income rose to $33.4 billion, and it ended the year with over $42 billion of cash in hand. Amazon has stated that as a result of the pandemic, the company fulfilled three years' volume of forecasted growth in about 15 months. However, due to global economic recession and high inflation in the United States, Amazon is reducing its employment at the beginning of 2023 and its **market value** went down by 51%, leaving $834 billion at the end of 2022, the biggest slump ever since 2000. After an adjustment of 2023, Amazon is gaining its market presence around the world.

Ali's B2C business

Alibaba Group is China's largest ecommerce company, operating online commerce businesses domestically and internationally. Among its many businesses, aliexpress. com focuses on its international B2C exporting business while Lazada[2] focuses on B2C business in Southeast Asia where there is a population of 600 million people. Lazada is also one of the largest online shopping websites in Southeast Asia, targeting Indonesian, Malaysian, Filipino and Thai users. Since 2016, it has become Alibaba Group's flagship ecommerce platform in Southeast Asia and the most popular ecommerce platform in

---

① http://finance. sina. com. cn/tech/2021-03-04/doc-ikftpnnz1572549. shtml, 5-3-2023.

② 莱赞达.

Indonesia. In addition to the exporting business, Tmall global and Koala are conducting importing B2C business.

In fact, Ali's B2C exporting is mainly conducted by Lazada, AliExpress, Trendyol, Daraz. For the last quarter of 2022, Alibaba's **retail revenue** is 14.64 billion Chinese Yuan, up 26% **year on year (YoY)**, see Figure 2-5, mainly from Turkey's ecommerce giant Trendyol. Alibaba acquired Trendyol in 2018 and increased its capital by $350 million in April 2021, raising its **shareholding ratio** to 86.5%. On January 9, 2023, Alibaba announced that it would invest more than $1 billion in Turkey. When Turkey was hit hard by the earthquake on 6 Feb, 2023, the business was affected. Daraz covers Pakistan, Bangladesh, Sri Lanka, Nepal, Myanmar and its business is rising.

	Three months ended December 31,		
(in RMB Mn, except percentages)	**2021**	**2022**	**YoY %**
International commerce retail	11,606	14,644	26%

Figure 2-5　Alibaba's B2C cross-border ecommerce[1] in 2021 and 2022

Besides Amazon and Alibaba, eBay, Newegg, Shopee, Shopify, SheIn, etc. are also well-known popular B2C platforms. There are quite a lot of local ecommerce platforms in most countries as well[2]. Germany, Russia, Singapore alike all have their own local popular platforms serving local people. Amazon, eBay conducts its global business locally and provide products for global customers. For example, Shopee, starting from Singapore, is the fastest growing ecommerce platform in Southeast Asia. Since its establishment in 2015, its business has spread to more than 10 countries, including Malaysia, the Philippines, Thailand, and Vietnam. Shopee is a preferred platform for Chinese goods to Southeast Asia. Due to global economic recession in the year of 2022, Shopee started to shrink its global business and refocus on south-East Asia countries.

In China, jd.hk, pinduoduo, vipshop.com, xiaohongshu etc. are also popular B2C importing cross-border ecommerce platforms.

2. 2. 4　Forms of Operation in B2C　B2C 运作实践

There are typically five sub-types of online B2C business forms that most companies employ to target consumers.

---

[1]　https://zhuanlan. zhihu. com/p/609194276, 5-03-2023.

[2]　See more in the reading material.

1. Direct sellers. This is the most common model in which people buy goods from online retailers. These may include manufacturers or small businesses or simply online versions of department stores that sell products from different manufacturers directly to sellers.

2. Online intermediaries. In a broad sense, these could be **liaisons** or **go-betweens** who don't actually own products or services but put buyers and sellers together. Sites like Expedia[①], Trivago[②], and Etsy[③] fall into this category. In a narrow sense, some sellers on taobao.com offer goods from manufacturers to customers by using the platform and get a **commission** from revenues.

3. Advertising-based B2C. This form uses free content or advertising to get visitors to a website. Those visitors, in turn, come across digital or online ads. Large volumes of web traffic are used to sell advertising, which promotes goods and services. We will cover advertising in chapter 3.

4. Community-based B2C. Sites like Facebook, Tiktok, etc. which build online communities based on shared interests, help marketers and advertisers promote their products directly to consumers. Websites typically target ads based on **users'** **demographics** and geographical location.

5. **Live broadcasting** B2C: Live broadcasting started from China and now is on its trial way to the world. Some fashion brands, various knowledge-sharing accounts or apps, book-reading clubs, or even Yoga clubs extend their service and sell **peripheral products** by doing live broadcasting. It has become a unique and attractive way in TikTok broadcasting. Big companies like Amazon and Facebook have tried this method. It is functioning in **branding**.

2. 2. 5　B2C and Mobile Purchasing　B2C 和移动购买

Decades after the ecommerce boom, B2C companies are continuing to eye a growing market: mobile purchasing. With smartphone apps and online traffic growing year over year, B2C companies have shifted attention to mobile users and capitalized on this popular technology. Throughout the early 2010s, B2C companies were rushing to develop mobile apps, just as they were with websites decades earlier. Take Wish as an example. As a great

---

① The biggest online travel agent started from the United States and entered China in 2007.

② The biggest hotel search engine started in Germany in 2005.

③ An American ecommerce platform originally selling handicrafts.

fashion direct-selling platform in North America, it focuses on its mobile app users and has achieved great success in mobile B2C ecommerce during the few years from 2015 to 2022. Success in B2C model is predicated with continuous evolving on consumers' appetites, opinions, trends, and desires etc.

Mobile Platform: Wish and SheIn[①]

Unlike Amazon and Alibaba, whose business could be done through computers and mobile devices, Wish and SheIn are mobile cross-border ecommerce apps, whose business is conducted only through mobile devices, mainly smart phones.

Founded in the United States in 2011 by Peter Szulczewski and Danny Zhang, engineers from Google and Yahoo, Wish is a cross-border B2C mobile ecommerce platform focusing on **second-tier and lower-tier market** (the so-called **sinking market** which is dominated by low-income group of people). It is also the most popular mobile commerce site in the United States. 92% of its customers are mobile users. It focuses on a few vertical **niches**, such as mother and baby, electrical appliances, clothing, and other products.

In fact, it is until 2013 that Wish successfully transformed into a cross-border ecommerce company. Through years of development, it has become the largest mobile e-commerce platform in North America and the sixth largest e-commerce platform in the world. Although Wish is a cross-border e-commerce company of the United States, most of the merchants are from China, so the Chinese headquarters was established in Shanghai in 2014. As a matter of fact, many cross-border e-commerce platforms hope to expand market planning with the help of Chinese enterprises.

SheIn is a China-headquartered cross-border ecommerce company started as early as in 2008[②], selling **fast-fashion products** mainly to customers in North America. It gained its popularity in the year of 2015 when venture capital joined in. SheIn has been working as an Internet fast fashion platform promoting its own **DTC brand**, see Figure 2-6.

---

① https://baijiahao. baidu. com/s?id=1686227572020428744&wfr=spider&for=pc, 8-2-2023; https://hy. chnmc. com/EMBA/zl/2022-09-28/12412. html, Jan-2-2023.

② https://baijiahao. baidu. com/s?id=1731404338077821536&wfr=spider&for=pc, 5-3-2023.

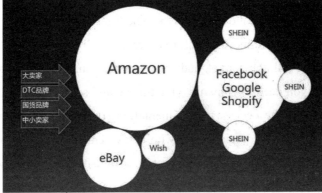

Figure 2-6   Wish, SheIn and their market share in the United States

Wish and SheIn have become a role model for mobile ecommerce and represent the future trend of ecommerce. A chunk of ecommerce platforms are transforming themselves toward m-commerce. They are boasting the following advantages:

1. Precise customers: Both SheIn and Wish's main market is North America, with a relatively concentrated customer base. The platform provides personalized products by using complex **algorithm** and analyzing **consumer behavior** and **preferences**. Sellers on the platform can conduct **precision marketing**. Every consumer could be entertained by browsing products to their own preferences.

2. Convenience: Convenience means you can get what you want whenever and whereever you need it. Due to great functions through the easy use of apps, it brings great convenience. An increasingly large number of customer transaction orders come from mobile terminals, and the potential of mobile terminals is still huge.

3. Great **logistics and delivery** system: Wish's logistics are Wish HUB (mainly for remote places in east and south China), Wish post (which could be slow), Wish Express

(an overseas warehouse model), A+ logistics plan (for markets of great potential but less developed countries and areas). SheIn has also established its multi-channel **flexible supply chain** system based on IT technology and tried to offer the most efficient delivery service. SheIn currently has three types of warehouses in the world, namely **domestic central warehouse, overseas transit warehouse** and **overseas operation warehouse**[①].

2. 2. 6   How to Start Your B2C Business 如何成为 B2C 零售商

If you want to be an online shop owner on amazon.com or aliexpress.com, for example, make sure you do your research before you start. And start with a small, narrow focus to ensure that you have room to grow.

You usually follow the following patterns. The first step is about providing goods and services (It isn't as easy as it may seem. It requires a lot of research about the products and services you wish to sell, the market, audience, competition, as well as traffic cost). Once that's determined, you need to come up with a name and set up a legal structure, such as a corporation and get the necessary documentation (**taxpayer numbers**, licenses, and permits). Next, set up an ecommerce site with a payment gateway. For instance, a small business owner who runs a dress shop can set up a website promoting their clothing and other related products online and allow customers to make payments with a credit card or through a payment processing service, such as PayPal or other payments.

Marketing is critical in selling goods and services. Business maintenance needs a lot of professional skills and continuous advertisement. It is advisable to keep everything simple at the beginning and make sure you use as many channels as you can to market your business and establish public relations, so it can bring **revenue** to your investment. All ecommerce platforms offer perfect service for a seller who wants to step into cross-border ecommerce business. For instance, Shopify is an expert in helping DTC sellers build their own platforms. Anyway, don't rush to the cross-border ecommerce market and preparation work is always the best starting point.

2. 3   Business to Business (B2B) Model   B2B 模式

2. 3. 1   Definition 定义

Business-to-business (B2B), also called B-to-B, is a form of transaction between

---

① https://baijiahao. baidu. com/s?id=1733580694566699700&wfr=spider&for=pc. Jan-2-2023.

businesses (companies), such as one involving a manufacturer and wholesaler, or a wholesaler and a retailer. Business-to-business refers to business that is conducted between companies, rather than between a company and individual consumer. B2B transactions often entail larger quantities, greater specifications, and longer **lead times**. The company placing the order may also have a need to set **recurring goods** if the purchase is for recurring manufacturing processes.

2. 3. 2   Global Development of B2B   B2B 全球发展现状

Although China has a great development in the field of online retail (B2C) in recent years, the United States, Japan and South Korea rank among the top three in the field of business-to-business non-retail (B2B). Among them, **the sales volume** of B2B e-commerce in the United States is as high as US $8.3 trillion, ranking first in all countries and making about 38% of the global B2B market volume (US $21.84 trillion), see Figure 2-7.

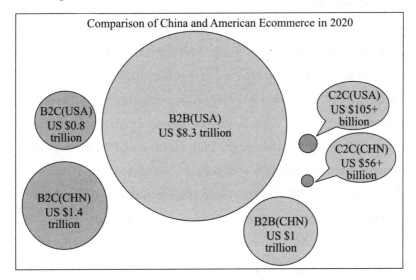

Figure 2-7   A comparison of ecommerce between China and the United States.
Source: United Nations Conference on Trade and Development 2021

B2B ecommerce dwarfs all other modes for American ecommerce business in Figure 2-7. Though China's B2C ecommerce volume exceeds that of the United States, America's B2B ecommerce exceeds that of China greatly. Taking B2C and B2B together, the United States ranks first in the whole volume of ecommerce, with more than $9 trillion; Japan ranks second, with more than $3 trillion; China ranks third, with more than $2 trillion. South Korea ranks fourth, with more than $1 trillion, followed by Britain, France, Germany, Italy, Australia and other countries, where the e-commerce market size is less than US $1 trillion.

2. 3. 3　Global Marketers of B2B　B2B 全球大公司

In a broad sense, business-to-business transactions are commonplace for firms in manufacturing. Samsung, for example, is one of Apple's largest suppliers in the production of iPhone. Apple also holds B2B relationships with firms like Intel, Panasonic and **semiconductor producer** Micron Technology[①]. B2B transactions are also the backbone of the automobile industry. Many parts are manufactured independently, and auto manufacturers purchase parts to assemble automobiles. Tires, batteries, electronics, hoses and door locks, for instance, are usually manufactured by various companies and sold directly to automobile manufacturers. Service providers also engage in B2B transactions. Companies specializing in property management, housekeeping, and **industrial cleanup**, for example, often sell these services exclusively to other businesses, rather than individual consumers.

As to the B2B ecommerce platforms in a narrow and typical sense, we have the following great platforms.

Alibaba.com

Alibaba.com is China's earliest B2B cross-border trade platform, with more than 150 million **registered members** around the world, publishing 300,000 cross-border **sourcing** every day. See Figure 2-8. Founded in 1999, Alibaba.com (known as international station) is the first business segment of Alibaba group. Alibaba international station has become one of the main platforms to promote the digitalization of Chinese foreign trade. Like many ecommerce platforms, Alibaba.com collects commission from online sellers which could be as high as 150,000RMB/year. The commission varies with different categories. Besides that, platform advertising contributes part of its revenue.

Beside Alibaba.com, dhgate.com also provides China-made products for small-and-medium enterprises to foreign enterprises at a small batch or small purchase. It adopts a small wholesale model. Similarly, its revenue comes from commission and advertisement service. Different cross-border ecommerce platforms collect different commission rate at different stages for different markets. Different platforms vary their product/categories and may have their own unique webpage arrangements.

---

① Micron technology is an American semi-conductor leading company founded in 1978, producing DRAM (Dynamic Random Access Memory) used in computers and mobile devices and NAND flash memory.

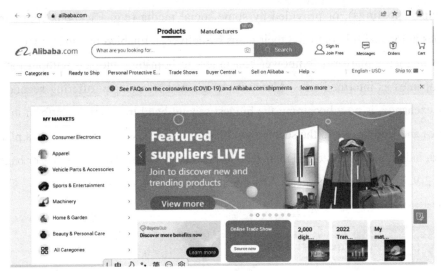

Figure 2-8　Alibaba.com

2.3.4　B2C vs. B2B　B2C 和 B2B 的区别

As mentioned above, the business-to-consumer model differs from the business-to-business (B2B) model. In B2C model, individual consumers are end-users, and in B2B model, the end-users are companies. While B2C consumers buy products for their personal use, B2B businesses buy products for their companies. Large purchases, such as mechanic equipment, generally require approval from those who head up a company. This makes a business' purchasing power more complex than that of the average consumer.

Unlike the B2C business model, pricing structures tend to be different in the B2B model. With B2C, consumers often pay the same price for the same products. However, prices are not necessarily the same in B2B model. Businesses tend to negotiate prices and payment terms. The volume of B2B business is much bigger than that of B2C.

2.4　Consumer to Consumer (C2C) Model　C2C 模式

C2C ecommerce provides a way for consumers to sell their products or services to others with the help of platform provider. Established companies used to be the only entities that can sell things, but ecommerce platforms such as digital marketplaces connect consumers with other consumers who can **list** their own products and execute their own sales. These C2C platforms may be auction-style **listings** (e.g. eBay auctions) or may warrant further discussion regarding the item or service being provided (e.g.

Craigslist[①] **postings**), or provided by some social media (e.g. Facebook Marketplace provides individual sellers to sell their items by delivery). Enabled by modern technology, C2C ecommerce platforms empower consumers to both buy and sell without the need of companies as intermediaries. Mercari[②], originated from Japan offering second-hand goods exchange, is now becoming the biggest second-hand transaction platform in North America and Europe. As to the second-hand fashion circle, Poshmark serves as a platform for both individual sellers to sell their second-hand or even new apparel, shoes or bags, see Figure 2-9. The platform charges a 20% commission for every deal.

Figure 2-9　C2C platforms: Mercari and Poshmark

Today, C2C commerce face competition from third party sales as that on Amazon or Alibaba. Third-party sales on Amazon have skyrocketed and Alibaba is operating a similar global C2C marketplace. Besides, on-demand service companies such as Uber, Airbnb, Didi, Meituan, can also be considered as C2C platform providers. EBay started as a C2C company and evolved into a B2C platform requiring sellers to be a company instead of an individual seller.

2.5　Mobile Ecommerce 移动电商

Different from B2B, B2C and C2C, mobile ecommerce comes to be a hot cake just because of the special device which is so convenient that there is no compare to match it. Mobile ecommerce, also known as m-commerce, involves using wireless handheld

---

① Cragslist. org, American's hottest classified advertising website established by Craig Newmark, is also the first classified advertising website in the world. It is also one of America's favorite websites. Some people sell their old cars here, some people rent their favorite houses here, some people find jobs here, some people find someone to help with their computers here, and others find their girlfriend here.

② 煤炉.

devices like cellphones and tablets to conduct commercial transactions online, including the purchase and sale of products, online banking, and paying bills. Mobile commerce is an increasingly large subset of electronic commerce, a model where firms or individuals conduct business over the Internet. Mobile ecommerce could be B2B, B2C and C2C ecommerce and B2C retail ecommerce is gaining popularity. When B2C retail ecommerce is done through mobile devices, it is retail m-commerce.

2.5.1 Global Development 全球发展

Retail m-commerce revenues reached almost $2.8 trillion worldwide in 2020, growing by 32%, in part due to the Covid-19 pandemic. Retail m-commerce is anticipated to continue to grow and reach almost $4.5 trillion by 2024, as consumers become more and more accustomed to using mobile devices to purchase products and services. See Figure 2-10. But other forms of ecommerce may go down because of the pandemic. For instance, mobile digital travel sales declined significantly in 2020 due to the Covid-19 pandemic but are expected to gradually begin to grow again once the pandemic eases.

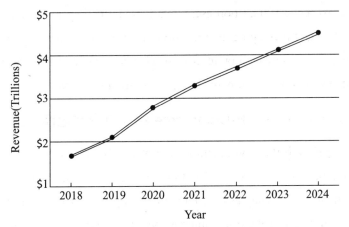

Retail m-commerce revenues surged by over 30% in 2020 and are expected to continue to grow to almost $4.5 trillion by 2024.
SOURCES: Based on data from eMarketer, Inc, 2020h.

Figure 2-10   The worldwide growth of retail m-commerce (Laudon &Traver, 2022)

Factors that are driving the growth of m-commerce include the increasing amount of time consumers are spending using mobile devices, larger smartphone screen sizes, greater use of responsive design enabling websites to be better optimized mobile checkout and payment, and enhanced mobile search functionality. In addition to those, the increased wireless handheld device computing power, a proliferation of m-commerce applications, and the broad resolution of security issues are contributing to it too. A variation of m-commerce known as conversational ecommerce involves the use of chatbots on mobile messaging apps such as Facebook Messenger, WhatsApp, Snapchat and Slack as a tool for companies to engage with consumers.

M-commerce activity is on the rise. According to market research company Statista, mobile commerce sales in the United States are an estimated $431 billion in 2022. Nearly 97% of Americans own a cell phone, and 85% of them own a smartphone, which is up from 35% in 2011, according to the Pew Research Center.

In China, Questmobile, a domestic third-party data agency, released *The 2021 China Mobile Internet Annual Report*[①]. According to the report, as of December 2021, China's mobile shopping industry flourished, with the number of users exceeding 1.1 billion. The user stickiness continued to increase under the diversified mode. Among them, the net growth of monthly active users of ecommerce platform, online banking, local life, payment and settlement, map navigation, browser, **efficient office** and **smart home** ranked the top eight, while the net growth of monthly active users of ecommerce, online banking and local life all exceeded 100 million users. In addition, the time spent on short video has surpassed that of instant messaging, and has become an industry that occupies the longest Internet time of people, showing a rapid growth. This is also one of the reasons behind the development of cross-border ecommerce live broadcasting in China.

2.5.2 M-Commerce vs. E-Commerce 移动电商和电商

Ecommerce refers to the buying and selling of goods and services over the Internet. Ecommerce may be conducted via a desktop computer, laptop, smartphone, or tablet. However, ecommerce is typically associated with a computer in which a user has access to internet connection. Conversely, m-commerce specifically refers to transactions done via a smartphone or mobile device. With m-commerce, users can transact anywhere provided there's a wireless internet provider available in that area.

M-commerce transactions tend to be done with a few clicks, while ecommerce done via a tablet, laptop, or desktop might involve more time and exploring a company's website.

2.5.3 Convenience of Mobile Commerce 移动电商的便利

The range of services offered by mobile commerce is growing. For example, digital

---

① 上海国际贸易平台, http://service. sh-itc. net/articleds/dianzisw/dsyjbg/202202/1527130_1. html. Jan-2-2023.

payment like PayPal, Apple Pay and Alipay, WeChat Pay let customers make in-store purchases without the inconvenience of swiping cards. The **portability** of mobile devices helps businesses extend their reach to their customers through mobile commerce. Coupons and discounts can be sent from retailers to customers. Personalized shopping experiences can also connect the retailer with their client. And during the mid-to-late 2010s, social media platforms, such as Meta (formerly Facebook), Twitter, Pinterest, and Instagram, launched "buy buttons" on their mobile platforms, enabling users to conveniently make purchases from other retailers directly from these social media sites. Besides that m-commerce apps allow **location tracking** via GPS to offer their customers help in finding items in their store. Security can also be enhanced using m-commerce apps since multi-factor **authentication** can be done, including **biometrics** such as fingerprints and **retina scans**.

Although there are many benefits of m-commerce to retailers and consumers, ecommerce is still not as prevalent among Americans as china. Only 15% of American adults use only their smartphone for their Internet connection, which means they have a broadband or cable service provider, while 77% own a computer.

2.6　Social Ecommerce 社交电商

Today's world is a social media era. Social e-commerce is ecommerce that is enabled by social networks and online social relationships. Social ecommerce is often intertwined with m-commerce, particularly as more and more social network users access those networks via mobile devices. The growth of social e-commerce is being driven by a number of factors, including the increasing popularity of social sign-on (signing onto websites using your Facebook or other social network ID), network notification (the sharing of approval or disapproval of products, services, and content), online collaborative shopping tools, social search (recommendations from online trusted friends), and the increasing prevalence of integrated social commerce tools such as Buy buttons, Shopping tabs, marketplace groups, and virtual shops on WeChat, Tiktok, Facebook, Instagram, Pinterest, YouTube, and other social networks.

Social e-commerce is still in its infancy. But with social media and networks playing an increasingly important role in influencing purchase decisions and driving sales, it has been proved to be good in building brand image and increasing traffic. Total social commerce revenues worldwide in 2020 were estimated to be around $90 billion (Business Wire, 2020).

2.7　Local Ecommerce 本地电商

Local e-commerce, as its name suggests, is a form of ecommerce that is focused on engaging the consumer based on his or her current geographic location. Local merchants use a variety of online marketing techniques to drive consumers to their stores. Local ecommerce is the third prong of the mobile-social-local ecommerce wave and fueled by an explosion of interest in local on-demand services such as Uber, which grew in the United States to over $125 billion in 2020.

Pinduoduo, established in September 2015, is a mainstream ecommerce application product of domestic mobile Internet, and it focuses on C2M (customer to Manufacture) **group shopping**. Its users can buy goods at a lower price by initiating group shopping with friends, family, neighbors, etc. Pinduoduo is now spreading its business around the world including the United States, Canada, New Zealand, Australia. U.K.(Temu) at the beginning of 2023 and Southeastern Asia countries (The Philipines) by the way of localizing its business and is gaining market presence in these places.

2.8　The Situation of Cross-border Ecommerce 跨境电商现状

Due to the rapid development of information technology and the internet economy, the number of global internet users has grown rapidly in the past decade, and online shopping has become increasingly popular. The COVID-19 has prompted traditional sellers to expand online, and more and more enterprises, brands and new retail platforms have entered e-commerce marketplace. The global retail e-commerce market has almost tripled in volume from 2014 to 2022. The growth rate reached 25.7% in 2020, 17.1% in 2021, and slowed down in 2022. In 2021, global retail e-commerce sales were approximately $5.2 trillion. EMarketer predicts that this number will increase by 56% in the coming years, reaching approximately $8.1 trillion by 2026. On the other hand, challenges are everywhere.

1. A slow **growth rate** of global e-commerce sales

The growth rate of global e-commerce sales reached 12.2% in 2022, and the subsequent growth of e-commerce sales is slowing down. Big tech companies home and abroad begin to restructure the company or lay off workers. For example, Amazon announced a 18,000 layoff in order to live through a hard time and its market value shrank a half during the end of 2022 and bounced back in the first half year of 2023.

2. The rebound of physical stores

Some bubbles in ecommerce are breaking and governments are encouraging the brick-and-mortar stores for the purpose of balancing local businesses and global business, and recovery of economy. Anti-globalization is still on the rise while China is practicing some local and regional economic agreements and economic belts.

3. Emerging opportunities in southeast Asia and Latin America

Several countries from the Asia Pacific and Latin America regions become most of the 10 countries with the fastest growth rate of ecommerce. The emerging cross-border markets in Latin America and the Asia Pacific region, especially in Southeast Asia, are the biggest opportunity for cross-border sellers. See Figure 2-11.

4. A steady growth rate of online consumers

In the year of 2022, the number of global online shoppers was about 2.56 billion, with a yearly increase of only 3.4%, the lowest increase in history. In developed areas like Western Europe and North America, the growth of buyer is slow. India, Indonesia, Brazil and some other emerging markets dominate the number of new online shoppers in the world.

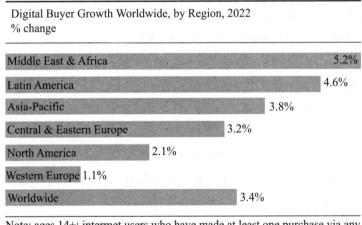

Digital Buyer Growth Worldwide, by Region, 2022
% change

Middle East & Africa	5.2%
Latin America	4.6%
Asia-Pacific	3.8%
Central & Eastern Europe	3.2%
North America	2.1%
Western Europe	1.1%
Worldwide	3.4%

Note: ages 14+; intermet users who have made at least one purchase via any digital channel during the calendar year, including online, mobile, and tablet purchases
Source: eMarketer, Jan 2022

Figure 2-11　Digital buyer growth worldwide in 2022

In brief, digital transformation is the general trend and most businesses would be electrified. Ecommerce could take the basic form of B2B, B2C, and C2C. With the development of computing technology, big data, AI, VR, IOT, and 5G technology, there are evolving some subtypes like mobile-commerce, local e-commerce and social commerce, etc. Globally speaking, B2B business exceeds B2C business while B2C is growing greatly. China has the biggest B2C market while the United States boosts an enormous B2B market.

📖 Words and Phrases 词汇和短语

intermediary 中间商

channel partner 渠道合作商

distributor 经销商

objects 商品；交易客体

inventory 存货

replenish 补货

intangible goods 无形商品

templates 样板；模型；标准

platform model 平台模式

categories 商品品类

platform+direct operating model 平台＋自营模式

direct operating model 自营模式

comprehensive platform model 综合性平台模式

general products/categories 通用产品/目录；一般产品/目录

vertical platform model 垂直平台模式

niché market 细分市场

dotcom boom 泡沫经济；网络泡沫化

the end-user-as-customers 消费者作为终端用户

Gross Merchandise Volume (GMV) 商品交易总额

behemoth 巨头

apparel 服装

disrupter 颠覆者

operating income 营业利润

net income 净收入

capitalize 利用……获利

market value（股票）市值

retail revenue 零售收入

year on year (YoY) 同比

shareholding ratio 控股比

liaisons 中间商

go-betweens 中间商

commission 佣金

traffic 流量

users demographics 用户特征

live broadcasting 直播

peripheral products 周边产品

branding 品牌推广

second-tier-and-lower-tier market 二级及以下市场

sinking market 下沉市场

niches 细分市场

fast-fashion products 快时尚产品

DTC brand 直接面对消费者的品牌；DTC 品牌

algorithm 算法

consumer behavior 消费者行为

preferences 个人偏好

precision marketing 精准营销

logistics and delivery 物流和配送

flexible supply chain 柔性供应链

domestic central warehouse 国内中心仓

overseas transit warehouse 海外转运仓

overseas operation warehouse 海外运营仓

taxpayer numbers 纳税号

revenue 营业收入

lead times 生产时间；研制周期；交付周期

recurring goods 经常购买的商品；复购品

the sales volume 销售收入

semiconductor producer 半导体生产商

industrial cleanup 工业清理

registered members 注册用户

sourcing 网络采购

list *v.* 发布产品；上架产品；上市 *n.* 产品

listing 产品页面，平台上上架的产品（每个商品对应的一个链接）

posting 帖子

efficient office 高效办公

smart home 智能家居

portability 便携性

location tracking 定位

authentication 授权

biometrics 生物计量学；生物测定学

retina scans 视网膜扫射

group shopping 团购

growth rate 增长率

 Exercise 练习

I. Reflections and Critical Thinking Questions.

1. What are the classifications of cross-border ecommerce?

2. Why B2C is currently widely conducted on mobile devices?

3. Which business model would have a great potential in cross-border ecommerce?

4. What is the relationship of mobile ecommerce, social ecommerce, local ecommerce?

II. True or False

1. Alibaba.com is an importing B2B ecommerce platform. (　　)

2. Walmart, as a typical direct seller model, offers more categories to consumers with the lowest price. (　　)

3. Vertical platforms focus on a niché market and often has its own stand-alone platform. (　　)

4. B2C model is the most popular ecommerce model and has the greatest GMV. (　　)

5. China has the biggest B2C market while America has the biggest B2B market value. (　　)

6. Just like Alibaba group, Amazon enjoys both B2B and B2C business. (　　)

7. Wish is one of the most successfully operated mobile ecommerce platforms in the world. (　　)

8. Compared to B2C business, the prices in B2B model could be negotiable and often lower than that in B2C. (　　)

9. Some cross-border ecommerce platforms conduct both B2C and C2C business. For example, Amazon allowed its C2C business on its platform. (　　)

10. With the development of m-commerce and social ecommerce , ecommerce would have much more greater market share in the next few years. (　　)

11. Anti-globalization would bring a negative impact to the development of ecommerce and more governments are supporting physical stores to support their national industry. (　　)

12. Pinduoduo, working as a local ecommerce, is also a social ecommerce. (　　)

III. Noun Explanation

1. B2B　B2C　C2C　DTC

2. mobile ecommerce, social ecommerce, local ecommerce

3. aliexpress.com, alibaba.com, amazon.com

IV. Reading and Critical Thinking

For vibrant, competitive internet businesses, look to emerging markets

(Economist, 8-12-2021)

A decade ago, the relentless expansion of American internet giants promised world domination. With their vast home market affording them "economies of scale" (规模经济), the likes of Amazon, PayPal and Uber looked destined to monopolise the screens of everyone from Californian charmers to Kalahari farmers.

Today America still rules the global tech industry, broadly defined, accounting for 71% of the market value of listed firms. Nonetheless a different pattern has emerged in the part of the technology industry that focuses on providing internet services to consumers. Here, activity is more dispersed and less American. The trend has been highlighted this year by a rush of flotations (大量发行股份) of emerging-market internet firms.

Instead of a few monoliths (巨 头), three different categories of business have formed. Using a taxonomy (分类学) first drawn up by Asia Partners, an investment company, you can define the first group as the **global** platforms. These still dominate in services where minimal physical presence is required, in particular search, social media and cloud computing. Giants like Alphabet and Facebook (now Meta) generate just over half their sales outside America and

———————————

① 　https://zhuanlan. zhihu. com/p/442815042, 19-7-2022.

are among tech's most international businesses.

A second category has become important in some places: the (protected) **national champion**. Russia has favoured home-grown outfits in e-commerce and fintech (金融科技).

The third digital type—local heroes—is prevalent across much of the rest of the world. In Asia and Latin America **local and regional** companies often rule in e-commerce, gaming, digital payments, ride-hailing, food delivery and other app-based services. Examples from South-East Asia include Sea, Grab and GoTo; South Korea has Kakao and Coupang; and Argentina has Mercado Libre. In India giants including Reliance and Tata aim to promote super-apps that provide a range of services, even as specialists, such as Zomato (a Food recommendation platform in India), a delivery firm, are scaling up.

Typically, these firms operate in markets (where it is useful to be on the ground), or (where local tastes are what count). In South-East Asia supply chains are highly decentralised, rewarding such knowledge. In fintech regulatory differences make it harder for international groups to thrive. Activity is booming. India's Unified Payments Interface, a system which connects banks and non-banks to make cheap and immediate payments, recorded about $100bn of transactions in October, more than four times the amount in the same month two years ago. Mynt, a startup that provides mobile payments and loans, has just become the Philippines' first-ever "unicorn" (独角兽), meaning that it is valued at over $1bn.

These businesses have been helped by a surge in the availability of capital, especially as global investors search for alternatives to China, of the $342bn spent on takeovers (收购) of emerging-market tech firms so far this year, 71% came from economies outside China, the highest share in 11 years. Emerging-market tech companies outside China issued $53bn in equity markets (股票市场) so far in 2021, more than twice the previous record. Venture-capital outfits (人马、团队) that once focused on America, and maybe China, are scouring the planet looking for startups.

The success of the third type of internet firm is cheering. They boost competition and innovate to solve local problems, such as mapping cities without registered property. In contrast to American and Chinese firms, they come with little to no geopolitical baggage and are creating clusters of software developers and seasoned investors around the world who may go on to create another generation of startups. Local pension funds no longer have to put money to work on Wall Street in order to get exposure to the digital economy.

Inevitably, there are risks. Some countries may be tempted to shelter their local heroes from competition, or limit how much outsiders can disrupt vested interests (既得利益) at home. Local expertise may not travel well. Capital markets can be unforgiving—share prices in India's Paytm, a payments firm, have tumbled after a botched (糟糕的) listing (上市) last month—and rising interest rates (利率) will make capital more expensive. When the supply of capital dries up, groups still struggling to make money could be in trouble.

Even so, the odds have receded of a global army of smartphone users all tapping an identical set of apps on their screen. Variety (多样化) should flourish instead, and that is to be welcomed.

Critical Thinking and Questions:

1. What are the 3 different categories of business drawn up by Asian Partners? What are the features of them?

2. In this article, the author thinks "among the three types of internet firm, the third type is cheering" (underlined). Do you agree with the author? Why and why not?

3. If you are the venture capitalist, what are the factors you may consider when you decide to invest in a new market?

4. At the end of the article, the author says: variety is welcome in the development of ecommerce. What does variety mean in the situation? And what are the odds and risks in introducing variety for cross-border ecommerce?

More Resources:

1. Global Cross-Border E-Commerce - Part 1(Keynote speech from Amazon)[①] (21: 24)
2. Reading: What Is B2B, and How Does It Differ From B2C and DTC?[②]

Keys-2

---

① https://www. bilibili. com/video/av969653008/, 6-1-2023.

② https://www. businessnewsdaily. com/5000-what-is-b2b. html, 6-1-2023.

Chapter 3

Cross-border Ecommerce Marketing
跨境电商营销

Objectives

1. Know consumer behaviour in marketing

2. Understand various channels of marketing

3. Understand strategies of marketing

4. Master modes of marketing

5. Master pricing methods of marketing

Open Case: Watch the videos and answer the questions

1. What is marketing? (2:36)

1) What does marketing include according to the video clip?

2) What are the cumulative functions of marketing?

3) Do you agree on the definition of marketing?

2. Amazon advertising: how to optimize on mobile. (3:19)

1) How do ads look on mobile?

2) How to optimize sponsored product?

3) How to optimize sponsored brands?

视频资源链接

Marketing is of critical value for the final completion of cross-border ecommerce. Any company that does marketing is called a **marketer**. The objective of marketing is to build customer relationships so that a firm can achieve more revenues at a certain price by offering superior products or services and by communicating the brand's features to customers. Cross-border ecommerce marketing could be both online marketing and offline marketing. Offline marketing could be the same as the traditional one, while online marketing is different from traditional marketing in that the nature of the medium is different and its capacities are more empowering than the traditional one. Cross-border ecommerce marketing is more personalized, participatory, interactive, **peer-to-peer**, and **communal**.

Marketing starts from studying **consumer's behaviour** and **User Persona** (or **user's profile)**. Consumer behaviour often follows a certain pattern, which is useful for marketers to do marketing. This is also true for cross-border ecommerce marketers for whom customers are the core of business. With the development of cross-border ecommerce, **the cost of consumer acquisition** is increasingly high. Whoever gets the greatest number of consumers would be more likely successful.

3.1 Consumer Behaviour and Customer Retention
消费者行为和顾客留存

The purpose to study consumer behaviour is to model and understand the behaviors of online-shopping consumers and build a strong relationship with customers in the time of internet and electronic commerce. The purpose of figuring out models of consumer behaviour is attempting to predict or explain what consumers buy and where, when, how much, and why they buy what. The ideal result is that if consumer's decision-making process can be expected, firms would have a better idea on how to market and sell their products to consumers.

3.1.1 Consumer Behaviour 消费者行为

There are usually social, psychological, and economical factors hiding behind consumer's behaviour. Figure 3-1 shows one of the consumer behaviour patterns in the internet age. Consumers experience 5 stages in the process of deciding what to buy: awareness of needs, searching more information, evaluating various alternatives, purchase and post-purchase behaviours: sharing, commenting, complaining, or returning, etc. It is the post-purchase behaviours that decide whether a consumer is loyal to a product or not. A successful marketing would either attract new customers, enhance the image of brand, or increase **user stickiness** to the brand, and thus increase **brand affinity and loyalty**.

Figure 3-1   Consumer behaviour in cross-border ecommerce

For online shopping, it is of critical importance to firstly understand why people choose to buy online rather than in a **physical store**. Price is too often an important consideration. Convenience and **availability** may be the second reason for they could save time and energy by browsing online products with a narrow time of 5 minutes. There are often more online categories available for consumers to choose from and to compare price. So, an overall cost reduction is often considered to be the major reason for choosing online shopping.

In understanding online shopper's behaviour, marketers should also know the consumers' **clickstream behaviour**. Clickstream behavior refers to the **transaction log** that consumers establish as they move on the Web, from search engine to a variety of sites, then to a single site, then to a single page, and then, finally, to a decision to purchase. Clickstream marketing takes maximum advantage of the Internet environment when shopping and firms could conduct precision marketing accordingly.

3. 1. 2　Customer Retention Strategies 顾客留存策略

Building a strong relationship with customers, increasing user loyalty or **customer stickiness** to a brand are the important objecitves of customer retention in marketing. In order to get customer retention, firms use **personalized advertising** with the help of **advanced algorithm**.

3. 1. 2. 1　Personalized Advertising 个性化广告

Personalized advertising is a kind of one-to-one, interest-based marketing based on a precise and timely understanding of customer needs, targeting specific marketing messages to these individuals. A recent survey found that almost 95% of marketers surveyed were implementing some form of personalization for online customer interactions. Of those using personalization, 97% reported a lift or improvement as a result (Laudon & Traver, 2022).

Personalized advertising involves using consumers' **personal profile** to adjust the advertising messages delivered to them online. The intent is to increase the efficiency of marketing and advertising, and to increase the **revenue streams of firms** who are in a position to behaviorally target visitors[①]. Take search engine as an example. If you are

---

① 　根据行为定位顾客。

visiting a jewelry site, you would be shown jewelry ads. If you enter a search query like "pearls", you would be shown text ads for pearls and other jewelry. This is taken one step further by advertising networks, which could follow you across thousands of websites and come up with an idea of what you are interested in as you browse, and then display ads related to those interests. For instance, if you visit several baby's clothing sites within the course of a few hours, you will be shown ads for baby's clothing on most other sites you will visit subsequently, regardless of the sites' subject content.

What we described above is called **search engine advertising**. Search engine advertising has turned out to be one of the most effective online advertising formats. Why is search engine advertising proved to be so effective? The reasons are that when users enter a query into a search engine, it reveals a very specific intention to shop, compare, and a great possibility to purchase. When ads are displayed at these very moments, they are 4 to 10 times as effective as traditional ads. In total, the database of words in searching websites contains very precise and real needs and intentions of users at a certain moment. This **treasure trove** of various intentions, desires, likes, wants, and needs is owned by big search engines like Google, Microsoft Bing, Baidu and to a lesser extent, Yahoo and this is also one of the main revenue resources for search engines websites.

3. 1. 2. 2　Customization 顾客定制广告

In the personalization process of marketing, **customization**, as an extension of personalization, emerges. Customization means changing the product and service—not just the marketing message—according to **user preference**s. It means it is the users who actually present their needs and think up the innovation, and help create the new product. It is especially true in the economy of **a steady market capacity** where there is little room to draw new customers and where there is **a saturated market**.

Customerized service can help reduce consumer frustration, cut the number of abandoned shopping carts, and increase sales. So a website's approach to customer service can significantly help or hurt its marketing efforts.

3. 2　Classifications of Marketing 营销分类

Just as mentioned above, marketing is regularly done online and offline. See

Table 3-1. Online marketing often goes hand in hand with offline marketing in cross-border ecommerce. Online transaction could be driven by offline **branding** and shopping, while online research may influence offline purchases. Offline marketing media could heavily influence online behaviour.

Offline marketing means traditional marketing through the means of TV, newspaper and magazines, etc. Its main function is more about **brand anchoring** than sales promotion in modern times.

Table 3-1　Channels and stages of marketing used in cross-border ecommerce

stages of consumer behavior	awareness of needs	search	evaluation of alternatives	purchase	post-purchase behaviour
offline marketing channels	mass media: TV, radio, print media, social network[①]	cataloges: print ads, mass media, sales reps, store visit, social network	reference group: KOL, mass media, product raters, store visit, social network	promotions, direct mail, mass media, print media	warranties, service calls, parts and repair, consumer groups, social network
online marketing channels	targeted display ads: Email ads, social media[①]	search engine: online catalog, site visit, email inquiry, social networks	search engine: online catalog, site visit, product review, social networks, user evaluation	online promotion, discounts, email, flash sales	consumption community, newsletter, Email, online update, social network

NB: Social network includes physical social interactions on a certain party while social media is often virtual (Laudon & Traver, 2022)

As a matter of fact, online marketing and advertising dominant cross-border ecommerce. It includes company website, traditional online marketing, social marketing, and mobile advertising, see Table 3-2. Traditional online marketing includes search engine marketing, **display advertising, direct email advertising** and **affiliate marketing** (which is popular in the West). We will discuss these channels in the following part.

Table 3-2　Types of marketing in cross-border ecommerce (Laudon & Traver, 2022)

ecommerce marketing	type	channel	function	example
offline marketing	TV, newspaper, magazine	CCTV, New York times, Elle	Inform, brand anchoring	Xiaomi, Legend, Apple

ecommerce marketing	type	channel	function	example
online marketing	traditional online marketing	company website,	anchor site	bydauto.com aliexpress.com
		email direct mailing,	permission marketing	big retailors
		search engine marketing,	query-based intention marketing	Baidu; Google; Bing; Yahoo; Zhihu
		display marketing	interest- and context-based marketing	Baidu; Google
		affiliate marketing	targeted marketing Brand extension	Amazon
	social marketing	social network, microblog, blog/ forum (visual/video/ game)	conversation; news; updates; community; share; engage; inform; identification	Facebook;WeChat; Xiaohongshu; TikTok; Instagram weibo.com blog.sina.com
	mobile marketing	App mobile site	visual engagement; quick access; news; update	Alibaba SheIn Wish

3.3   Main Channels of Marketing 主要营销渠道

3.3.1   Website Marketing 网页营销

For cross-border ecommerce sellers, the firm's website is the first step to start marketing and a major tool for establishing the initial relationship with its customer. The website performs four important functions for a firm: establishing the brand identity and consumer expectations, informing and educating the consumer, shaping the customer experience, and anchoring the brand in an ocean of marketing messages coming from different sources, thereby driving sales revenue.

The first function involves identifying the differentiating features of the product or service in terms of quality, price, product support, and reliability and creating expectations in the user of what it will be like to consume the product. For instance, Tesla's website focuses on green electronic battery technology and long miles per **charge** for an **electronic vehicle**. The expectation created is that if you buy a Tesla, you'll be experiencing the latest automotive technology and the highest **mileage**.

Websites also function to anchor the brand online, acting as a central point where all the branding messages that emanate from the firm's multiple digital presences, such as Facebook, Twitter, mobile apps, or e-mail, come together at a single online location.

Aside from branding, websites also perform the typical functions of establishing commercial presence by informing customers of the company's products and services. Websites, with their online catalogues and associated shopping carts, are important elements of the online customer experience. A great website would bring great customer experience for more customers.

3. 3. 2　Search Engine Marketing 搜索引擎营销

Search engine marketing (SEM) refers to the use of search engines to build and sustain brands, to support direct sales to online consumers. The most often used search engine is Google and Baidu.

In the last five years, advertisers have aggressively increased online spending and cut **outlays** on traditional channels. In 2017, for the first time, the amount spent on online advertising worldwide exceeded the amount spent on television advertising worldwide, and by 2024, television advertising is expected to account for only about 24% of total ad spending (eMarketer, 2021).

Companies spent an estimated $614 billion on all forms of advertising in 2020, down about 4.5% from 2019, due to the impacts of the Covid-19 pandemic. An estimated $340 billion of that amount was spent on online advertising (paid messages on a website, app, or other digital medium). The top three digital advertising platforms in terms of worldwide estimated ad revenues in 2020 were Google (about $99 billion), Facebook (about $79 billion, including Instagram), and Alibaba (about $31 billion) (eMarketer, 2020i, 2020j, 2020k). Paid research advertisement ranks first in marketing in the United States in 2020.

3. 3. 2. 1　Functions of Search Engine Marketing 搜索引擎营销的功能

Search engines are often thought of as mostly direct sales channels focused on making sales in response to advertisements. While this is a major use of search engines, they are also used more subtly to strengthen brand awareness, **drive traffic** to other websites or blogs to support **customer engagement**, to gain deeper insight into customers' perceptions of the brand, to support other related advertising (for instance, sending consumers to local dealer sites), and thus support the brand indirectly.

Search engines can also provide marketers insight into customer search patterns, opinions customers hold about their products, top trending search keywords, and what their competitors are using as keywords and the customer response. For example, the **click-through rate** for search engine advertising is generally 1%–4% (with an average of around 2%) and has been steady over the years. The top four search engines worldwide are Google, Baidu, Microsoft Bing, and Sohu (eMarketer, 2020r). In cross-border ecommerce, marketers set the priority in advertising on these important platforms and the cost of marketing on these search engines is experiencing a steady increase.

3. 3. 2. 2   Types of Search Engine Marketing 搜索引擎营销的类型

Search engine marketing (SEM) could be **paid search** and **organic search.** Paid search is known as search engine advertising and sometimes referred to as **Pay-Per-Click (PPC) search**, and organic search is given when a product is good and lucky enough to be listed high in the search engines without paying for the privilege. When search engines performe unbiased searches of the Web's huge collection of web pages and derive most of their revenue from banner advertisements, it is called organic search because the inclusion and ranking of websites depends on a more or less "unbiased" application of a set of rules (an algorithm) imposed by the search engine. The effect of organic search is built on a long-time accumulation of **branding** and is slow in getting new customers.

Since 1998, search engine sites slowly transformed themselves into digital yellow pages, where firms pay for inclusion in the search engine index, pay for keywords to show up in search results, or pay for keywords to show up next to other vendors' ads. It is paid research marketing or paid search advertising which is often conducted by Pay-Per-Click search ads.

3. 3. 2. 3   Keyword Advertising 关键词广告

Pay-per-click search ads are a primary type of search engine advertising. Keyword advertising is a primary type of SEM based on PPC. In order to do keyword advertising, merchants must purchase keywords through a bidding process at the search sites like Google and Baidu. When a consumer searches for that bought word of the company, their advertisement shows up on the page, either as a listing on the very top of the page, or as a small text-based advertisement on the right. The more the merchants pay, the higher the rank and greater the visibility of their ads on the page. Generally, the search engines do not exercise editorial judgment about quality or content of the ads although they do monitor the use of language. In addition, some search engines rank the ads in terms of product popularity and goods quality rather than merely the money paid by the advertiser so that the **rank of the ad** depends on both the amount paid and the number of clicks per unit time.

Search engine advertising is considered as an ideal targeted marketing technique: at precisely the moment a consumer is looking for a product, an advertisement for the product is presented. Consumers benefit from search engine advertising because ads for merchants appear only when consumers are looking for a specific product. Thus, search engine advertising, for example, Google AdWords and Baidu, saves consumers energy and reduces search costs (including the cost of transportation needed to do physical searches for products). So, search engine advertising is a consumer-take-the-initiative strategy which does not disturb or invade consumer's line of vision and energy, just like paper ads or **banner ads**. The advertisement appears only when the consumers want to have it when searching. It is more kind of a respectful ad for customers without invading too much into user's life.

3. 3. 2. 4　Search Engine Optimization 搜索引擎优化

Search engine optimization (SEO) is the process of improving the ranking of web pages with search engines by altering the content and design of the web pages and sites. Because search engines like Baidu and Google have their own algorithms to capture the words or pictures on the websites and they are improving their methods continuously. The most appropriate content and words or pictures would appear first. Search engine marketing has been proved to be very effective in increasing revenue, and companies often try to optimize their websites continuously for search engine recognition. The better optimized the page is, the higher a ranking in search engine result **listing**s, and the more likely it will appear on the top of the page in search engine results. By carefully selecting keywords used on the web pages, updating content frequently, and designing their website so it can be easily read by search engine programs, marketers can improve the impact and return on investment in their web marketing programs. Just as mentioned above, big search engine firms like Google and Baidu develop and update their algorithms to improve search results and user experience and make profits by offering paid advertising.

3. 3. 3　Display Ad Marketing 展示广告营销

Display ads include a handful of different types of ads, including banner ad, **rich media ad,** and video ad, etc. Trillions of display ads are served annually on desktop and mobile devices. The top four display ad companies in 2020 were Facebook (including Instagram), Google, Twitter, and Baidu, which together were expected to account for almost 55% of worldwide display ad revenue.

3. 3. 3. 1 Banner Ad 横幅广告

As one form of display ad, banner ads are the oldest and most familiar form of display marketing. They are also the least-effective and the lowest-cost form of online marketing. A banner ad displays a promotional message in a rectangular box on the screen of a desktop computer or mobile device. A banner ad is similar to a traditional ad in a printed publication but has some added advantages. When clicked, it brings potential customers directly to the advertiser's website, and the site where the ad appears can track the user's behavior on the site. The ability to identify and track the user is a key feature of online advertising. Banner ads often feature video and other animations.

3. 3. 3. 2 Rich Media Ad 富媒体广告

Rich Media Ads are ads of complex visual effects that employ interactive features to engage users, such as animations (moving graphics), or elements that trigger new content experiences, such as ad expansion, where the ad expands to a size bigger than its original size, or video play. They are more effective than simple banner ads. For instance, one research report that analyzed 24,000 different rich media ads with more than 12 billion impressions served in North America over a six-month period found that exposure to rich media ads boosted advertiser site visits by nearly 300% compared to standard banner ads. Viewers of rich media ads that included video were six times more likely to visit the advertiser's website, by either directly clicking on the ad, typing the advertiser's **URL(Uniform Resource Locator)**, or searching.

3. 3. 3. 3 Video Ad 视频广告

Video ads are TV-like advertisements that appear as **in-page video commercials** before, during, or after a variety of content. Video ads are expected to be the fastest growing form of online advertisement over the next five years. The rapid growth in video ads is due in part to the fact that video ads are far more effective than other display ad formats. For instance, according to research analyzing a variety of ad formats, **in-stream video ads** had click-through rates 12 times that of rich media and 27 times that of standard banner ads (MediaMind, 2012). Research indicates that interactive digital video has even greater impact than typical, non-interactive video formats, with interaction rates three to four times higher, and brand awareness heightened by more than 50% (Interactive Advertising Bureau, 2014).

3.3.4　Email Direct Marketing 电子邮件营销

Email direct marketing (EDM) was one of the first and most effective forms of online marketing communications. Email direct marketing messages are sent to an opt-in audience of Internet users who, at one time or another, have expressed an interest in receiving messages from the **advertiser**. By sending email to an opt-in audience, advertisers are targeting interested consumers. By far, **in-house email lists** are more effective than purchased e-mail lists. Due to its comparatively high response rates and low cost, email direct marketing is still considered as a common form of online marketing communications, especially in some western countries.

Other benefits of email marketing include its mass reach, the ability to track and measure response, the ability to personalize content and tailor offers, the ability to drive traffic to websites for more interaction, the ability to test and optimize content and offers, and the ability to target by region, demographic, time of day, or other criteria.

Although companies spend a relatively small amount of money on email marketing when compared to search engine and display ad marketing, email marketing still packs a punch with solid customer response. Click-through rates for legitimate email depend on the promotion (the offer), the product, and the amount of targeting, but average around 3%-4%. Despite the deluge of spam mail, email remains a highly cost-effective way of communicating with existing customers, and to a lesser extent, finding new customers. Mobile devices have contemporarily become the predominant method for accessing email.

Email marketing and advertising is inexpensive and somewhat invariant to the number of mails sent. The cost of sending 1,000 emails is about the same as the cost to send 1 million. The primary cost of email marketing is for the purchase of the list of names to which the email will be sent. This generally costs anywhere from 5 to 20 US dollar cents a name, depending on how targeted the list is. Sending the email is virtually cost-free. In contrast, the cost to acquire the name, print, and mail a 5×7-inch direct mail post card is around 75 to 80 cents a name.

While email marketing is often sales-oriented, it can also be used as an integral feature of a multi-channel marketing campaign designed to strengthen brand recognition.

Relevancy in the form of behavior-based triggers, segmentation, personalization, and targeting remain major themes in email marketing.

Although email can still be an effective marketing and advertising tool, it faces challenges: spam. Software tools are used to control spam and eliminate many emails from users' mailboxes, and there exists poorly targeted purchased email lists. In a word, Email works well for maintaining customer relationships but poorly for acquiring new customers.

3.3.5　Affiliate Marketing 联盟营销

Affiliate marketing is a type of **performance-based marketing** (pay-for-performance) in which a business rewards one or more affiliates for each visitor or customer brought by the affiliate's own marketing efforts. Affiliate Marketing industry has four core players: the advertiser[1](also known as "merchant" or "retailer" or "brand"), the network (which contains offers for the affiliate to choose from and also takes care of the payments), the **publisher** (also known as "the affiliate") and the customer[2]. In affiliate marketing, a firm pays a commission, typically anywhere between 4% to 20%, to other websites (including blogs) for sending customers to their website.

Visitors to an affiliate website typically click on ads and are taken to the advertiser's website. In return, the advertiser pays the affiliate a fee, either on a per-click basis or as a percentage of whatever the customer spends on the advertiser's site. Paying commissions for **referrals** or recommendations long predated the Web. For instance, Amazon has the world's largest affiliate program, called **Amazon Associates**[3]. Participant sites receive up to 10% commission on sales that their referrals generate. Affiliates attract people to their blogs or websites where they can click on ads for products at Amazon. Members of eBay's Partner Network affiliates program can earn between 1% and 6% depending on the type of product. Amazon, eBay, and their large ecommerce companies with affiliate programs typically administer such programs themselves. Smaller ecommerce firms who wish to use affiliate marketing often decide to join an affiliate network (sometimes called an affiliate

---

① An advertiser is the one who advertises for his own products, while a publisher owns an advertising platform and does advertising on behalf of the shoppers (or advertisers) who do business on the publisher's platform.

② https://encyclopedia. thefreedictionary. com/affiliate+marketing, 14-03-2023.

③ https://www. awyerwu. com/3147. html, 14-03-2023.

broker), such as CJ Affiliate[①] and Rakuten Linkshare[②], which acts as an intermediary. Bloggers often sign up for Google's AdSense program to attract advertisers to their sites. They are paid for each click on an ad and sometimes for subsequent purchases made by visitors.

3.3.6　Social Media Marketing 社交媒体营销

Social media marketing involves the use of online social networks and communities to build brands and drive sales revenues. There are several kinds of social networks, from Facebook, Twitter, Pinterest, Instagram, and WeChat, to social apps, social games, blogs, and forums. In 2020, companies spent about $90 billion worldwide on social network marketing and advertising. Even so, that represents only about 26.5% of the amount spent on all online marketing.

Social networks offer advertisers all the main advertising formats, including banner ads, short **pre-roll and post-roll ads** associated with videos, and **sponsorship** of content. Having a corporate Facebook page is in itself a marketing tool for brands just like a web page. Many firms, such as Coca-Cola, have shut down product-specific web pages and use Facebook pages instead.

Blogs can also be used for social marketing. Blogs have been around for a decade and are a part of the mainstream online culture. In the United States, 30 million people write blogs and around 85 million read blogs. Blogs play a vital role in online marketing. Although more firms use Facebook, Instagram and Twitter, these sites have not replaced blogs, and in fact often point to blogs for long-form content. Because blog readers and creators tend to be more educated, have higher incomes, and be opinion leaders, blogs are ideal platforms for ads for many products and services that cater to this group of audience. Because blogs are based on the personal opinions of the writers, they are also an ideal platform to start a **viral marketing** campaign. Advertising networks that specialize in blogs provide some efficiency in placing ads, as do blog networks, which are collections of a small number of popular blogs, coordinated by a central management team, and which

---

①　It is the largest and most powerful comprehensive advertising alliance in the world. Founded in 1998, it is a wholly-owned subsidiary of Valueclick, a listed company in Nasdaq, USA.

②　It is one of the top three online marketing alliances in the world. Linkshare is based on Pay-Per-Action (i.e. PPA) advertising, with hundreds of top advertisers including Wal-Mart, J. P. Morgan, AT&T, American Express, Apple, Avon and other Fortune 500 companies. At the same time, it also has more than 10 million websites. LinkShare was acquired in September 2005 by Rakuten, the largest e-commerce company in Japan, at a price of $425 million in cash.

can deliver a larger audience to advertisers.

Influencer marketing is an important form of social media marketing that began initially with bloggers and has since expanded to a wide variety of social networks. An influencer could be a **key opinion leader (KOL)** or **key opinion consumer (KOC)**. Influencer marketing uses endorsements and product mentions from people who have dedicated followers on social media and who are viewed by those followers as trusted experts or celebrities. Brands seek to **leverage** the trust influencers built up with their followers and translate recommendations from influencers into sales.

Viral Marketing

Viral marketing is the mode of social marketing making use of the widespread of Internet. Just as affiliate marketing involves using a trusted website to encourage users to visit other sites, viral marketing is a form of social marketing that involves getting customers to pass along a company's marketing message to friends, family, and colleagues. It's the online version of word-of-mouth advertising, which spreads even faster and further than in the real world. In the offline world, next to television, word of mouth is the second most important means by which consumers find out about new products. And the most important factor in the decision to purchase is the face-to-face recommendations of parents, friends, and colleagues. In viral marketing, millions of online consumers are "influencers" who share their opinions about products in a variety of online settings.

In addition to increasing the size of a company's customer base, customer referrals also have other advantages: they are less expensive to acquire because existing customers do all the acquisition work, and they tend to use online support services less, preferring to turn back to the person who referred them for advice. Also, because they cost so little to acquire and keep, referred customers begin to generate profits for a company much earlier than customers acquired through other marketing methods. There are a number of online **venues** where viral marketing appears. E-mail used to be the primary online venue for viral marketing ("please forward this e-mail to your friends"), but venues such as WeChat, TikTok, Facebook, Pinterest, Instagram, Twitter, YouTube, and blogs now play a major role.

3. 3. 7   Mobile Marketing 移动营销

It is with the widespread of mobile devices that **mobile marketing** comes into its own. Mobile is now a required part of the standard marketing budget. Mobile marketing includes the use of display banner ads, rich media, video, **native advertising**[①], games, e-mail, text messaging, in-store messaging, **Quick Response (QR)codes**, and couponing etc.

Apps on mobile devices constitute a marketing platform that did not exist a few years ago. Apps are a non-browser pathway for users to experience the Web and perform a number of tasks from reading the newspaper to shopping, searching, and buying. Apps provide users much faster access to content than do multi-purpose browsers. Apps have begun to influence the design and function of traditional websites as consumers are attracted to the look and feel of apps, and their speed of operation, etc.

Marketing on the mobile platform has exploded and constituted over 70% of the overall $340 billion spent on online marketing worldwide in 2020. In 2020, spending on all forms of mobile marketing was estimated to be about $250 billion, and it is expected to increase to over $420 billion by 2024 (eMarketer, Inc. , 2020w). Several factors are driving advertisers to the mobile platform, including much more powerful devices, faster cellular networks, wireless local networks, rich media and video ads, and growing demand for local advertising by small businesses and consumers.

Most importantly, mobile is where the eyeballs are now and increasingly will be so in the future: about 3.5 billion people have access to Internet at least some of the time from mobile devices. All the above-mentioned models of advertising could be completed on mobile advertising and there are overlaps among all these models of advertising.

3. 4　Theories in CBEC Marketing 跨境电商营销理论

With the development of ecommerce, new theories emerged from business practices and in turn guided the marketing of cross-border ecommerce. The most popular one may be funnel marketing.

3. 4. 1　Sales Funnel Marketing 销售漏斗营销

Sales Funnel Marketing (pipeline marketing) perceives marketing in an order of time sequence or stages, see Figure 3-2. Marketing happens in different phases: awareness, interest, consideration, intent, evaluation, and the final purchase phase. During each step

---

① A philosophy of advertising by using various content-based articles, comments, videos, pictures, etc. to do advertising in a natural way, https://wiki. mbalib. com/wiki/%E5%8E%9F%E7%94%9F%E5%B9%BF%E5% 91%8A, 12-2-2023.

of the journey, marketers must stay in contact and keep their **leads** engaged and interested. The goal of marketing funnel[①] is to eventually take the leads to the bottom of the funnel. In the first stage, marketers spread brand awareness about their products and services to generate leads that will hopefully, eventually, become new customers. At this point, they will attract as many leads as possible, and then narrowing them down as they go through the marketing funnel. Funnel marketing focuses on the steps of actions taken by marketers or sellers and represents the quantity and **conversion rates** of **prospects** through the pipeline stages. It's called a "funnel" because of its shape: wide at the top as prospects enter, then increasingly narrow as they are disqualified or decide not to buy. A funnel report can tell you, for example, of the 100 leads you received last quarter, what percentage of them advanced through each stage of your pipeline. In the process of getting more customers, **lead generation marketing** is what marketers put great effort on to achieve an ideal effect.

A sales funnel report is important for sales leaders because it can help them forecast sales based on current **lead volume** and identify where deals are getting stuck so they can improve their process and better coach their team. It measures conversion rates through the sales process and is widely accepted and used in ecommerce marketing.

Awareness
Primary Tools: Content marketing, Social Media, Paid Advertisements, SEO/SEM, Public Relations

Interest
Primary Tools: Landing Pages, E-books, Newsletter, Free Tools, Case Studies, Retargeting

Decision
Primary Tools: Sales Pages, Free Consultation, Trust Signs, Promotions, Free Trials, Demos, Email Marketing

Action
Primary Tools: Payment System, Shopping Cart，Reviews and Referrals

Infographics by Amber Creative   http://ambercreative.sg

Figure 3-2   Sales marketing funnel

---

① https://blog. taboola. com/effectively-top-funnel-marketing, 6-1-2023.

3. 4. 2　Long Tail Marketing 长尾营销

Long Tail Marketing comes from long tail theory when *Wired Magazine* writer Chris Anderson coined the phrase in 2004, see Figure 3-3. In terms of popularity and usefulness, the highly popular goods are head and the long tail is formed by not so popular goods and niche products in the map. The long tail describes statistical distributions characterized by a small group of events of high amplitude and a large group of events with low amplitude. Taking Hollywood movies as an example: there are a few big hits and also thousands of films that no one has ever heard about. It's the legion of niche products that make up the long tail. Anderson claimed that the Web would change the rules: no matter how much content you put online, thanks to online search, social networks and recommendation engines, someone, somewhere will show up to buy it.

The theory has implications for marketers and product designers. In the long tail approach, online merchants, especially those selling digital goods, should build up huge libraries of content because they can make significant revenues from niche products that have small audiences. A former Amazon employee famously outlined the "long tail" nature of the company: now we sell more books that could not be sold in the past than those that could be sold in the past.

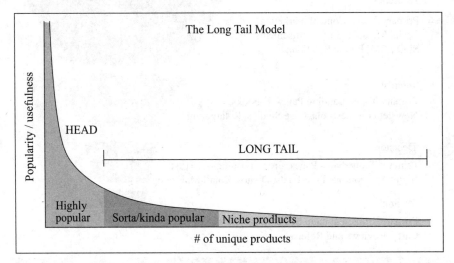

Figure 3-3　Long tail marketing

Google is the most typical "long tail" company. Its growth process is the process of commercializing the "long tail" of advertisers and publishers. Millions of small businesses and individuals have never advertised before or have never advertised on a large scale. They are so small that advertisers disdain them, and even they never thought that they could advertise. But Google's AdSense has lowered the threshold of advertising: advertising is no longer unattainable; it is self-made, cheap, and anyone can do it. On the other hand, for thousands of blog sites and small-scale commercial websites, placing advertisements on their own sites has become a simple task. At present, half of Google's business comes from these small websites rather than ads placed in search results. Millions of small and medium-sized enterprises represent a huge long tail advertising market. Nobody can predict how long this long tail will be.

3.5   New Practice in Marketing 营销实践

Some practices appeared only a few years ago and are popular in a certain market and facing improvement in the trial-and-error process.

3.5.1   Private Traffic Marketing 私域流量营销

Public traffic and **private traffic** are divided according to the range of its audience. For private traffic, you own the traffic by yourself (or your firm) and a repeated use does not increase the cost. For public traffic, it is one-time traffic purchased from other platforms. Typical Public traffic usually lies in big companies like Google, Facebook, Baidu, Taobao, Jingdong, Pinduoduo, Meituan, TikTok, Kuaishou, Xiaohongshu, Bilibili, etc. Private traffic comes from some APPs, official websites, **applets**, official accounts (such as an enterprise of WeChat account), WeChat personal account, **WeChat moments**, WeChat friends, etc. For instance, with the start of WeChat community marketing, traffic is transferred to personal WeChat account or enterprise WeChat account, and traffic is converted through activities, promotions, private small talks, etc. Private traffic could be converted into company revenue more easily, which is attained with a low cost and yields a high conversion rate.

3.5.1.1   Livestreaming Marketing 直播营销

Among private traffic marketing, the most popular one in China is **livestreaming marketing**. Livestreaming started and bloomed in China where it produced ecommerce **anchors** and a livestreaming economy. Live broadcast marketing refers to the marketing method of producing and broadcasting programs on the scene of a physical store or a studio by an anchor. This marketing activity takes the live broadcast platform as the carrier to achieve the purpose of improving the brand or increasing the sales volume of the enterprise. It is also one of the ways to establish DTC (direct to customer) brand. Live broadcast marketing is a specific product of the present situation because of technical improvements including the development of mobile network and popularization of smart equipment and device.

3.5.1.2　Development 发展状况

Livestream broadcasting is spreading into the world like a wildfire. 2016 is recognized as the first year of **live broadcast**. In that year, more than 300 online live broadcast platforms emerged in China, and the number of live broadcast users also increased rapidly. When the majority players focused on live game and entertainment at first, mogo.com (mushroom street literally in Chinese) was the first to introduce live broadcast to e-commerce. In March 2016, the live broadcast function of mogo.com was launched. Thus, it has become a "live broadcasting+ content + e-commerce" platform. Soon, Taobao.com, WeChat, jd.com, douyin.com and kuaishou.com joined them and there emerged a boost of live broadcasting.

3.5.1.3　Features 特色

Live marketing meets the needs of both firms and individuals and embodies its own features.

1. Live broadcast marketing takes the form of **event marketing**. In addition to its own advertising effect, the news effect of live broadcast content is often more obvious and explosive. An event or a topic can be relatively easy to spread and attract attention.

2. It can reflect the accuracy of the user group. When watching live video, users need to enter the play page together at a specific time. However, due to the limitation of broadcast time, this group of loyal and accurate target groups can be identified and captured.

3. It is a real time interaction with users. Compared with traditional TV, one of the advantages of Internet is that it can meet more diverse needs of users. It is not only a one-way viewing, but also a platform of interaction by sending a barrage of **roasting words and phrases** freely or comment on it. Whoever likes it will directly give flowers and rewards, and even use the power of public opinion to change the program process. The authenticity and three-dimensional nature of this interaction can only be fully displayed during the live broadcast.

4. There is an in-depth communication and emotional resonance. In this fragmented

era and decentralized context, people may have little interactions in their daily life, especially in the emotional level. Live broadcastcan gather a group of people with the same interests together, focus on common hobbies, influence each other, and reach a high point in emotional atmosphere. If the brand can make a proper contribution in atmosphere, its marketing effect will be enormously effective.

3. 5. 2   Product Crowdfunding and Presale 产品众筹和预售

Product crowdfunding is based on the characteristics of Internet e-commerce. It refers to a unique marketing that consumers (or investors) invest their funds in product developers (producers, as well as fund raisers) to develop a product (or service). When the product (or service) is successfully developed, it starts to be sold to the orderers and then for external sales, according to the agreement. This is a new market development and marketing method in which the manufacturer provides the developed products (or services) to investors (customers). It can be considered as a small-scale collective group purchase mode for future products with special needs of consumers with common needs.

Presale is a product crowdfunding in a small scale. Online sellers advertise their new products, a new **down coat**, for example, and take orders from customers who are interested in it. The presale period may last 7 or 10 days before winter is really coming. It is good for sellers to produce the customerized coat and collect **advance**. On the other hand, sellers could reduce the inventory to zero. For new buyers, they could get a latest style coat at a low price. Once the product is proved successful, the seller would produce more and sell at a normal price. Instagram tried this method on some limited editions of some famous brand clothes and named it as **limited edition drops**. It has been one of the successful marketing methods for some well-known and high-end brands.

3. 5. 3   Big Data Marketing 大数据营销

With the popularization of digital life, the total amount of global information is showing explosive growth. **Big data marketing** refers to the marketing process of collecting a large amount of behavioral data through the Internet to help advertisers find out the target audience first, so as to predict and deploy the content, time, form, etc. of advertising, and finally complete the advertising process. All the above-mentioned advertising models could be and are conducted with the help of big data in the new technology era.

3. 5. 4　Content Marketing 内容营销

Content marketing creates a content campaign for a brand and then tries to secure **placement** on a variety of websites. Examples of content include articles, **infographics**, case studies, interactive graphics, white papers, and even traditional press releases. The aim of content marketing is to introduce more visitors to a company's website, improve the organic search ranking and brand engagement via social media platforms like Facebook or other channels such as WeChat account, etc.

In the future, businesses are expected to see a rise in video content as a way to market products and services to their users. These kinds of videos aim to be engaging, informative, and fun, while also including product links throughout. With just a few simple clicks, the viewer can purchase your advertised product straight from the video. Some video formats include: **testimonials**, **demos**, educational/informative videos, etc. Video content advertising may be presented on Facebook, Instagram, YouTube, TikTok and other popular social media platforms.

3. 6　Pricing Strategies in Marketing 营销定价策略

Pricing is an integral part of marketing strategy. Marketers use different pricing strategies to get the biggest market share, the most revenue or the biggest profit.

3. 6. 1　Freemium 免费

Free products are often used at the primary stage. **Freemium** is only a pricing strategy. The freemium pricing model is a cross-subsidy online marketing strategy where users are offered a basic service for free, but must pay for **premium** or add-on **service**s. The people who pay for the premium services hopefully will pay for all the free riders on the service. For example, Skype, as one of the most popular internet phone provider in the United States, uses a freemium model: millions of users can call other Skype users on the Internet for free, but there's a charge for calling a land line or cell phone.

3. 6. 2　Versioning 版本差异化

Versioning is to create multiple versions of the goods and selling essentially the same product to different market segments at different prices. Versioning means the price of products depends on the value to an individual consumer. Consumers are segmented into various groups who are willing to pay different prices for various versions. Versioning often goes like this: A reduced-value version is offered for free, while premium versions is offered at higher prices. A "reduced-value version" might be less convenient to use, less comprehensive, slower, less powerful, and offer less service than the high-priced versions. Just as there are different General Motors car brands appealing to different market segments (Benz, BMW, BYD, Cadillac, Buick, Chevrolet, and GMC), and within these divisions, hundreds of models from the most basic to the more powerful and functional, so can information goods be "versioned" in order to segment and target the market and position the products.

Versioning is widely used in the realm of information goods, online magazines, music companies, and book publishers offer sample content for free, but charge for more powerful content. The New York Times, for instance, allows you to read a certain number of articles a month online for free, but if you want to read more, you must have a digital subscription. Some websites offer "free services" with annoying advertising, but turn off the ads for a monthly fee.

3.6.3   Bundling 捆绑销售

"Ziggy" Ziegfeld, a vaudeville entrepreneur at the turn of the twentieth century in New York, noticed that nearly one-third of his theater seats were empty on some Friday nights, and during the week, matinee shows[①] were often half empty. He came up with an idea for bundling tickets into "twofers" : pay for one full-price ticket and get the next ticket free. Twofers are still a Broadway theater tradition in New York. They are based on the idea that (a) the marginal cost of seating another patron is zero, and (b) a great many people who would not otherwise buy a single ticket would buy a "bundle" of tickets for the same or even a slightly higher price.

Bundling offers consumers two or more goods for a price that is less than the goods would cost when purchased individually. The key idea behind the concept of bundling is that although consumers typically have very diverse ideas about the value of a single product, they tend to agree much more on the value of a bundle of products offered at a fixed price. In fact, the per-product price people are willing to pay for the bundle is

---

① A matineeshow is an afternoon performance. While not every show has an afternoon slot, most do, and you can catch top London matineeshows playing every day, https://www. londontheatredirect. com/tickets/matinee-shows-in-london-west-end, 12-02-2023.

often higher than when the products are sold separately. Bundling reduces the variance (dispersion) in market demand for goods.

3. 6. 4 Dynamic Pricing 动态定价

Dynamic pricing holds the opinion that the value of a good is equal to what the market is willing to pay (it may have nothing to do with its cost sometimes). With dynamic pricing, the price of the product varies, depending on the demand characteristics of the customer and the supply situation of the seller.

There are different kinds of dynamic pricing mechanisms. For instance, auctions have been used for centuries to establish the instant market price for goods. Auctions are flexible and efficient market mechanisms for pricing unique or unusual goods, as well as commonplace goods such as computers, flower bundles, and cameras.

Yield management (revenue management) is a kind of dynamic pricing which is different from auctions. In auctions, thousands of consumers establish a price by bidding against one another. In yield management, managers set prices in different markets, appealing to different segments, in order to sell excess capacity. It is in essence a price discrimination. Airlines exemplify yield management techniques. Every few minutes during the day, they adjust prices of empty airline seats to ensure at least some of the 50,000 empty airline seats are sold at some reasonable price—even below marginal cost of production. Amazon and other large online retailers frequently use yield management techniques that involve changing prices hourly to stimulate demand and maximize revenues. Amazon can also track shopping behavior of individuals seeking a specific product, such as a laser printer. As the consumer searches for the best price, Amazon can observe the offering prices on other websites, and then adjust its prices dynamically so that when the user visits Amazon again, a lower price will be displayed than all other sites visited.

Surge pricing is a kind of dynamic pricing used firstly by Uber. Uber uses a dynamic pricing algorithm to optimize its revenue, or as the company claims, to balance supply and demand. Prices have surged from two to ten times or higher during storms and popular holiday periods. Critics say this is kind of like rubbering customers in emergency.

A third dynamic pricing technique is **flash marketing**, which has proved extraordinarily effective for travel services, luxury clothing goods, and other goods.

Using e-mailor dedicated website features to notify loyal customers (repeat purchasers), merchants offer goods and services for a limited time (usually hours) at very low prices. JetBlue has offered $14 flights between New York and Los Angeles. Deluxe hotel rooms are flash marketed at $1 a night.

Words and Phrases 词汇和短语

marketer 公司；（营销）公司

peer-to-peer 对等（的）；个人对个人（的）

communal 共享的

consumer's behaviour 消费者行为

User Persona 用户画像

user's profile 用户资料，用户画像

the cost of consumer acquisition 获客成本

customer retention 顾客留存

user stickiness 用户粘性

brand affinity and loyalty 品牌吸引力和忠诚度

physical store 实体店

availability 便捷

clickstream behaviour 点击（流）行为

transaction log（交易过程中的）行为记录

customer stickiness 顾客粘性

personalized advertising 个性化广告

advanced algorithm 高级算法

personal profile 个人资料

revenue streams of firms 企业的收入流（源）

search engine advertising 搜索引擎广告

treasure trove 宝藏

customization 客制化服务

user preference 客户偏好

a steady market capacity 存量市场

a saturated market 饱和的市场

branding 品牌打造；品牌营销

brand anchoring 品牌定位；品牌导航

display advertising 显示广告

direct email advertising 直邮广告

affiliate marketing 联盟广告

charge 充电

electronic vehicle 电动汽车

mileage 里程

Search Engine Marketing (SEM) 搜索引擎营销

outlays（启动新项目的）开支；费用；

increase traffic 引流

customer engagement 顾客参与度

click-through rate 点击率；点进率

paid search 付费搜索

organic search 自然搜索

Pay-Per-Click (PPC) 按点击付费

rank of the ad 广告竞价排名

listing 排名

display ad 展示广告

banner ad 横幅广告

rich media ad 富媒体广告

URL 统一资源定位符

in-page video commercial 业内视频广告

in-stream video ad 插播视频广告

Email Direct Marketing (EDM) 电子邮件营销

advertiser 广告主

in-house email lists 行业内部邮箱地址

affiliate marketing 联盟营销

performance-based marketing (pay-for-performance) 基于效果的营销（按效果付费）

publisher（广告）发布商；流量主

referrals 推荐

Amazon Associates 亚马逊联盟营销

pre-roll ad 前贴片广告（视频播放前播放的广告）

post-roll ad 后贴片广告

sponsorship 赞助（广告）

viral marketing 病毒营销

influencer marketing 网红营销

key opinion leader (KOL) 关键意见领袖

key opinion consumer (KOC) 关键意见消费者

leverage 利用……获益

venues 渠道，场合

native advertising 原生广告

Quick Response (QR) codes 二维码

sales funnel marketing (pipeline marketing) 销售漏斗营销

marketing funnel 营销漏斗；销售漏斗

leads 潜在客户

conversion rates 转化率

prospects 潜在客户

lead volume 潜在客户量

lead generation marketing 潜在客户生成营销

Long Tail Marketing 长尾营销

private traffic marketing 私域流量营销

public traffic 公域

private traffic 私域

applets 小程序

WeChat moments 微信朋友圈

livestreaming marketing 直播营销

anchor 主播

DTC brand DTC 品牌

an event marketing 事件营销

live broadcast 直播

roasting words and phrases 吐槽语言

product crowdfunding 产品众筹

presale 预售

down coat 羽绒服外套

advance 定金；预付款

limited edition drops 限量版预售

big data marketing 大数据营销

content marketing 内容营销；软文广告

placement 排名

infographics 信息图表

testimonials（鉴定书、客户评价等）证明材料

demos 样品展示

freemium 免费

premium service 优质服务

add-on service 增值服务

versioning 版本差异化

bundling 捆绑销售

dynamic pricing 动态价格

yield management 收益（率）管理

surge pricing 动态定价

flash marketing 秒杀（价）营销

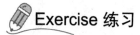 Exercise 练习

I. Reflections and Critical Thinking Questions.

1. As an online consumer, what is your consumer behaviour?

2. What are the strategies used to get a better customer retention?

3. What does a traditional online marketing include?

4. What are the functions of search engine marketing?

5. Social media marketing and mobile marketing stand for the trend of marketing in CBEC. How would a marketer improve the two?

6. Long Tail Marketing is widely used in business, what is the best strategy for a retail platform according to Long Tail Marketing?

7. While live broadcasting is popular in China, it is not as popular in the United States. What are the possible reasons for this?

8. What are the pricing strategies used in cross-border ecommerce?

II. True or False

1. The purpose of online marketing is mainly to increase user stickiness. (   )

2. A firm's website is the first step to start marketing. (   )

3. Search engine advertising has turned out to be one of the most effective online advertising formats. (   )

4. In order to have a good marketing effect, a company should first use search engine marketing. (   )

5. Customization in marketing is especially good for a saturated market. (   )

6. An advertisement on TV is a way of online marketing. (   )

7. Keyword advertising is a primary type of search engine advertising. (   )

8. Search engine advertising is a traditional and popular way of online advertising for products. (   )

9. Email advertising works well in introducing new customers. (   )

10. Facebook pages could serve as a web page for some companies' products. (   )

11. Blogs work as an important online marketing tool because bloggers are offering long-form content and they are more professional. (   )

12. With the widespread of mobile marketing, apps have taken the place of browsers as a main access to content. (   )

13. Livestreaming is gaining popularity around the world. (   )

14. Many companies use freemium as a pricing strategy, whose purpose is to draw people to pay for the premium service. (   )

15. Expensive stuff like Deluxe hotel rooms use flash price as a strategy to promote its marketing and increase the loyalty of customers. (   )

III. Nouns Explanation

1. Search engine advertising & search engine optimization

2. Display ad marketing; rich media ads; content marketing; direct email marketing; affiliate marketing

3. Social marketing&mobile marketing

4. Funnel marketing; longtail marketing

5. private traffic marketing; livestreaming marketing; presale

6. Dynamic pricing; surge pricing; flash pricing

IV. Reading and Critical Thinking

Passage 1

Fake Commodities in Livestreaming[①]

Luo Yonghao, founder and chief executive of smartphone company Smartisan Technology, forwarded a statement posted by his livestreaming firm on Chinese microblogging platform Weibo on Tuesday, apologizing for selling fake and shoddy (劣质的) products after the wool sweaters they sold during a livestream on the platform last month turned out to be non-wool. According to the statement, the firm will make a triple repayment to more than 20, 000 customers who bought the fake products.

The post (帖子) soon became a trending topic on Chinese social media, with related hashtags[②] viewed over 300 million times as of Thursday.

Luo hosted his first e-commerce livestream earlier this year, ending with transactions of over 110 million yuan in just three hours.

Livestreaming e-commerce is a new business model that has combined entertainment with consumption and has become popular among consumers in recent years. The ads and sales on livestreaming platforms get extra attention, especially during big shopping promotions, such as the recently concluded "Double 11" shopping extravaganza (狂欢).

However, soon after the shopping frenzy (狂欢), the China Consumers Association exposed several cases that reflected a different side of the story. According to the association, Li Jiaqi's livestreams received complaints for not allowing consumers to return the products. Wang Han, a host on Hunan TV, was accused of being involved in creating fraudulent (欺骗的) sales revenue, and Li Xueqin, a newly rising influencer known for a variety talk show, for using bots (网上机器人) during her livestream.

China has tightened the management of livestreaming platforms.

On July 1, the China Advertising Association issued a regulation, and on November 6, the State Administration for Market Regulation published an instruction on regulating livestream sales events, clarifying the responsibilities and obligations of the involved bodies.

On November 13, the Cyberspace Administration also published a drafted regulation on the registration, marketing catalogs and protection of minors in such livestream events.

---

① 21 世纪英文报, 2020-12-18.

② 微博, Twitter, Facebook 等的主题标签, 以 # 开头, 后面通常是短语或词组, 如 #alibaba。

In the newly issued rules by the National Radio and Television Administration, livestreaming shows should be clearly classified, based on their content, as music, dance, singing, fitness, or games, among other categories.

In fact, regulations about livestream sales have already been made since it became an important part of e-commerce.

Passage 2

Brands and Marketing, the Serious Business of Being a Social Influencer[①]

It is a sure sign that a hot trend has reached the mainstream when the tax authorities catch up. This week China promised a tax-evasion crackdown on social-media influencers, who are paid by brands to promote products online to armies of followers. One of the big stars, Viya, a 30-something fashionista (时尚达人) known as the live-streaming queen, has already been fined $210m for not declaring her income. The size of that levy shows the sheer scale of the industry, which accounts for 12% of online sales in China. Outside China, influencers are also likely to have an enduring role in ecommerce (see Business section). For all firms with brands—and together those brands are worth over $7trn—it is time to realise that influencing is more than just a hobby.

The use of personal endorsements (担保、背书) used to be about harnessing existing celebrity power. Elizabeth Taylor touted Colgate-Palmolive's shampoo in the 1950s, and Michael Jordan's deal in 1984 with Nike revolutionised both basketball and branding. Influencers turn the logic on its head: selling things helps make them more famous. Through curated (精选的、策划的) feeds of clipped videos and filtered photos they offer recommendations to consumers, mingled with glimpses into their daily lives that give their artifice (诡计) an aura of authenticity. Sometimes they disclose how they are paid. Often, they do not.

Initially dismissed as credulous Gen-Z folk who had mistaken posting selfies for having a job, these entrepreneurs have become a big business, boosted further by the ecommerce surge from the pandemic. Total spending on influencers by brands could reach $16bn this year. Whereas the number of wannabe (想成名的) influencers outside China is in the millions, an elite of under 100,000 of them who have over 1m followers each get the bulk of revenues and the front seats at fashion shows.

---

①　Leaders, economist, 2022-04-02.

Their staying power suggests that they add value in several ways. They can save money: Elon Musk is an honorary influencer whose raucous (尖利刺耳的) online presence lets Tesla do without any conventional advertising (General Motors blew $3.3bn on it in 2021). Influencers' networks reach new audiences, particularly younger shoppers. Global brands can localise their appeal by cutting deals with them. In China local shopping festivals and style sensibilities matter, so transplanting marketing campaigns from the West does not work. And influencers are technologically proficient in a way that old-style brand ambassadors never were. They are quick to adapt to newer platforms like TikTok and to the ever-changing algorithms of older ones like Instagram.

Yet one-third of brands do not use influencers. They worry about tarnishing their reputation. Having a swarm of freelance advocates is riskier than the command-and-control campaigns of the "Mad Men" era. And the industry is a Wild West, awash with fraud and manipulation.

Despite this, ignoring influencers is a mistake. Their share of digital advertising budgets is still low at perhaps 3%, but it is rising fast. The boundary between entertainment and ecommerce is blurring. And the most popular marketing strategy of the 2010s—ads targeted through Google and Facebook—is under threat as new privacy standards, including on Apple's iPhone, make it harder to spy on potential customers.

To get the most out of influencers, brands should set a clear strategy. They should expect more regulation on consumer protection: China's crackdown may also include limits on spending and content rules. The guiding principle should be to use only influencers who disclose to their audiences that their posts are paid. As the Wild West phase ends, brands should also embrace new analytical tools that help them gauge (计算) the performance of influencers, sorting the con-artists (骗子) from the stars. It used to be said that only half of all advertising spending worked, but it was impossible to know which half. Now brands can control only half of what influencers say, but they may be able to calculate 100% of the value they add.

Critical Thinking and Questions:

1. What is live broadcasting and what are the benefits of it?

2. Why some brands don't use influencers and livestreaming according to the author?

3. What kind of words and expressions did the author use to express his opinion about

branding, marketing and livestreaming? What is his opinion on livestreaming?

4. What kind of regulations should be taken by the platform and government, enterprises or even an individual to cope with the problems of fake products online in cross-border ecommerce?

5. How about the future development of livestreaming in China and around the world?

More Resources:

1. 7 分钟看懂 search engine marketing[①].

2. Marketing Strategy 专项课程 - 4. The Marketing Plan[②].

3. Pricing Strategy An Introduction[③].

4. Mosh 完全版 HTML/CSS 课程 [④].

Keys-3

① https://v. qq. com/x/page/g07873wwv4i. html: 12-3-2023.

② https://www. bilibili. com/video/BV1u7411i7Wf/?p=29, 12-3-2023.

③ https://www. bilibili. com/video/BV1354y1a7eu/, 12-3-2023.

④ https://www. bilibili. com/video/BV1bX4y1N74d/?p=44, 12-3-2023.

Chapter 4

Logistics and Supply Chain in Cross-border Ecommerce
跨境电商物流和供应链

Objectives

1. Know logistics and logistics management

2. Know supply chain and supply chain management

3. Master the differences between logistics management and supply chain management

4. Master the logistic modes used in cross-border ecommerce

5. Understand 3PL and 4PL

Open Case: Watch the video and answer the questions

What is logistics management? (Watch the first 4 minutes among all 8:50.)

1. What's the difference between supply chain and logistics according to the video?

2. What are the 7 Rs of logistics?

3. What are the 4 functions of logistics?

4. What are the two key elements in the value proposition of logistics?

5. What are the goals of logistics?

视频资源链接

Logistics, derived from old French logisticque, is a compound word composed of Logis (the same as Lodge, means settling down, boarding house, hotel, mountain forest hut) and the Greek suffix -istikos. (-ics, means theory). It was originally a temporary place for hunters or business travelers to stay, and it extended to food, accommodation and material stacking and distribution. Another saying says that it originally referred to the arrangement of the army's vehicles and horses. That is logistics in the modern sense. With the development of modern information technology and ecommerce, logistics is imbued with rich meaning and content. The term is now used widely in business sectors, particularly by companies in the manufacturing sectors, to refer to how resources are handled and moved along the supply chain. We start from the most basic concepts: logistics and **supply chain**.

4.1　Logistics and Supply Chain 物流和供应链

The two are closely intertwined in the process of goods transportation and contributing to ecommerce cross-border transaction.

4.1.1　Logistics and Logistics Management 物流和物流管理

Logistics is the process of planning and executing the efficient transportation and storage of goods from the point of origin to the point of consumption. The goal of logistics is to meet customer requirements in a timely, cost-effective manner. It is also an overall process of managing how resources are acquired, stored, and transported to their destination. It revolves around the transportation and management of physical resources, see Figure 4-1.

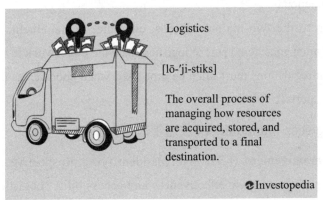

Figure 4-1　Logistics is more about transportation and warehousing[1]

Many companies specialize in logistics, providing the service to manufacturers, retailers and other industries with a large need to transport goods. Some own the full gamut of infrastructure, from jet planes to trucks, warehouses and software, while others specialize in one or two parts. FedEx, UPS, TNT and DHL are well-known third-party international logistics providers.

Typically, large retailers or manufacturers own major parts of their logistics network. Most companies, however, outsource the function to third-party logistics providers (3PLs, see more at 4.5.1).

---

① https://www. investopedia. com/, 14-2-2023.

4. 1. 1. 1　Functions of Logistics 物流的功能

Transportation and **warehousing** are the two major functions of logistics.

Transportation management focuses on planning, optimizing and executing the use of vehicles to move goods between warehouses, retail locations and customers. The transportation is multimodal and can include ocean, air, rail and road transportations. Logistics companies typically use **transportation management system (TMS)** software to help meet the demands of transport-related logistics.

Warehousing, or warehouse management, includes such functions as **inventory management** and **order fulfillment**. It also involves managing warehouse infrastructure and processes — for example, in a **fulfillment center**, where orders for goods are received, processed and fulfilled (shipped to the customer). Most companies use **warehouse management system (WMS)** software to manage the flow and storage of goods and track inventory. Most vendors of **enterprise resource planning (ERP)** software offer TMS and WMS modules, as well as more specialized components for inventory management and other logistics functions.

In addition to the two main functions, customer management, or global trade management, is often considered part of logistics since the **paperwork** to show compliance with government regulations must often be processed when goods cross national boarders or enter shipping ports[①].

4. 1. 1. 2　Logistics Management 物流管理

Logistics management (LM) involves identifying prospective distributors and suppliers and determining their effectiveness and accessibility. Logistics managers are referred to as logisticians. The goal of logistics management is to have the right amount of resources or input at the right time, getting it to the appropriate location in proper condition, and delivering it to the right customers. Take natural gas industry as an example, logistics management involves managing the pipelines, trucks, storage facilities, and **distribution centers** that handle oil as it is transformed along the supply chain. An efficient supply chain and effective logistical procedures are essential to reduce costs and to maintain and increase efficiency. Poor logistics leads to untimely deliveries, failure to meet the needs of clientele, and ultimately causes the business to suffer.

---

① https://www. techtarget. com/searcherp/definition/logistics, 14-2-2023.

As to the philosophy of logistics management, **lean logistics** is one of the guiding theories. Lean logistics originated from Toyota Motor Corporation of Japan. Its core is to eliminate any waste, including inventory, and develop a series of specific methods around this goal. It evolved from the concept of lean production and is the application of lean thinking in logistics management, reflecting the idea of continuous improvement and excellence every day. Lean logistics is to minimize waste while providing satisfactory customer service. The basic principles are that: (1) It starts from the perspective of customers rather than enterprises or functional departments to study what can produce value. (2) It determines the necessary steps and activities in the supply, production and distribution of products according to the needs of the entire value stream. (3) It creates a flow of value-added activities without interruption, detour, waiting and backflow. (4) It creates value driven only by customers. (5) It constantly eliminates waste and pursues perfection. This philosophy is closely related with **integration value preposition**.

4. 1. 2　Supply Chain 供应链

A supply chain[1] is a network of individuals and companies who are involved in creating a product and delivering it to the consumer, see Figure 4-2. It is a network link of relative parties participating logistics of products. Links on the chain begin with the producers of the raw materials and end when the van delivers the finished product to the end user.

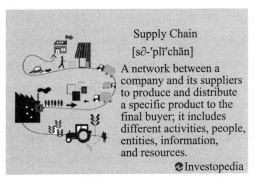
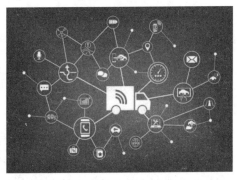

Figure 4-2　Supply chain[2]

A supply chain includes every step that is involved in getting a finished product or service to the customer. The steps may include sourcing raw materials, moving them to production,

---

①　This definition is defined in a narrow sense from the perspective of ecommerce. From the perspective of a whole country, a comprehensive consideration is closely related to a nations' supply chain safety, risk and strategy.

②　https://www. investopedia. com/terms/s/supplychain. asp, 14-2-2023.

then transporting the finished products to a distribution center or retail store where they may be delivered to the consumer. The **entities** involved in the supply chain include producers, **vendors**, warehouses, transportation companies, distribution centers, and retailers. The supply chain begins operating when a business receives an order from a customer. Thus, its essential functions include product development, marketing, operations, **distribution networks**, **finance**, and customer service, etc. Supply chains cover everything from production to product development to the information systems needed to direct these undertakings.

COVID-19 pandemic brought great damage to the supply chain and affected nearly every sector of the economy. Supplies of products of all kinds were delayed due to ever-changing restrictions at national borders and long **backups** in ports. At the same time, demand for products changed abruptly. Shortages developed as consumers hoarded essentials like toilet paper and baby formula. Masks, cleaning wipes, and hand sanitizers were suddenly in demand. Shortages of computer chips delayed the delivery of a wide range of products from electronics to toys and cars. Due to a relatively complete supply chain, the pandemic brought less damage to China than to other countries and the supply chain is rebounding back to its pre-covid, level at the end of 2022.

4.1.3 Supply Chain Management 供应链管理

Supply chain management (SCM) is the management of the flow of goods and services and includes all processes that transform raw materials into final products. It involves the active **streamlining** of a business's supply-side activities to maximize customer value and gain a competitive advantage in the marketplace. It is also the optimization of a product's creation and flow from raw material sourcing to production, logistics and delivery to the final customer.

SCM encompasses the integrated planning and execution of processes required to manage the *flows* of business, materials and goods, information and financial capital (the so-called 4 flows) in activities that broadly include demand planning, **sourcing**, production, **inventory management** and storage, transportation — or logistics — and returning **excess or defective products**, etc. Supply chain management relies heavily on business strategy, specialized software and collaboration. Because it's such an expansive, complex undertaking, each partner — from suppliers to manufacturers and beyond — must communicate and work together to create efficiencies, manage risk and respond to change quickly.

Facing global climate change and social development, **supply chain sustainability** has aroused more concerns. It covers environmental, social and legal issues and is closely related to corporate social responsibility and ESG (Environment, Social responsibility and corporate Governance) which evaluates a company's efforts on the environment and social well-being. It has become one of the major concerns for today's companies involved in cross-border ecommerce.

The concept of logistics has been transforming since the 1960s. The increasing intricacy of supplying companies with the materials and resources they need, along with the global expansion of supply chains, has led to a need for supply chain management. When supply chain management is effective, it could lower a company's overall costs and boost its **profitability** and increase **velocity**. If one link of the supply chain breaks, it can affect the rest of the chain. Supply chain management represents an effort by suppliers to develop and implement supply chains that are as efficient and economical as possible.

Typically, SCM attempts to control or link the production, shipment, and distribution of a product. By managing the supply chain, companies can cut excess costs and deliver products to the consumer faster. This is done by keeping a tight control of a company's production and inventories, distribution, sales, and the inventories of vendors. Some international companies, according to *The Gartner Global Supply Chain Top 25 in 2022*, like Cisco system and China's Lenovo, have great modern supply chain management capacity, see Figure 4-3. Cross-border ecommerce giant Alibaba Group ranked no.25 in the chart and Amazon is gaining more influence in supply chain management. Cross-border ecommerce is more closely related with the development of future supply chain.

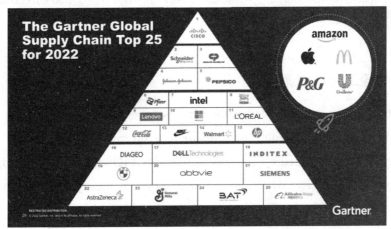

Figure 4-3　Top 25 supply chain companies[1]

---

[1]　http://www. gkong. com/item/news/2022/06/107899. html, 14-2-2023.

4. 1. 4 Differences and Similarities between LM and SCM
物流管理和供应链管理的异同

Logistic management could be seen as a part of supply chain management, contributing one *flow* in the 4 *flows* of supply chain. Firstly, they share commonalities:

1. Both revolve around the same flow of goods and services, from suppliers to manufacturers, to wholesalers, and finally to retailers or consumers.

2. Both share the same goal of meeting customer satisfaction by offering the best service in the greatest efficiency and lowest cost.

3. In accordance with the flow of goods and service, flows of information and fund are essential for the successful conduct for both. They are heavily and digitally internet and information-based.

They show differences mainly in the following aspects:

1. Logistics management refers to the activities related to product distribution within a company / organization, so it is task-based. While supply chain management is a net-based term that focuses on a wider range and is used to describe the whole business concept. It may start from the source of the product to its delivery to consumers, including all internal and external supply chain processes, covering logistics and transportation.

2. The primary consideration of the two shows difference. For logistics, it is to provide on-time delivery, and customer satisfaction is the primary consideration. For supply chain management, it focuses on the process to optimize the supply chain for gaining competitive advantage. Part of the chain may not be so cost-effective, but the whole chain is highly effective.

4. 1. 5 Logistics Engineering and Logistics Management
物流工程和物流管理

The two belong to different areas though closely related to logistics with the former focuses on technology side and the later focuses on management aspect. Logistics technology is mostly studied by students of **logistics engineering** with an engineering degree (engineering course) while logistics management is mostly studied by humanities and management majors with a management degree in universities or colleges.

Logistics engineering refers to the theories and methods related with logistics in the field of natural science and social science, as well as the general terms of facilities, equipment, devices and processes used in logistics activities. Logistics technology includes both *hard* logistics technology and *soft* logistics technology. Hard Logistics technology refers to the technologies of various mechanical equipment, transportation tools, **station facilities**, electronic computers and communication network equipment that are involved in organizing the material flow.

Soft Logistics technology refers to the systems of engineering technology, **value engineering technology** and **distribution technology** used to form a high-efficient logistics system. Technologies like **EDI** (electronic data Interchange), **RFID** (Radio Frequency Identification), barcode, **GPS** (global positioning system), **GIS** (geographic information system) and **cloud computing** are advanced applications in the field.

Logistics management mainly includes enterprise resource planning (ERP), material requirement planning (MRP), distribution requirement planning (DRP), logistics resource planning (LRP), **order point technology** and **just in time (JIT)** in production and inventory. JIT is a **stockless production** or **zero inventory** used especially in supermarket system.

In the modern era, the technology boom and the complexity of logistics processes have spawned logistics management software. And specialized logistics-focused firms expedite the movement of resources along the supply chain. One of the reasons that large online retailers like Amazon have come to dominate the retail landscape is the overall innovation and efficiency of their logistics along every link of the supply chain. Manufacturing companies choose to outsource the management of their logistics to specialists or manage logistics internally based on its cost-effectiveness and efficiency.

4.1.6　Reverse Logistics 反向物流

Regularly, logistics forwards goods to another country. In cross-border ecommerce, if a customer wants to return his goods due to various reasons, a backward logistics comes into being. It is called **reverse logistics**[1]. Reverse logistics experiences the same process of transportation and faces the same problems of customs clearance in both countries, which means the cost of logistics would be doubled. Due to high cost in reverse logistics, sellers or platforms would rather discard or destroy the excess goods produced in returning process. And there are environmental and social issues during the process. There are various definitions on reverse logistics and it could be defined

---

[1]　https://baike. baidu. com/item/%E9%80%86%E5%90%91%E7%89%A9%E6%B5%81/1198691?fr=aladdin, 21-2-2023.

from a narrow and a broad sense.

In a broad sense, reverse logistics is the process of planning, managing and controlling the effective flow of raw materials, inventories, final products and related information from the place of consumption to the starting point for the purpose of value recovery or reasonable disposal. The objects of reverse logistics are diverse, including used package, processed computer equipment, return of unsold goods, mechanical parts, etc. In short, reverse logistics covers the whole process from the recovery of returned, used, outdated, or damaged products or packages from customers to the final disposal. Reverse logistics is also the coordination of the complete, effective and efficient use of products and materials throughout the product life cycle.

The main contents of reverse logistics include four aspects:

(1) The purpose of reverse logistics is to regain the value of waste products or defective products, or to properly dispose of the final waste.

(2) The objects of reverse logistics are products, and containers used for product transportation, packaging materials and related information, etc. They flow from the end of the supply chain to the corresponding nodes along the channels of the supply chain.

(3) The activities of reverse logistics include recovery, detection, classification, remanufacturing and scrapping of the above objects.

(4) Although reverse logistics is the physical flow of goods, just like regular **forward logistics**, reverse logistics is also accompanied by the flow of funds, information and commodities.

In China, a narrow sense of reverse logistics is used. It is called **returned logistics**. In *the Logistics Terminology of the National Quality Standard of the People's Republic of China*[①] implemented on August 1, 2001, reverse logistics is referred as "returned logistics". It refers to the physical flow of goods formed by the repair and return of unqualified goods and the return of packaging containers used for turnover from the consumer to the supplier (seller). For example, it includes the reverse flow process of recycling pallets and containers used for transportation, receiving the returned goods from customers, collecting containers, raw material leftovers, and defective work-in-progress products in parts processing, etc.

---

① 《中华人民共和国国家质量标准物流术语》。

4. 1. 7   Top Shipping Logistic Companies 头部运输物流公司

In business world, logistics could be realized by shipping companies, **freight forwarder**, flight companies, international railway companies etc. Ocean transportation is the dominant way of logistics. It is necessary to have a general idea on the biggest shipping companies who are undertaking the main task of international logistics.

According to data provided by YCharts[1], as of September 10, 2020, **MAERSK** is an integrated transport and logistics firm with a revenue of $38.3 billion. The Denmark-based MAERSK operates a worldwide fleet of **tankers**, **supply ships**, **terminals**, and other vessels. In addition, the company also explores for and produces oil and gas and operates industrial businesses[2].

Nippon Yusen Kabushiki Kaisha (NYK) is the second largest and a transportation and logistics company facilitating services between international and domestic ports based in Japan. The company's primary businesses include **container transportation**, **cruise lines**, **specialized carriers**, and logistics, etc.

The third largest shipping company comes from China. COSCO SHIPPING Holdings is a shipping service company offering container and **bulk shipping**, **terminal operations**, and related services around the world.

Other international shipping companies like the Hong Kong-based Orient Overseas and the Israeli firm ZIM are popular shipping companies offering logistics and transportation services.

4. 1. 8   Maritime Container Transportation 海运集装箱运输

Just like traditional international trade, ocean container transport is still the most popular one. Maritime container transportation, also known as containerized transportation, is a popular mode of transportation carrying big quantities in international trade. The basic unit of international standard container is **TEU**. TEU(Twenty-foot Equivalent Unit**)** and **FEU**(Forty-foot Equivalent Unit**)** are two basic box types. The standard dimensions of a 20ft container are 8 feet in width, 8.6 feet in height and 20 feet in length, and that measurement is known as a TEU. One 40ft container is roughly two TEUs.

---

[1]   YCharts is a financial software company providing investment research tools including stock charts, stock ratings, and economic indicators in Chicago, USA.

[2]   https://www. investopedia. com/10-biggest-shipping-companies-5077534, 14-2-2023.

Container transportation has many advantages, such as facilitating the **mechanization** of port operations, thus improving the **loading and unloading efficiency**, greatly shortening the time of ships in the port, speeding up the turnover rate of ships, saving packaging costs, reducing cargo damage, and facilitating the connection of different transportation lines and vehicles, and carrying out door-to-door transportation. Container transportation rose in the 1930s and developed after World War II. The appearance of maritime container makes container transportation flourish.

More than 100 countries and regions in the world have formed a container transport network, with more than 400 container ports and more than 10,000 **berths**. All major routes have been containerized. Shanghai port, Ningbo port, Shenzhen port and Guangzhou port in China are among the top ten container ports in the world.

4.1.9　Duet Clearance in Ocean Transport 海派双清

In China's cross-border ecommerce, customs clearance is often a critical step in both export and import. In ocean transport, it is often conducted by the way of "maritime customs duet clearance", or "maritime duet customs clearance door to door". It refers to a one-stop logistics service for goods exported by sea from the port of departure to the port of destination, including one-stop services such as export customs declaration at the port of departure, maritime transportation, customs clearance at the port of destination and post port delivery.

Take export to the United States as an example. The price quoted is all inclusive, including the cost of domestic customs clearance and U.S. customs clearance. Among them, the domestic **trailer**, packing, **booking**, **customs declaration**, tax payment, customs clearance, container delivery and fulfillment in the destination country are basically handled by a **freight forwarder**. It is simple, direct and can save excessive transshipment. The customs clearance in American ports is carried out on the basis of a whole container, and very few customs clearance will be carried out in less than a container. Therefore, in the case of **bulk cargo consolidation**, once there is a problem with one shipment, the whole container of goods will be detained and then wait for release for a long time. Therefore, before the shipping to the United States arrives at the port, it is necessary to prepare the relevant data and customs clearance documents in advance and pay attention to the rules and regulations related to customs clearance.

4.2　Factors Influencing Logistics Freight 物流运费的影响因素

Logistics has long been *the pain point* that hurts the development of goods transportation, especially for those **huge piece (HP)**, **big-ticket item,** awkward length cargo or **heavy cargo** in the process of cross-border ecommerce for there are many uncertainties arising during the process and fees are charged based on weight, measurement and length, etc. The top three costs of cross-border ecommerce logistics are labor cost, international transportation cost and warehouse rent cost. Quite often logistic fees make up the major part of a quoted price for a certain products like clothes, dog's leash, etc. For the **freight**, it is calculated in the following way: total freight=domestic transportation fee (both at the importing country and the exporting country) + international transportation freight.

4.2.1　Freight Charge 运输费用

Logistic freights (rates) could be calculated on the basis of Weight, Volume (measurement) or Value. They charge differently for different countries based on physical distance, quantity of goods, modes of transportation, etc. Different companies publish their standard of freight to the public regularly.

As to cross-border transportation cost, it often includes two parts: domestic transportation cost and international transportation cost. Domestic transportation cost includes the transportation cost in importing country and exporting country. Cross-border transportation cost, no matter it is ocean, air, rail or road, makes up a main part of freight charge. A cross-national-border logistics is often called **First leg transportation** which could make up the largest share in freight. For articles of low value, such as **apparel** or dog's leash, the cost of product may be as low as $3-5 while the transportation cost may be more than 10 dollars. Occasionally, the cost of cross-border transportation, especially air transportation, could make up to 90% of a **quoted price**.

Different express companies and online cross-border platforms offer different **logistic freight rate**. Amazon has its FBA (Fulfillment by Amazon) system which is more expensive but fast and convenient for delivery service. Similarly, JD logistics offers logistic service for its own goods, while Cainiao logistics under Alibaba integrates several logistics companies into one logistic system. No matter what pattern it is, a general rule is that the faster, the more expensive. For international **commercial express**, like UPS, DHL, FedEx, their freight rate is way higher than **post services** which is often slower and cheaper. For airmail, it is the most expensive and the fastest, which is suitable for expensive and urgent goods like medical supplies and apple mobile phones, etc.

4.2.2　Flexibility and Resilience in Supply Chain 供应链的柔性和韧性

Today's ecommerce tends to be small: small quantity in purchasing and small adjustment happens all the time with a high turnover rate. With the development of modern technology, informationization is necessary for logistics service suitable to meet the flexibility and distribution of logistics. A comprehensive logistic matching service system is dynamically suitable for offering various service for different areas and different requirements. Goods should be delivered to consumers by using the most appropriate express in the most efficient and cost-saving way.

In cross-border ecommerce, products serve as either functional or innovative purpose for consumers. **Functional products** are those necessities that people use for everyday life. Vendor could offer them in a large quantity online and the needs are steady. While **innovative products** are those that meet a fashion or a trend and the needs is unpredictable. For example, some products become popular suddenly over a night and many followers would emerge after a few days. For different products, **efficient supply chain** is suitable for functional products and **responsive supply chain** is appropriate for innovative products which no one could predict. A flexible and resilient supply chain could meet both needs of functional goods and innovative goods.

4.2.3　JIT in Transportation and Fulfillment 运输和配送中的即时制

Just in Time means timely production, transportation and delivery in different situations. Logistics timeliness refers to the period from the time when the order is placed to the time when the goods are received. A strict requirement in timely logistics means a high logistics price. Timeliness is one of the key factors to be considered in logistic fees. For instance, On June 24,2020, **Zim Integrated Shipping Ltd**. (an Israel shipping company) opened the ecommerce express ship Zex route from Yantian Port in Shenzhen, China to Los Angeles Port in 12 days. The cross-border logistics time for exports from South China to ports in the west of the United States was reduced by about 20%. The ocean shipment from Ningbo China to Los Angeles, USA would last about 25-40days. **China Railway Express (CR Express)** offered the supply of medical protection materials to European countries during the covid-19 pandemic in 14-22 days and there are an average of over 10,000 freight trains every year since 2020 starting from China to European countries. While the ocean transport from south China to Europe would usually cost 35-40 days.[①]

4.3   Logistics Modes in Cross-border Ecommerce
跨境电商物流模式

4.3.1   China Post Air Parcel/Mail 中国邮政大 / 小包

China Post air mail is an international postal parcel business service carried out by China Post. It belongs to the category of postal air mail and is an economical international express service program. Post service takes subsidies from government and thus provides services at a low price. It can be sent to postal outlets in more than 230 countries and regions around the world. Similarly, Postal parcels belong to the operation of the post office and enjoy the priority of loading and delivery to the door. For critics of using postal service in cross-border ecommerce, it takes too much advantage of national resources and may plague some local governments to allocate subsidies to post office. However, the delivery speed is low and there are requirements and restrictions on weight and size. Because of the low fees, air mail dominants China's international logistics for small parcels. For parcels over 2kg or lengthy and irregular items, China post air parcel is more appropriate.

4.3.2   International Commercial Express 国际商业快递

The 4 big international expresses are UPS, FedEx, DHL and TNT. TNT has been acquired by UPS in 2012, see Figure 4-4. EMS is China's biggest express. It offers fast and convenient service with a high price.

The 5 big expresses conduct delivery and logistics business between two or more countries (or regions). Their business is about the delivery of letters, commercial documents and articles from one country to another country (or region). Parcels are to be inspected and released through border ports and customs between countries. After arriving at the destination country, it needs to be transshipped and then goes through the Last-mile delivery to the final customers.

---

① http://www. shuishangwuliu. com/xiaofangjiusheng/150875. html, 6-1-2023.

In China, **EMS (express mail service)** is dominant in transporting cross-border parcels and has a lot of business around the world. EMS provides international mail express service under the leadership of **the Universal Postal Union**. As this is a business under the name of a state-owned company, it enjoys priority in customs clearance, release and other segments.

Figure 4-4　International commercial express

4.3.3　Overseas Warehouse 海外仓

While the pandemic has attacked the business of global physical stores, and more and more consumers in various countries have turned to online shopping, Chinese enterprises have enhanced the **localization-oriented operation** of overseas warehouses, not only meeting local needs for employment and consumption, but promoting the development of local warehousing, logistics and ecommerce industries.

Overseas warehouse is considered to be one of the key elements to drive the growth of foreign trade. Data provided by the Ministry of Commerce shows that Chinese businesses now operate more than 1,900 overseas warehouses, covering a total floor area of 13.5 million square meters. Almost 90 percent of those facilities are in North America, Europe and South-east Asia. The development of overseas warehouses will help the country's brands go global, explore international market and improve efficiency of value chains.

Overseas warehousing enables quicker customs clearance and faster delivery, with some offering one- or two-day delivery services in destination countries. Exporters can also optimize their inventories and minimize possible losses from unmarketable goods within the warehouses, which can provide **amenities** such as localized return and repair services and improve the shopping experience for consumers.

Overseas warehouse is usually built by big third-party logistics companies or big ecommerce platforms. The purpose is to help micro, small and medium-sized enterprises to go global, drive Chinese brands and products from startups and innovative companies to grow their **market presence**. For example, Okorder.com, a cross-border e-commerce platform under the China National Building Material Group Co. Ltd (CNBM), has established an overseas warehouse in the Jebel Ali Free Zone in Dubai, the United Arab Emirates (UAE). With an area of 52,000 square meters, the warehouse sells products from various companies, including building materials, machinery and equipment, to over 10 countries in the Middle East and North Africa, such as Saudi Arabia, the UAE, and Algeria etc.

Modern overseas warehouses have automated assembly lines, three-dimensional warehouses, intelligent robots, and other facilities to increase goods storage efficiency and parcel sorting speed. Some new technologies like RFID[①](Radio Frequency Identification) are used to improve efficiency. Many international companies have established overseas warehouses and the competition is intense. FBA owns the leading overseas warehouses and is a model for others to follow.

4.3.4   Logistics Special Line 国际物流专线

For places where overseas warehouse is not available, a regular specialized carrier is appropriate. The cross-border logistics special line is generally used to transport goods to foreign countries by chartering plane, and then send them to customers through cooperative local logistics companies. It is a popular logistics mode. Popular logistics special lines are mainly serving the most developed ecommerce market like the United States, Europe, Australia and Russia. Yanwen logistics special line to Russia is a famous Chinese line.

The advantage of special logistics line is that it can collect large quantities of goods to a specific country or region, and reduce costs through **scale economy effect**. Therefore, its price is generally lower than that of commercial express. In terms of timeliness, special line logistics is slightly slower than commercial express, but much

---

① It is a technology of remote identification of objects by using radio waves. It is devised with the development of semiconductor. A RFID tag is widely used in Walmart supermarket and objects could be recorded without calculating in person. It is widely used in airport and other logistics system. In 2003, ISO standardized low-frequency RFID tags for animal identification and data collection and initialized standardized RFID systems for various applications. In 2004, American Food and Drug administration approved implanting RFID tags in humans and the use of m-chip cryptography for privacy. https://www. doc88. com/ p-6621321551421. html, 7-11-2022.

faster than postal parcels.

4.3.5　Frontier Warehouse 边境仓

Frontier Warehouse is a warehouse which is rented or built along the border of the neighboring country of the target country due to political factor or tariff policies. Goods are transported to the frontier warehouse in advance through various logistics, and the goods are delivered from the warehouse after receiving customer orders through the Internet.

Frontier Warehouse can be either absolute border warehouse or relative border warehouse. For absolute border warehouse, two countries are adjacent, and the warehouse is set up in the cities adjacent to the buyer's country and in the seller's country. For example, for cross-border ecommerce transactions between China and Russia, the warehouse is set up in Harbin or other Chinese cities along the Sino-Russian border.

Relative border warehouse means that when the two parties of cross-border ecommerce transactions are not adjacent, the warehouse is located in the border city of the neighboring country. The relative border warehouse is a frontier warehouse for the buyer and an overseas warehouse for the seller. For example, in order to do exporting business to Brazil, some logistics companies build warehouse in Peru which is neighboring Brazil.

4.3.6　Logistics of Bonded Area and Free Trade Zone 保税区与自贸区物流

Logistics in both **bonded area** and **free trade zone** are also popular business for cross-border goods in China. Bonded area, also known as the low tariff free zone, tax protected warehouse, is an area set, approved and governed by the customs. It subjects to the supervision and management of the customs and can store goods for a long time. **Comprehensive bonded area** is an economic area approved by **the State Council** and subject to special supervision by the customs. Bonded area enjoys less priority than the comprehensive bonded area. The would-be-exported goods could not get tax refund in a bonded area while in a comprehensive bonded area, the would-be-exported goods could be tax-refunded once goods entered the comprehensive area. Both areas enjoy the same policy in importing goods.

In 1990, Shanghai Waigaoqiao had China's first bonded area. Goods transported into the bonded area may be stored, modified, classified, mixed, exhibited, processed and manufactured. Foreign goods can freely enter and leave the bonded area and re-export abroad without paying customs duties. Goods entering the customs frontier need to pay customs duties, and tax can be refunded only after goods leaving the country. Before the emergence of the pilot Free Trade Zone, bonded area was the most open-up place in China.

Free trade zone (FTZ) is a special area designated by a country or region in order to promote the development of foreign trade, which unilaterally gives special duty preference and regulatory policies. China free trade zone refers to a multi-functional **Special Economic Zone** set up in and outside China, with **preferential tariff** and special customs supervision policies as the main means and **trade liberalization and facilitation** as the main purpose. China free trade zone is an important move of Chinese government to strive to build an upgraded version of China's economy. Its core is to create an international business environment that conforms to international practices and has international competitiveness for both domestic and foreign capital. China (Shanghai) pilot free trade zone is the first free trade zone in China, and also the first batch of free trade zones set up in China and outside the customs boundary. From September 2013 on, China has approved 21 pilot free trade zones.

In terms of geographical location, the pilot free trade zone is a combination of existing bonded areas; In terms of policy, the pilot free trade zone is an all-round upgrade of the existing bonded zone. The pilot free trade zone implements the policy of **"outside the customs and inside the national boundary"** and the bonded area implements the policy of "inside the customs and within the boundary". In brief, the free trade zone implements "tax refund for entering the zone" and the bonded area implements "tax refund for leaving the country".

4. 4　3PL, 4PL and Logistics Alliance
第三方物流、第四方物流和物流联盟

In cross-border ecommerce, there is a strong demand for a market-oriented, highly efficient, low-cost, differentiated, and sustainable supply chain with the help of modern information technology, comprehensive logistics and financial system. It evolves with an **integration arrangement**. Logistics companies may pursue the lowest single point cost, such as the lowest overseas warehouse and the lowest sea transportation, but they may not resolve problem from the perspective of a whole map. It is not only to minimize the cost of a single section, but to optimize the whole chain. The whole supply chain system evolves from 1PL, 2PL, 3PL, to 4PL and logistics alliance under the value proposition of integration, see Figure 4-5.

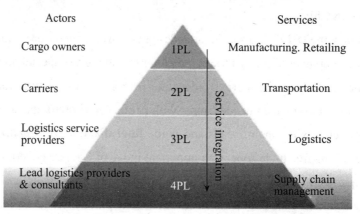

Figure 4-5　Evolvement of logistics and supply chain

4. 4. 1　Third Party Logistics (3PL or TPL) 第三方物流

With the development of information technology and the trend of economic globalization, more and more products are produced, sold, consumed, and circulated in the world, and the logistics activities are increasingly complex. However, the organization and operation mode of the first- and second-party logistics cannot fully meet the needs. At the same time, in order to participate in the world competition, enterprises must establish core competitiveness, strengthen their supply chain management, reduce logistics costs, and outsource logistics activities that are not their core business. Therefore, the third-party logistics came into being.

In the term "the third-party logistics", the third-party grows out of the "first party"—the **shipper (the seller) and the "second party"—the consignee (the buyer)**. It is neither a **consignor** nor a consignee, so it is called a third party. The third-party logistics enterprises undertake the logistics activities for the other two parties as an independent enterprise. Instead, it provides professional logistics services through cooperation with the first party and the second party. It does not own goods and does not participate in the purchase and sale of goods. As a matter of fact, it provides customers with a series, personalized and information-based logistics agency service constrained by contracts.

Third party logistics is also known as outsourcing logistics or contract logistics. It is a professional logistics company with substantial assets that provides logistics-related services to other companies, such as transportation, warehousing, inventory management, order management, information integration, fulfillment and added value service, or cooperates with relevant logistics service providers to provide more **one-stop service**s. The third-party logistics is also the service provided by the middleman in the logistics channel. The middleman provides all or part of the logistics services required by the enterprise in the form of a contract within a certain period. A third-party logistics provider is a company that manages, controls and provides logistics services for external customers. They do not occupy a place in the product supply chain. They are only the third party, but serve the product supply chain by providing a whole set of logistics activities.

The third-party logistics has a history of about 10 to 15 years. In the United States, the third-party logistics industry is considered to be in the development stage of the product life cycle. In Europe, especially in Britain, it is generally believed that the third-party logistics market has reached a certain degree of maturity. The proportion of using third-party logistics services in Europe is about 76%, and that in the United States is about 58%, and its demand is still growing. Research shows that 24% of non-third-party logistics service users in Europe and 33% in the United States are actively considering using third party logistics services. Some industry observers have estimated the size of the market and said that the entire third-party logistics industry in the United States has a market size equivalent to US $420 billion. The recent potential logistics market in Europe is estimated to be about US $950 billion.

There is a great potential for the third-party logistics market in the world. Most of the third-party logistics service companies have developed from the traditional "internal logistics" industry, such as warehousing, transportation, air transportation, sea transportation, freight forwarding and logistics department within the enterprise. They have achieved success by providing unique services according to different needs of customers. At present, there are hundreds of third-party logistics suppliers in the United States. Most of them are not third-party logistics service companies at the beginning, but gradually develop into the industry. Most of the service contents of the third-party logistics are concentrated in the traditional transportation and storage categories.

4.4.2　The Fourth-party Logistics 第四方物流

The Forth Party Logistics (4PL) is developed on the basis of 3PL. The concept of

4PLwas first proposed by Dow Baukness of **Accenture**[①]. Accenture defines "the fourth party logistics" as a supply chain **integrator**. It mobilizes and manages its own resources, capabilities and technologies as well as those of complementary service providers to provide a comprehensive supply chain solution. Therefore, the fourth party logistics is a supply chain integrator that provides comprehensive supply chain solutions. It may operate in a light-asset pattern.

The fourth party logistics has many advantages: provide customers with perfect services closest to their requirements; provide a comprehensive supply chain solution; use the information resources, management resources and capital scale of the fourth party to create a low-cost information application platform for enterprises. It can provide enterprises with low-cost information technology.

3PL mainly provides users with substantial and specific logistics operation services. The main disadvantage is that the technical level is not as advanced, and there are few value-added services for customers. On the contrary, 4PL specializes in logistics supply chain technology. It has rich experience in logistics management, supply chain management technology, information technology, etc. The fourth party logistics focuses on reducing the operating costs of enterprises through the optimization and integration of the entire supply chain. The idea of 4PL must be realized and verified by the actual operation of 3PL; 3PL is eager to get guidance from 4PL in optimizing the supply chain process and scheme. Therefore, only by combining the two can we provide better and comprehensive logistics operations and services.

A genuine "fourth party" usually embodies the following features: 1. provide better solutions or consolidation solutions. 2. be familiar with the resources of logistics sub-sectors and supporting industries. 3. able to integrate resources in various fields on the basis of solutions, jointly establish rules of business operation, and solve logistics or supply chain problems.

4.4.3　Logistics Alliance 物流联盟

Alliance is an organizational form between independent enterprises and market transactions. It is a relatively stable and long-term contractual relationship between enterprises for the needs of their own development in some aspects. Logistics

---

① An Ireland-headquartered high-tech company established in 1989 and ranked 78 in Fortune 500 in 2020.

alliance is a strategic alliance of enterprises based on logistics cooperation. It refers to a loose network organization formed by two or more enterprises through various agreements and contracts to achieve their own logistics strategic goals. They work in a complementary way in their own core businesses, jointly undertake risks and share benefits. In modern logistics, it is self-evident that whether to establish logistics alliance is one of the strategies for logistics enterprises. Compared with 3PL and 4PL, logistics alliance could offer more services of setting a certain standard for logistics and thus formed their own brand and logistics service standard, which distinguish their alliance from other logistics companies.

We must acknowledge the fact that the level of logistics is still in its infancy in China. Under the guidance of the 20th National Congress of the Communist Party of China, the 14th Five-Year Plan (2021-2025) has set a goal of establishing a modern logistics system. According to it the logistics industry is required to pay more attention to lowering costs and enhancing information capability. Logistics and supply chain is increasingly of great strategic value to our country. Developed countries, like Germany, UK, USA, etc. , have their own national safety strategy concerning modern supply chain.

📖 Words and Phrases 词汇和短语

logistics 物流

supply chain 供应链

warehousing 仓储

transportation management system (TMS) 运输管理系统

inventory management 存货管理

order fulfillment 订单配送

fulfillment center 配送中心

warehouse management system (WMS) 仓库管理系统

enterprise resource planning (ERP) 企业资源管理

paperwork 文书工作

logistics management 物流管理

distribution centers 配送中心

lean logistics 精益物流

integration value preposition 整合（思维）价值理念

entities（参与的）主体

distribution networks 配送网络

finance 融资；金融

backups 阻塞

supply chain management (SCM) 供应链管理

streamlining 流线型优化；流程优化

sourcing 资源组合；采购

inventory management 存货管理

excess or defective products 剩余或缺陷产品

supply chain sustainability 供应链可持续性

profitability 盈利能力

velocity 速度；效率

logistics engineering 物流工程

station facilities 站场设施

value engineering technology 价值工程技术

distribution technology 配送技术

EDI (electronic data interchange) 电子数据交换

RFID (radio frequency identification) 射频识别

GPS (global positioning system) 全球卫星定位系统

GIS (geographic information system) 地理信息系统

cloud computing 云计算

order point technology 订货点技术

just in time (JIT) 准时制（生产方式 / 物流）

stockless production 无库存生产方式

zero inventories 零库存

reverse logistics 逆向物流

forward logistics 正向物流

returned logistics 回收物流

freight forwarder 货代；货物代理人

MAERSK 马士基公司

tankers 油轮

supply ships 补给船；运输船

terminals 场站（如机场、火车站、码头等）

Nippon Yusen Kabushiki Kaisha（NYK）日本邮船株式会社

container transportation 集装箱运输

cruise lines 邮轮

specialized carriers 专线（运输）

bulk shipping 散货运输

terminal operations 场站运营

the pain point 痛点

huge piece (HP) 大件

big-ticket item 昂贵件

heavy cargo 重大件

freight 运费

first leg transportation 头程运输

apparel 服装

quoted price 报价

logistic freight rate 物流运费率

commercial express 商业快递

post services 邮政服务

flexibility and resilience in supply chain 柔性供应链

turnover rate 换手率；周转率

functional products 功能性产品

innovative products 创新型产品

efficient supply chain 有效性供应链

responsive supply chain 反应型供应链

Zim Integrated Shipping Ltd. 以星综合航运有限公司

China Railway Express (CR Express) 中欧班列

maritime container transportation 海运集装箱

TEU 20 英尺标准箱；标箱

FEU 40 英尺箱

mechanization 机械化

loading and unloading efficiency 装卸效率

berths 停泊位

duet clearance in ocean transport 海派双清

trailer 拖车；挂车

booking 订舱

customs declaration 海关申报

freight forwarder 货代

bulk cargo consolidation 散货拼柜

EMS (express mail service) EMS 邮政快递

the Universal Postal Union 万国邮政联盟

China Post air mail 中国邮政小包

China Post air parcel 中国邮政大包

bonded area 保税区

free trade zone 自贸区

comprehensive bonded area 综合保税区；综保区

the State Council 国务院

Free Trade Zone (FTZ) 自由贸易区

Special Economic Zone 经济特区

preferential tariff 优惠税

trade liberalization and facilitation 贸易自由化、便利化

outside the customs and inside the national boundary 境内关外

localization-oriented operation 本地化运营

amenities 便利设施

customs clearance 清关

scale economy effect 规模经济效应

Frontier Warehouse 边境仓

third party logistics (3PL) 第三方物流

shipper 发货人

consignee 收货人

consignor 发货人

one-stop service 一站式服务

integration arrangement 整合思维

Accenture 埃森哲咨询公司

integrator 集成商

omni-channels 全渠道

the forth-party logistics 第四方物流

logistics alliance 物流联盟

Exercise 练习

I. Reflections and Critical Thinking Questions.

1. What are the differences and similarities between logistics management and supply chain management?

2. What are the logistic modes in China's cross-border ecommerce?

3. What are 3PL and 4PL?

4. What do you think of the significance of supply chain for China?

II. True or False

1. Logistics is about goods transportation from the starting point to the final destination. (　　)

2. Medical supplies and Apple mobile phones which are urgently needed could be transported by commercial express like FedEx or UPS. (　　)

3. Cross-border ecommerce ocean transport is mostly done in the way of containers. (　　)

4. Double clearance of the customers is suitable for all countries. (　　)

5. Parcels in China post air mail is much safer than that in China post ail parcel. (　　)

6. A mahogany chair could be delivered to the United States through China post airmail. (　　)

7. Bonded area and the comprehensive bonded area enjoy the same tariff policy while comprehensive bonded area is bigger than bonded area. (　　)

8. Overseas warehouse represents the philosophy of localization operation. (　　)

9. Logistics special line is oriented to a big market where there are a big group of consumers. (　　)

10. Third party logistics is irrelevant to both the consignor and the consignee. (　　)

11. The 3PL could be an outsourcing process of logistics service for sellers on cross-border ecommerce platforms. (　　)

12. The fourth party logistics is developed on the basis of the third party logistics. (　　)

III. Nouns Explanation

1. Logistics, supply chain, logistics management and supply chain management

2. Duet clearance in ocean transport

3. China Post air mail; China Post air Parcel

4. bonded area; comprehensive bonded area; free trade zone

5. overseas warehouse and frontier warehouse

6. 3PL, 4PL, logistics alliance

IV. Reading and Critical Thinking

E-commerce logistics: Formula races[①]

When it comes to delivery, Chinese tech titans take divergent routes

In 2019 RICHARD LIU told couriers (快递员) working for JD.com that the Chinese e-commerce giant he founded would cancel their base pay after a 2.8bn yuan ($438m) loss the previous year, its 12th consecutive one in the red. Riders(快递员) would make only a commission on deliveries. If the company did not cut back on spending, Mr. Liu warned, it would go bust(破产) in two years.

Far from collapsing, two years on JD Logistics, JD.com's delivery division, is on a roll, fuelled by a boom in Chinese e-commerce. Its parent company's revenues jumped by 39%, year on year, in the first quarter, to 203bn yuan. On May 26th Pinduoduo, an upstart rival that also offers customers delivery by JD Logistics couriers, reported quarterly sales of 22bn yuan, 239% higher than a year ago (2020).

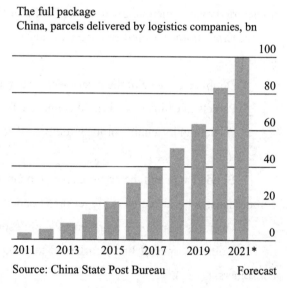

The full package
China, parcels delivered by logistics companies, bn

Source: China State Post Bureau   Forecast

The State Post Bureau expects logistics companies to deliver more than 100bn parcels this year (2021), twice as many as in 2018. Overall spending on logistics in China is projected to hit 16trn yuan in 2021 and surpass 19trn yuan by 2025. That would make it the world's largest market. The logistics business has also avoided the worst of the crackdown against Chinese big tech, which has seen firms such as Alibaba and Tencent (which owns a large stake in JD.com) taken to task by the Communist authorities over their growing power.

---

① Economist—Business, 29-5-2021.

Domestic and foreign investors have been pouring money into the industry, say lawyers working on deals involving such businesses. JD Logistics has attracted investments from big private-equity groups such as Sequoia China (红衫中国) and Hillhouse Capital (高瓴资本). The market buzz around the firm is as frenetic as the pace at which its 190,000 workers fulfil and ferry orders. On May 21st it raised $3.2bn in Hong Kong's second-largest initial public offering this year. Its shares are scheduled to begin trading on May 28th. The company's backers are betting that its Amazon-like approach of creating a fully integrated delivery network has more mileage than a similar offering from SF Express, a stodgier (古板的) incumbent similar to FedEx, or a rival model championed by Alibaba, which has plumped (变大) for a more distributed system.

JD Logistics is the only large Chinese delivery service to grow out of an e-commerce parent. It became a separate entity from JD.com in 2017, in part so that it could take orders from other online retailers. It still delivers the bulk of JD.com's packages but a large chunk of its revenues now comes from orders outside the group. By owning much of its technology, lorries and warehouses, and directly employing staff, the firm has been able to ensure faster delivery times while monitoring quality. It operates China's largest integrated logistics system, covering a good's entire journey and including a fully autonomous fulfilment centre in Shanghai and driverless vehicles. The system can also flip into reverse, sending customer feedback to product designers that, JD Logistics claims, helps it produce better products and bolster brands.

Contrast that with Cainiao, in which Alibaba has a controlling stake. It does not own many of the logistics assets in its network. Instead it allows around 3,000 logistics companies employing some 3m couriers to plug into its platform. Its aim is to integrate and streamline (整合) the vast delivery resources that already exist across China, rather than build its own. The company has teamed up with most large logistics services—and taken investments from them as well. Alibaba, for its part, has bought minority stakes in several large operators as a means of exerting more influence over the industry. Cainiao is not publicly listed and does not disclose many operational details or, for that matter, how exactly it makes money.

In terms of revenues, both JD Logistics and Cainiao trail (效仿) SF Express. Similarly to JD Logistics, that firm operates its own network. It still leads the market in "time-definite" delivery, a service that requires couriers to pick up and drop off parcels on a rapid, predetermined timetable. Like FedEx in America but unlike JD and Cainiao, it did not emerge from the tech industry, so lacks its rivals' technological chops (优势).

Which model emerges victorious will ultimately depend on which best controls costs, thinks Eric Lin of UBS, a bank. JD Logistics may have to lower prices further as it tries to get more business beyond JD.com. Analysts predict it could lose a combined 12bn yuan over the next three years, and turn a profit only in 2024. SF Express is spending heavily to try to match JD's and Cainiao's tech prowess. Its share price has fallen by around half since it issued a profit warning in April; it is expected to record a net loss of at least 900m yuan in the first quarter. Jefferies, an investment bank, points to SF Express's troubles as a clear sign of an ongoing price war.

In the long run Cainiao's asset-light model may enable it to keep spending in check. But for the time being it, too, is thought to be having trouble containing costs. Like its rivals it must fend off new specialist competitors offering cut-price services in areas like cold-chain and last-mile delivery. Average delivery prices in America have increased by about 5% annually in recent years, according to Bernstein, a broker. In China they have been falling at an average rate of 10% for the past decade. As China's online shoppers get their goods ever more quickly, investors may need to brace for longer waiting times before their logistics returns finally arrive.

Critical Thinking and Questions:

1. What is logistics and what are the functions of logistics?

2. What are the features of JD Logistics, Cainiao logistics and SF Express according to the paper?

3. What are the predicaments for JD logistics, SF Express and Cainiao's model in the last two paragraphs?

4. How to develop better logistics for China's cross-border ecommerce?

More Resources:

1. 10 Biggest Shipping Companies[①].

---

① https://www. investopedia. com/10-biggest-shipping-companies-5077534, 14-2-2023.

2. Third-party logistics a standout sector amid robust economic recovery[1].

3. 京东物流美国"洛杉矶 3 号仓"正式投入使用，新京报，2023-02-21[2].

4. 京东物流持续发展海外基础设施建设，金融界，2023-01-22[3].

Keys-4

[1]　http://www. chinadaily. com. cn/a/202105/07/WS60949bc9a31024ad0babc6a8. html, 14-2-2023.

[2]　https://baijiahao. baidu. com/s?id=1758443226115862933&wfr=spider&for=pc, 24-3-2023.

[3]　https://baijiahao. baidu. com/s?id=1755698232479416785&wfr=spider&for=pc, 24-3-2023.

Chapter 5

Cross-border Ecommerce Payment
跨境电商支付

Objectives

1. Know various types of payment for cross-border ecommerce

2. Master benefits of mobile payment

3. Master the flow chart of money in cross-border ecommerce

4. Know Alipay, WeChat Pay and PayPal, Apple pay, etc.

5. Understand the importance of fin-technology in the creation of cross-border ecommerce payment

Open Case: watch the video and answer questions

Video: Harmony + BUSD – payment solutions for cross-border finance (3:55)

Questions:

1. What are the strengths of blockchain in cross-border ecommerce?

2. What are the new generation of stable coins backed?

3. What is the present situation of stable coins?

4. What is Binance?

5. What are the procedures in international remittance in the case of Alice under the blockchain system?

视频资源链接

Getting revenue and profit is the backbone of cross-border business. In the year of 2020, the volume of online payments surged due to the Covid-19 pandemic and worldwide online payments from consumers represented a market of over $5 trillion. Third-party payment institutions and business firms that handle large volume of transactions (mostly the large banking and credit firms) would extract a certain percentage of money as a commission from the transactions (generally 2% – 5%) in the form of fees. Given the size of ecommerce market, competition for online payments is also spirited. New forms of online payment, at present, mobile payment, are expected to attract a substantial part of this growth.

Payment for traditional international trade is still largely based on traditional payments, that is, **remittance, collection, letter of credit**, etc. Remittance is preferable to a seller because the seller could get money directly from the buyer when business is conducted. As a popular form of remittance, 30% – 50% **T/T**[①]**(telegraphic transfer) advance payment** is welcome to start their business and secure money. Collection and letter of credit are complementary for cross-border business. In cross-border B2B ecommerce, payment is done by both traditional payment and online payment. While for B2C cross-border ecommerce, online money transfer is in dominance.

A lot of newly developed science and technology contribute to the emerging of new payments (mobile platform, e-wallet, **block chain technology**, **cryptocurrency** etc.), and new types of purchasing relationships (such as business conducted between individuals online) have created both a need and an opportunity for the development of new payment systems. With the emerging of ecommerce and the rapid development in encryption, computing and transmission technology (for example, the **Near-Field Communication (NFC)** technology started from Apple Pay in Oct. 2014), ecommerce payment varies a lot in different countries concerning payment traditions and internet & web infrastructures.

Ecommerce business in different places may adopt different payment systems. European mainland payment (for example, Klarna, Sofort and Giropay are used for ecommerce online payment in Germany[②]) is different from that of north Europe, where Trustly is widely used in Sweden; Latin American payment (mainly bank card, credit card or pay by cash) is different from the payment in North America (the United States and Canada are big users of PayPal, together with credit card like Visa card or Master card, etc.). Boleto is widely used in Brazil while Webmoney and Kiwi are popular local payment systems in Russia. Local markets like India, and countries in southeast Asia have their own electronic payment systems or even **cash on delivery (COD)**. For Example, as a new emerging cross-border ecommerce market, Indonesia users have a few ways to pay for online products. They may use third-party payment like Shopee Pay, OVO, Dana, Doku,

① There are often 3 forms of remittance: payment by T/T in advance; payment by T/T after shipping 7 days later or payment by T/T after customer receiving the goods; for example, an advanced payment of 30% as down payment, and the balanced will be paid off after shipping 7 days.

② https://zhuanlan. zhihu. com/p/200740617, 1-1-2023.

LinkAja, bank account transfer (the most popular way of paying), ATM transfer, personal internet banking, or even COD.[1] Credit card payment in Indonesia is still in the state of low **permeability**, and the percentage is estimated to be as low as 2%. While in Malaysia, online banking payment (for example, by using FPX[2]) and e-wallet (such as Boost, Grab Pay, and Touch'n Go eWallet) go hand in hand in practice. While in the Philippines[3], COD may be the most popular way of payment.

5. 1　Types of Electronic Payment 电子支付类型

Modern electronic payment is gaining popularity around the world with the widespread of cross-border ecommerce retailing. Classifications of e-payment could be very distinctive in different places. This chapter follows China's classification. According to the People's Bank of China, considering the medium used in electronic payment, it could be divided into the following types: **online payment**, telephone payment, mobile payment, **point of sale terminal transaction (POS)**, automatic teller machine (ATM) transaction and other electronic payments, see Table 5-1. And these types may be overlapped.

Table 5-1　Types of electronic payment

Types	subtypes	Example(s)	Areas or regions
Online payment	Online banking payment	Online account transfer	B2B business
	Third party payment	Alipay, WeChat Pay, Apple Pay, Google Pay, Samsung Pay	B2C business China, European countries, Middle East , Southeast Asia
Telephone payment	-		B2C business
Mobile payment	-	PayPal, Alipay, WeChat Pay, JD Pay	B2C business The United States, Canada, China
POS payment	-		B2C business
ATM payment	-		B2C business
Card-swiping payment	-	Debit card swiping Credit card swiping	B2C business
code scanning payment	-	QR Code Scanning	B2C business China
Cash on Delivery	-	Cash payment	Vietnam, the Philippines

---

[1]　https://zhuanlan. zhihu. com/p/479276877, 1-1-2023.

[2]　FPX is a real-time online payment gateway. It is similar to China UnionPay.

[3]　https://www. eservicesgroup. com. cn/news/84132. html, 1-1-2023.

5. 1. 1　Online Payment 线上支付

Online payment, in a broad sense, is based on the Internet, using a certain digital financial tool supported by bank to conduct financial exchange between buyers and sellers. It fulfills the functions of online money transfer, cash flow, fund settlement, **query statistics** etc. from buyers to financial institutions and merchants, thereby providing financial support for e-commerce services and other services. Payment could be completed through banks or through a third-party platform to pay for goods or services.

For cross-border ecommerce, online payment, especially **the third-party online payment** is skyrocketing during recent years and a lot of third-party payment companies are springing up and offering their services either locally or globally. Among them, **PayPal** is the most successful and widely used one around the world while in the biggest ecommerce market — China, **Alipay** and **WeChat Pay** are two dominant e-payment systems.

5. 1. 2　Telephone Payment 电话支付

Telephone payment is an offline form of electronic payment. It refers to the way that consumers can directly complete payment from their personal bank accounts through the banking system by using a telephone [fixed line telephone, mobile phone, **Personal Handy-phone System (PHS)**] or other similar terminal devices.

5. 1. 3　Mobile Payment 移动支付

Mobile payment is a new payment method that uses mobile devices to complete payment by wireless means. The mobile terminal used for mobile payment may be made for a product or service through a portable electronic device like a mobile phone, a **PDA (personal digital assistant)** or a tablet. Mobile payment could be done either online or offline. If you pay by Apple Pay at a Macdonald store, the payment is offline payment. If you pay for online shopping through the internet by using your mobile phone, it is online mobile paying.

Besides, **Mobile P2P (peer-to-peer) payment** is gaining more popularity after the covid-19 pandemic in places of developed countries, China, wealthy Middle-east countries, East Asian and some Southeast Asian countries. If you buy some fruits at a street corner vendor and pay by scanning the QR code of WeChat or Alipay, it is one form of the most popular Mobile P2P payment. We will learn more later in this chapter.

5. 1. 4　Offline Payment 线下支付

Converse to online payment, there still exists offline payment in the transaction of cross-border ecommerce in some less developed countries or in areas where credit card payment is still in the primary stage or places where ecommerce just started at an early stage. For example, though Vietnam is a fast-growing economy in recent years and cross-border ecommerce is developing rapidly, Cash on Delivery payment is still prevalent there.

5. 2　Popular Practice in CBEC Payment 跨境电商主要支付实践

This part would focus on the small-sum transaction of retail ecommerce payment which is newly developed during the past decades and suited to cross-border ecommerce. As one of the most popular tools of online payment, credit card is popular in both North America and EU countries.

5. 2. 1　Credit Card Payment 信用卡付款

International credit card collection generally refers to international credit card online payment, which is generally used for small amount collection under US $1000 in B2C business. It is popular in North America and Europe where ecommerce market is well-developed. Credit card is mostly used for online retailing: the main categories are shoes and clothing, accessories, daily necessities, electronic products, health products, virtual games and ticket or hotel booking etc.

Cross border e-commerce websites can open **ports** for receiving credit card payments from overseas banks through cooperation with **international credit card organizations** such as Visa and MasterCard, or cooperate directly with overseas banks.[①] At present, **Visa, Mastercard, America Express, JCB (Japan Credit Bureau) and Diners Club** are the top five credit card brands in the world.

Its advantages are obvious. As the most popular payment method in Europe and the United States, the number of credit card users is large. The disadvantages are also obvious. The **access mode** is troublesome, the deposit is required, the charge is high, and the payment sum is small. With some illegal **black card**s spreading around, there is a risk of being refused to pay.

---

① All the credit cards are subjected to the supervision of the international credit card organization. Banks cooperate with credit card organization to issue their credit card.

5.2.2　Offshore Bank Account 离岸银行账户

Because of foreign currency control, Chinese mainland cross-border ecommerce firm would apply a Hong Kong company account in order to collect foreign currencies, and the HK account is thus called offshore bank account. A Chinese company could similarly open an account in other places like Singapore to conduct offshore business and reduce the risk of exchange rate fluctuation. Offshore accounts can be used to collect foreign currencies like US dollars, Singapore Yuan, or EU Euro etc., but not directly collect RMB. Offshore RMB is also a kind of foreign exchange. The commonly used foreign exchange is US dollars, Hong Kong dollars, Pounds, Euros, offshore RMB etc. And you can exchange foreign currencies into RMB and transfer it to domestic bank accounts. Offshore accounts enjoy great advantages of money transfer freedom, but at present, the threshold for opening offshore accounts is high, and it is difficult for small start-ups to open such accounts. Big and middle-sized enterprises engaged in international trade have a need to handle offshore accounts.

5.2.3　Mobile Payment 移动支付

Many banks have recently adopted fin-technology into their banking apps that allow customers to pay for online shopping or send money instantly to others directly from their bank accounts. In China, mobile payments are also made on site at stores by scanning a barcode on an app on your phone, accepting payments from convenience stores to large, multi-national retailers. Mobile payments work much the same as credit cards, without the need to reach for your wallet or purse.

Mobile payments first became popular in Asia and Europe before becoming more common in the United States and Canada. Early on, mobile payments were sent by text message. Later, technology enabled pictures of checks to be taken via cell phone camera and sent to the payment recipient. This technology eventually morphed into mobile check deposit capabilities for banking apps.

Since 2014, apps such as PayPal and Apple Pay were developed. They also allow users to simply tap their phone against a contactless credit card terminal, paying instantaneously. More Competitors follow Apple Pay. Companies like Google and Samsung, Alibaba and Tencent, released their respective mobile payment apps in the wake of Apple Pay's success. We have stepped into an age of mobile payment and life has been changed profoundly by mobile payment.

5. 2. 3. 1　Benefits of Mobile Payment 移动支付的益处

The most obvious benefit of mobile payments is the elimination of a physical wallet, which brings great convenience to its users. Not reaching and pulling out cash not only saves time but is safer as nobody is able to see the contents of your wallet or purse. Since individual security codes are generated by the mobile service for each transaction, this method of payment is significantly safer than using a physical card. Touch ID in the form of a fingerprint scan or **PIN (Personal Identification Number)** input makes mobile payments more secure than a physical credit card. Merchants usually will not check identification, so accepting mobile payments is a smart move for them as well, as they will not have to deal with fraudulent activity as much.

An additional benefit is privacy. When you are with other people, they are not able to tell what card you have. Users with low credit scores and credit cards with low limits and high **APRs (Annual Percentage Rate**[1]) might not want, say, an interviewer or partner to know these things, and mobile payments offer an additional level of personal privacy.

Mobile payment developed greatly on the base of NFC technology. Near-field Communication (NFC) is a short-range wireless technology that makes your smartphone, tablet, wearables, payment cards, and other devices even smarter. Near-field communication is the ultimate in connectivity. With NFC, you can transfer information between devices quickly and easily with a single touch—whether paying bills, exchanging business cards, downloading coupons, or sharing a research paper.

5. 2. 3. 2　Mobile Payment App 移动支付应用

Mobile payment apps like Apple Pay and PayPal's Venmo[2] have grown exponentially

---

[1]　According to the Consumer Financial Protection Bureau (CFPB), an APR is the price you pay for borrowing money. In other words, it's the yearly rate you'll pay if you carry a balance, and it can vary from lender to lender. For example, let's say that you have two credit cards. The APR of one card may be 10. 99% and the APR of another might be 15. 99%. Your credit score is taken into account by creditors when determining your APR, with a higher credit score generally resulting in a lower rate, https://www. nasdaq. com/articles/what-is-apr, 15-11-2022.

[2]　Venmo is an application software launched by PayPal. It is interesting and simple, and can be used for transfer between friends and consumption on e-commerce platforms. Users can also use their favorite Emoji to add notes to the transfer, or comment on friends' stories and like them. Venmo can easily check the financial status. The use of the balance, bank card account number, debit card or prepaid card are all free, but the use of credit card needs to charge 3% commission. Users can purchase, pay installments or transfer money to friends on Venmo, which can better avoid the demand for cash. In addition, Venmo users can choose to share what they have purchased on social networks, and then view and comment on the purchased goods in their feeds. Venmo is especially popular among young people. 25% of people under the age of 24 in USA in 2020 were using this app. They mainly pay for their friends.

since their launch. Users will find solace in their ease of use and exceptional security. Many big firms designed their apps for mobile payment, like Starbucks and others. The Starbucks mobile-pay app allows you to order on your way, and then just walk in (or drive-through) and pick up your order without waiting in line. Their mobile payment app had nearly 22 million active users as of the end of 2020. The app was rolled out to all stores in USA as early as 2011. Meanwhile, other merchants have been upgrading their credit card payment processing devices in order to enable more secure **EMV (ease of movement value)** technology, and many smartphones are ready for tap-and-pay use. Big companies like PayPal, Zelle, Cash App[①], and Google Pay offer popular mobile payment services.

American attitude on mobile payment is in sharp contrast to that of Chinese consumers, who have embraced a cash-free life. Millions of Chinese consumers use mobile payments. They use their mobile phones to pay for taxis and meal delivery, in Walmart stores, and at mom-and-pop market stands. Alipay, owned by Alibaba, is China's dominant mobile payment service. And WeChat Pay is the second. In China and in other developing nations, where many have never used a traditional bank, many newly minted consumers are avoiding banks and substituting with a mobile payment service. Alipay users can deposit their money in a money market account that pays the investor higher interest rates than traditional bank savings accounts.

5. 3　Electronic Payment in China 中国的电子支付

No other country in the world could see the prosperity of electronic payment like China. China also boosts the most developed e-payment system in ecommerce around the world. In the year of 2019 before the pandemic, China's value of third-party mobile transactions totaled over 226 trillion RMB while American consumers only reached about $110 billion via **proximity mobile payments**.

5. 3. 1　Flow Chart of CBEC Payment 跨境电商支付流程

A value chain is involved in the payment of cross-border ecommerce. Different parties and institutions cooperate closely in this fin-tech industry.

---

① PayPal has one of the largest international online payment transfer systems. Zelle is another one of the largest digital instant transfer platform in the United States. Cash app is another American multi-functional transfer and payment tool. They transfer and receive payment as long as you know the phone number, email or Cash App user name of the other party. You can transfer money instantly without adding friends in advance.

5. 3. 1. 1 Flow Chart of Importing Payment 跨境代付 / 境外收单业务

For cross-border ecommerce goods importing, a third-party payment institution is used to pay foreign currencies to **foreign vendors**. To be specific, when domestic consumers buy products through ecommerce platforms by paying local currency RMB, the third payment institution, working as an agent, would change RMB into foreign currencies, and pay foreign currencies to foreign online sellers. In this way, the foreign vendors could collect their own currency and get their revenue, see Figure 5-1.

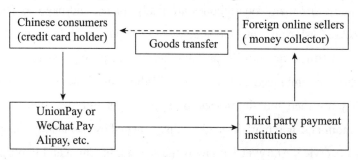

Figure 5-1 Chart of cross-border ecommerce payment in importing

5. 3. 1. 2 Flow Chart of Exporting Payment 跨境代收 / 外卡收单业务

For cross-border ecommerce, just like traditional overseas trade, selling goods, **acquiring orders** and getting revenue are the critical steps of ecommerce. When domestic sellers sell goods on cross-border ecommerce platforms to foreign consumers, the payment agent does the refinancing business by converting foreign currencies into local currencies and does the money settlement for sellers, see Figure 5-2. In the flow chart, payment institutions offer financial passages for the exchange of domestic currency and foreign currency and promote the conduct of foreign trade. There are mainly two types of payment institutions serving the function: the third-party payment platform and commercial bank.

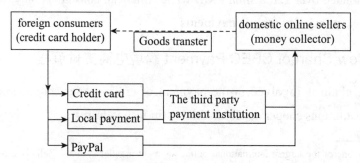

Figure 5-2 Chart of cross-border ecommerce payment in exporting

In Figure 5-2, for the third-party payment institution (platform), consumers should firstly register their name and their bank card. It is easy to use for both sides. Consumers could pay and sellers could collect their money with the service of the third-party payment system directly. For example, Chinese sellers on eBay could collect their payment by using PayPal (PayPal is a subdiary company of eBay) while Chinese consumers on eBay could pay easily through PayPal to buy their items through the platform. The main task of a third-party is to collect foreign currency and change the foreign currency to a certain local currency. In this case, PayPal is also a third-party payment institution (party). They make money by commission and other value-added service such as financing and data analysis and predication, etc.

In the flow chart, there are three ways of acquiring foreign currencies in cross-border ecommerce: by foreign bank cards, by overseas local payment and by PayPal. The first one, bank card payment, especially credit card payment, are popular around the world. In cross-border ecommerce, 70% ebusiness could be finished by credit card especially in developed countries. Overseas local payment is prevalent in some local development markets like Brazil (Boleto), Russia (Webmoney, Kiwi) and even Germany (SofortBanking). PayPal is widely used in as many as 200 countries and has a wide variety of as many as 100 currencies with 300 million users.

Many cross-border ecommerce platforms have a cooperative partnership with many international bank cards like American's Visa Card, Masters Card, American Express Card, Japan's JCB (Japan Credit Bureau) and China's Union Pay, etc. Consumers could bond their card to the platform and do the payment when buying. They even could pay by double currencies on some platforms. For example, you could pay US dollars and RMB to buy what you need on some websites. Some American consumers could buy goods on Lightinthebox by using their credit card or bank card.

The third-party payment institutions often cooperate with foreign commercial banks or other financial institutions to collect money for Chinese online sellers. Commercial banks are subjected to the rules and regulations of international bank card organizations. In practical business, once some well-known brands find some **knockoff or copycat commodities** being sold on some platforms, they might appeal to the **international card organizations** and the international bank card organizations would freeze the seller's bank account with the help of commercial banks and even punish some third-party platforms by fining or stopping cooperation. For example, one of the reasons of PayPal's stopping their cooperation with AliExpress and Dhgate is that they found some copycat products on these platforms and refused to offer payment service for them.

5.3.2 China's Electronic Payment Business Operation 中国电子支付业务运作

China has outpaced the rest of the world in electronic payments. China's electronic payment started from the year 2005. In 2022, more than 80% of adults use electronic payment. Electronic payment refers to the behavior of any institutions, units and individuals who issue payment instructions through electronic terminals to realize monetary payment and fund transfer in a direct or indirect way. In brief, electronic payment refers to the money payment or fund transfer through the network by various parties of electronic transactions, including consumers, manufacturers and financial institutions by using secure electronic payment means.

Electronic payment has experienced five stages in China: The first stage is that banks use computers to process business between banks and handle settlement. The second stage is the settlement of funds between bank computers and computers of other institutions, such as **payroll**. The third stage is to use network terminals to provide various banking services to customers, such as self-service banking. The fourth stage is to use the bank's sales terminal to provide automatic services to customers. The fifth stage, also the latest stage, is the electronic payment based on Internet. It integrates the electronic payment system of the fourth stage with the Internet, realizes **direct transfer settlement** through the Internet anytime and anywhere, and forms an ecommerce transaction payment platform. As two of the dominant payment tools in China, Alipay and WeChat Pay are gaining popularity with the development of cross-border ecommerce.

5.3.2.1 Alipay 阿里支付

In 2004, Alibaba created Alipay in response to widespread lack of trust between buyers and sellers on its platforms. In 2011, Jack Ma moved Alipay out of Alibaba's direct ownership into **Ant Financial**, a financial service holding company that Jack Ma controlled, but Alibaba continues to have a significant interest in Alipay. Alipay is the leader in domestic ecommerce mobile payment and one of the rising payments in cross-border ecommerce. It has also become a **life service platform** with 520 million real name users in China and the world. Alipay has covered 38 countries and regions.

Alipay is an **escrow-based system**, where funds moving from one party to another are held by Alipay until both sides of the transaction give their full approval. The system helped Alibaba gain the trust of Chinese consumers, and when smartphone adoption began to skyrocket in 2008, Alipay's share of China's mobile payments market also skyrocketed. Between 2010 and 2020, the number of mobile Internet users in China grew from about 265 million to over 835 million, and the percentage of the population that are digital buyers grew from about 17% of the Chinese population to almost 65%. In 2019, Alipay reached a milestone, with 1 billion active users worldwide, and by March 2020, it had reached 1.3 billion, with over 700 million using it on a monthly basis.

Alipay has begun to extend its business into other places, including Pakistan, South Korea, Malaysia, Thailand, and Singapore, since Chinese market has edged closer to full saturation. Alipay has also worked to ensure that Chinese citizens traveling abroad can use Alipay to pay for goods overseas.

As the company's **user base** has grown, Alipay has greatly diversified its offerings beyond online and mobile payment. Payments used to be Alipay's only focus. Now mobile payment is the gateway to a much larger array of financial products, all of which are as profitable as the original online payments business. For example, Alipay's *Yu'e Bao* money market fund is now one of the largest such funds in the world. Alipay users can quickly and easily invest in the fund with the same app they use to make payments at a restaurant or grocery store. Alipay also uses algorithmic assessments to offer loans both to individuals and to businesses. Its artificial intelligence-powered risk control engine has reduced Alipay's **fraud-loss rate** dramatically.

5. 3. 2. 2   WeChat Pay 微信支付

Just as Alipay arose from Alibaba and its lineup of ecommerce sites, WeChat Pay arose from the incredibly popular text and voice messaging service WeChat, operated by tech titan Tencent Holdings. WeChat boasts over 1.2 billion users and more than 800 million people reportedly use WeChat Pay every month. Like Alipay, payment is only a small portion of WeChat's larger ecosystem of services. WeChat offers social networking features that resemble Facebook's **News Feed**, featuring a comment system that is more tightly limited to close friends. WeChat can also be used to pay parking tickets, call an ambulance, translate from Chinese to English, pay bills, book train and air transportation, reserve hotel rooms, make charitable donations, and perform online banking with the WeBank online bank—it can even be used as a makeshift dating service. The sheer number of features offered by WeChat app has made it central to Chinese consumers' lives and has increased the likelihood that they will use the app to make mobile payments.

WeChat could deposit money that can be used to pay for goods and services or to send to others. In addition, WeChat also offers an extremely popular **"red packet" feature**, based on a long-standing Chinese tradition practiced on the Chinese New Year and other significant occasions. Using this feature, users can divide a predetermined amount of money into small virtual "packets" called *hongbao* and send them to a chatgroup, allowing members of the group to race to claim each packet. The red packet feature, which subsequently was also adopted by Alipay, has been a significant driver in the popularity of mobile person-to-person (P2P) transactions, with over 600 million people in China (half of the population) sending or receiving money via this mobile payment app in 2020.

WeChat made significant inroads against Alipay's dominance in the Chinese market. One technique it used to achieve this was partnerships with other prominent Chinese services, such as Chinese rideshare service *Didi Chuxing*, with whom WeChat Pay had **an exclusive partnership**. WeChat had a similar arrangement with *Meituan Waimai* **on-demand food delivery service**, which no longer accepted Alipay due to its partnership with WeChat. Walmart's Chinese outlets also did not accept Alipay for these reasons. With development in business, this way of exclusiveness is used less. More platforms are welcoming both Alipay and WeChat Pay and Meituan Waimai accepts both. Still, jd. com only accepts WeChat Pay due to its rival relations with Ali group.

WeChat has also sought partnerships with foreign businesses, such as Japan's Line messaging service. WeChat partnered with Line Pay in 2018 to make it easier for Chinese tourists in Japan to make mobile payments. WeChat has grown rapidly worldwide. In 2020, WeChat Pay could be used in 64 countries and regions. To that end, WeChat has developed a cross-border payment system in partnership with payment firm **Travelex** to allow Chinese tourists to shop overseas. Chinese customers of U.S. retailers can use Travelex Pay to purchase goods. Money in their WeChat Pay accounts is used to generate a digital gift card in U.S. dollars, which is then immediately spent to purchase the desired items. Many of the biggest U.S. retailers that are popular with Chinese tourists are participating in the plan. The appeal is that it helps tourists avoid having to carry a lot of cash. While the use of Chinese credit cards abroad can trigger large transaction fees for the exchange of foreign currency, which this method avoids.

WeChat and Alipay have both stated that their international expansion is focused on allowing Chinese travelers abroad to use the same features they are used to in China, but industry analysts suspect that both companies have greater ambitions for the U.S. market, which still lags far behind in mobile payment adoption compared to China. Read more in the exercise part of this chapter about Alipay and WeChat pay. In addition, JD Pay, another e-payment system developed under JD Group is also gaining influence in China and even the world.[①]

5. 4   International E-payment Business Operation
国际电商支付业务运作

Google and Apple are aspiring to become the preferred mobile payment platform in as many countries as possible worldwide. Other countries like India began to grow in mobile payment adoption at a faster rate; India had about 125 million mobile payment users in 2020, a distant second to China's 650 million, but India grew at a robust rate of almost 30% in 2020, with double-digit increases expected to continue until 2023. Nevertheless, only about 38% of Indian smartphone users and 13% of the population of India currently use mobile payments. Other countries in Asia-Pacific with heavy adoption of mobile payments include South Korea (about 40% of smartphone users), Japan (about 32%), Indonesia (about 23%), and Australia (about 20%). In many countries, the advent of **biometric authentication** has been a major driver of mobile payment adoption, since it greatly reduces the chances of identity theft and speeds up transaction at the point of sale.

5. 4. 1   PayPal 贝宝

Many people are familiar with using PayPal to send money to a buddy or complete an eBay transaction in the United States. Since its launch in 1998, PayPal has been growing fast in terms of customer use and revenue around the world. Over 100,000 people sign up for PayPal's service everyday, more than $1,000 goes through the PayPal financial engine every second and thousands of individuals and business from across the global come to PayPal looking for a solution to meet their online payment needs. PayPal is now available in over 200 countries and 100 currencies at the end of 2022. It is the world's fastest growing global currency exchange, and PayPal is creating a new standard in online payments. Over 70% cross-border users prefer to use this tool, according to Baidu encyclopedia. On 13 March 2023, PayPal officially entered China by acquiring 70% equity of a Chinese company Gopay[②].

---

① JD Pay + Melbourne Airport Partnership Announcement, https://www. wechat-pay. net/171. html, 17-2-2023.

② https://m. dachao. com/kuwanshuma/34962. html, 24-3-2023.

For the thousands of businesses opening online storefront, it is a fact that PayPal is becoming less of a nice-to-have payment option and more of a must-have. Small and large businesses are using PayPal not only as payment option, but also a stand-along payment solution. PayPal lends **credibility** to small businesses. By offering a payment service, where customers don't have to submit their credit card number over the Internet, merchants can instill confidence in users who are hesitant to buy from a site that they may have never visited or even heard of before. The strength of PayPal's brand has made a difference in helping many new businesses get off the ground and establish themselves in a massive online market. PayPal offers a high level of payment security, which is increasingly important.

5.4.2　Apple Pay 苹果支付

With the supportive power of telecommunication, e-payment business is becoming a big lucrative cake which attracts big tech business like Apple, Google, Samsung and Amazon etc.

Apple Pay is an NFC-based mobile payment released by Apple at the 2014 Apple Autumn New Product Launch, which was officially launched in the United States on October 20, 2014. Since its launch, Apple Pay has accounted for 1% of the transaction volume of the digital payment market. Two thirds of new Apple Pay users used this service many times in November 2014. Apple Pay users use Apple Pay 1.4 times a week on average. Apple launched the iOS personal transfer service in the fall of 2017. However, if users use credit cards in the transfer process, they need to pay an additional 3% service charge, which is the same as his competitors.

Apple Pay service was introduced to UK on July 14, 2015, which was the first time Apple Pay entered a foreign market. This service supports iPhone 6 and iPhone 6 Plus, as well as Apple Watch.

Apple and **China UnionPay** jointly announced that Apple Pay officially landed in China on December 18, 2015. China UnionPay cardholders can add their UnionPay cards to their iPhone, Apple Watch and iPad. On February 18, 2016, the number of bank cards of Apple Pay business in China was more than 38 million within 12 hours of its debut. On June 6, 2017, Apple iOS 11 was released, and Apple Pay supports friend transfer. On March 30, 2018, Apple officially launched the version of iOS 11.3 system, which supports the use of ***Beijing all-in-one card*** and ***Shanghai traffic card***. In May 2018, Apple Pay web payment technology entered China. From December 31, 2020, Apple Pay supports **"strong customer certification" (SCA)**.[①]

On February 3, 2023, South Korean financial department announced that Apple Pay could be introduced into South Korea. Today, Apple Pay can be used in most developed countries including European countries, Japan, Canada, Australia, etc.[②]

5. 4. 3　Google Pay, Samsung Pay, Amazon Pay
　　　　谷歌支付、三星支付、亚马逊支付

In order to compete with Apple Pay, big companies launched their payment platforms and apps based on the technology of NFC. On January 9, 2018, Google announced the integration of its existing payment service Android Pay and Google Wallet. The new payment platform is called Google Pay. Google Pay can be used in YouTube and Chrome, as well as some third-party applications in Android and Chrome, such as Airbnb, Dice, Fandango, HungryHouse, and Instaart etc.

Similar to Apple Pay, Samsung Pay offers mobile payment, electronic cash and membership card management service based on NFC and MST (Magnetic Secure Transmission) technology of Samsung Electronics in South Korea, which enables consumers to make payment with Samsung smart phones. Like Apple Pay, Samsung Pay does not need to use special non-contact terminal devices, and can be used directly on NFC-enabled readers and bank card readers. On March 29, 2016, Samsung and UnionPay held a press conference to officially launch the Samsung Pay mobile smart payment service in China.

Amazon Pay is currently widely used in the United States. Amazon platform has also been promoting Amazon sellers to use Amazon Pay. Amazon Pay allows consumers to use their Amazon account to pay for shopping.

Currently, a handful of cross-border ecommerce platforms develop their own e-payment system which goes hand in hand with their online goods transaction. For example, Shopee, a Singapore-based cross-border ecommerce platform, has established its own payment channel, Shopee Pay.

---

① Strong Customer Authentication (SCA) is a new regulatory requirement in Europe, aiming to reduce fraud and make online and offline payment more secure. To meet the SCA requirements, they need to build additional verification procedures. At least two of the following three elements should be used for authentication: first, password or PIN, second, telephone or token; third, fingerprint or face recognition. Payments that require "strong customer authentication" but do not meet the above criteria will be rejected by bank.

② https://support. apple. com/zh-cn/HT207957, 24-3-2023.

5.5　New Fin-tech 新金融科技

Because of the critical significance of money in both national economies and cross-border ecommerce platforms, technologies are widely used to secure the safe transfer of funds.

5.5.1　Blockchain Technology 区块链技术

Blockchain is a technology that enables organizations to create and verify transactions on a network nearly instantaneously without a central authority. Traditionally, organizations maintained their own transaction processing systems on their own databases, and used this record of transactions to keep track of orders, payments, production schedules, and shipping. With blockchain technology, when you place an order online, it enters into a transaction database as an order record. As the order works its way through the firm's factories, warehouses, shipping, and payments process, the initial record expands to record all this information about this specific order. You can think of this as a block of information that's created for every order and that grows over time as the firm processes the order. When the process is completed, the order fulfilled and paid for, the result is a connected chain of blocks (or linked records) associated with that initial order.

There are many risks in a distributive transaction database that shares transaction information among thousands of firms in cross-border ecommerce. A person or firm could enter a false transaction or change an existing transaction. **Imposters** could falsely claim a product has shipped when it has not. **Encryption** is used to avoid these risks. What makes a blockchain system possible and attractive is encryption and **authentication** of the participants, which ensures that only legitimate actors can enter information, and only validated transactions are accepted. Once recorded, the transaction cannot be changed.

There are benefits to firms using blockchain databases. Blockchain networks radically reduce the cost of verifying users, validating transactions, and the risks of storing and processing transaction information across thousands of firms. While a hurricane or earthquake can destroy a firm's private database, these events would disturb only a single **node** in the P2P network, while the records remain stored on all the other nodes in the network. Instead of thousands of firms building their own private transaction systems, and then integrating them with suppliers, shippers, and financial institution systems, blockchain offers a single, simple, low-cost transaction system for participating firms. Standardization of recording transactions is aided through the use of smart contracts. Smart contracts are computer programs that implement the rules governing transactions between firms (e. g. , what is the price of products, how will they be shipped, when will the transaction be completed, who will finance the transaction, what are financing terms, and the like). All the elements of a traditional legal contract can be monitored by a smart contract to ensure the terms are met by parties in the transaction.

The simplicity and security that blockchain offers has made it attractive for storing and securing financial transactions, medical records, and other types of data. Blockchain is a foundation technology for cryptocurrencies as well as supply chain management.

5. 5. 2　Cryptocurrencies 加密货币

Cryptocurrencies are purely digital assets that work as a medium of exchange using blockchain technology and cryptography. **Bitcoin** is the most prominent example of cryptocurrency in use today, but many other cryptocurrencies have emerged in the last few years. Cryptocurrencies have grown meteorically from no value at all in 2008, when Bitcoin was invented, to a market capitalization in the hundreds of billions of dollars.

Bitcoin was created by a mysterious figure or group known only by the pseudonym Satoshi Nakamoto in response to the worldwide financial crises that roiled world markets in the late 2000s. As opposed to traditional paper- and coin-based currencies, which are controlled by central banking systems in the countries that create them, Bitcoin is fully decentralized—no one controls Bitcoin. Instead, Bitcoin is managed through the use of blockchain, which automates the process of synchronizing the **ledger**. Even the most ardent skeptics of Bitcoin typically accept that blockchain technology has revolutionary potential in fields involving transactions between multiple entities.

Bitcoin and other cryptocurrencies, like **Ether**, represent the intersection of complicated technology, economics, geopolitics, and social dynamics. Proponents believe that cryptocurrencies represent the future of money; skeptics believe that collectively, they are destined for a narrow use at best, and a complete collapse at worst.

Cryptocurrencies are not supported by our government presently because of many issues it entails, primarily for the difficulties in government regulation. Cryptocurrencies and Bitcoin are characterized by its decentralized nature, which makes Bitcoin a major regulatory challenge for the government. In the traditional monetary system, countries can implement monetary policy and financial regulation through the central bank, but the emergence of Bitcoin challenges this system, as its decentralized nature makes it difficult for the government to effectively regulate and control. In addition, there are challenges of financial risk and market instability. Financial security and market stability have always been highly valued topics by government. The price volatility of Bitcoin is extremely high, and investors face extremely high risks. The government is concerned that this unstable factor will affect the stability of the entire financial market and may trigger systemic risks, thereby affecting the healthy development of the national economy. Besides that, there are illegal activities and money laundering issues. The anonymity of Bitcoin has become another factor that has attracted government attention. Cryptocurrency can be easily used for illegal activities such as drug trafficking, smuggling, and money laundering. The use of cryptocurrencies such as Bitcoin has increased the difficulty of tracking and cracking down on illegal activities.

Despite the ban on Bitcoin, China still maintains an open attitude towards the development and application of blockchain technology. China is actively developing and promoting digital renminbi, exploring the application of blockchain technology on the basis of legal tender.

5.5.3　Future of CBEC Payment 跨境电商支付的未来

In the near future, experts predict that the following trend may continue:

(1) Payment by credit and/or debit card remains the dominant form of online payment. Though Online payment volume surges in early 2020 due to the Covid-19 pandemic, the payment will not change much.

(2) Mobile retail adoption and payment volume skyrocket.

(3) WeChat and Alipay are two major online paying methods in China while PayPal remains the most popular alternative payment method online worldwide.

(4) Big ecommerce companies like Alibaba (Alipay), Tencent (WeChat Pay), Douyin (Douyin Pay), Baidu (Baifubao), Apple (Apple Pay), Google (Google Pay), and Samsung (Samsung Pay) extend their reach in mobile payment apps. There are quite a few third-party payments like LianLian Pay (Hangzhou, established in 2015), PingPong (Hangzhou, 2015), Airwallex (HK, 2015) in China and Payoneer (USA), Western Union (USA) are working actively in the field of cross-border ecommerce.

(5) There is a growing convergence in the online payments marketplace with large banks entering the mobile e-wallet and P2P payments market with apps.

📖 Words and Phrases 词汇和短语

remittance 汇款

telegraphic transfer 电汇（通过银行转账）

T/T advance payment 事前电汇付款；前 T/T

collection 托收

letter of credit 信用证

block chain technology 区块链技术

cryptocurrency 加密货币

Near-Field Communication（NFC）近场通信

cash on delivery (COD) 货到付款

permeability 渗透率

online payment 线上支付

exchange rate fluctuation 外汇波动

credit card payment 信用卡收款

point of sale terminal transaction (POS) pos 机终端支付

query statistics 查询统计

the third-party online payment 第三方线上支付

PayPal 贝宝支付

Alipay 支付宝

WeChat Pay 微信支付

telephone payment 电话支付

Personal Handy-phone System (PHS) 个人手持式电话系统（如本地小灵通）

PDA (personal digital assistant) 个人数码助理（如掌上电脑）

mobile P2P (peer-to-peer) payment 移动点对点支付

e-money 电子货币

fintech 金融科技

smart card 智能卡

Electronic Funds Transfer (EFT) 电子资金转账

electronic cash 电子现金

E-wallet 电子钱包

default rate 违约率

ports 端口

Visa 维萨卡

Mastercard 万事达卡

America Express 美国运通卡

JCB 日本信用卡株式会社卡；JCB 卡；吉士美卡；日财卡

Diners Club 大来卡

access mode 接入模式

black card（来源不明的）黑卡

offshore bank account 离岸账户

PIN (Personal Identification Number) 个人识别码

APRs (Annual Percentage Rate) 年利率

EMV (ease of movement value) 简易波动指标

proximity mobile payments 近距离移动支付

foreign vendors 外国商户

acquiring orders 收单

knockoff or copycat commodities 山寨货

international card organizations 国际卡组织

payroll（公司的）工资总支出；单位工资

direct transfer settlement 直接转移支付

Ant Financial 蚂蚁金服

life service platform 生活服务平台

escrow-based system 基于第三方保管的系统

user base 用户基础

fraud-loss rate 违约损失率

News Feed 新闻推送；动态消息

red packet feature 红包功能

an exclusive partnership 独家合伙

on-demand food delivery service 即时外卖服务

Travelex 通济隆（英国外币兑换专业机构）

biometric authentication 生物识别；生物认证（技术）；生物特征身份认证

credibility 信用

China UnionPay 中国银联

Beijing all-in-one card 北京一卡通

Shanghai traffic card 上海交通卡

Strong Customer Authentication (SCA) 强客户认证

imposters 骗子

encryption 加密（技术）

authentication 授权

node 节点

Bitcoin 比特币

ledger 分类账（技术）；分布式总账（技术）

Ether 以太币

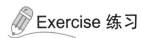 Exercise 练习

I. Reflections and Critical Thinking Questions.

1. What are the most popular ways of payment in cross-border ecommerce?

2. What are the advantages of mobile payment?

3. In cross-border ecommerce, payment follows a certain pattern. What are the patterns (flow chart) of payment in exporting and importing?

4. What do you think of the trends of ecommerce payment?

II. True or False

1. The third-party payment institution survives mainly with commissions from buyers or sellers in cross-border payment. (　　)

2. Telephone payment is one of the online e-payments according to People's Bank of China. (　)

3. Mobile payment is dominating international cross-border ecommerce payment. (　)

4. Mobile payment is the payment done through mobile phones. (　　)

5. The more developed an ecommerce market is, the more credit card payment is used. (　)

6. Commercial banks often get involved in cross-border ecommerce payment by cooperating with third-party payment institutions. (　　)

7. A Chinese consumer is buying foreign products through a cross-border ecommerce website. Under the scenario, for the third-party payment institution, it collects the consumer's RMB and changes it into foreign currency and pays for him. (　　)

8. China UnionPay bank card is subject to the administration of international card

organization. (　　)

9. Bank cards payment, especially credit card payment, is the most popular payment in the world. (　　)

10. Alipay's an escrow-based system which secures trust between online sellers and buyers and helps Alibaba gain the trust of Chinese consumers. (　　)

11. WeChat Pay worked exclusively with local service partners like *Didi Chuxing* and *Meituan Waimai*, which falled into the scope of unfair competition. (　　)

12. PayPal, as one of the largest online payment system, offers local service in different places. (　　)

III. Nouns Explanation

1. T/T advanced, off-shore account payment

2. PayPal, Alipay, WeChat Pay, Google pay, Apple Pay

3. Near-Field Communication (NFC), COD, PIN, QR Code

4. blockchain, cryptocurrencies, bitcoin

IV. Reading and Critical Thinking

Alipay and WeChat Pay, Lead in Mobile Payments[①]

With over 1.2 billion consumers worldwide expected to use a mobile wallet to make a proximity mobile payment (近距离移动支付) in 2021, it's no surprise that a slew of companies, including smartphone manufacturers and payment processing companies, are aggressively pursuing global expansion for their mobile payment products. Traditional U. S. tech giants like Google and Apple are aspiring to become the preferred mobile payment platform in as many countries as possible worldwide; however, Chinese tech companies Alibaba and Tencent have a commanding lead in this space, not Google and Apple.

China has over 58% of the world's users of proximity mobile payments in 2021— a total of over 680 million people and an increase of 10% from 2019. Proximity mobile payments are those that take place at the point of sale, where the person paying for a good or service uses their phone in tandem with (同时) NFC (near field communication), QR codes (quick response code), Bluetooth, or other, similar technology to make a payment. Not every country has embraced proximity mobile payments, but China has proved to be the perfect environment for them to catch on. In Western countries like the United

---

① Kenneth C. Laudon, Carol Guercio Traver, E-commerce 2021–2022: business. technology. Society (17th edition) [M]. Pearson Education Limited, UK, 2022.

States and European countries, credit cards are still in widespread use and have been for many years, as are other payment systems tied to banks, such as debit cards and checks. However, China has bypassed credit cards completely in favor of mobile payment apps. There are only 0.31 credit cards per capitain in China, compared to 2.5 credit cards per capita in the United States.

In 2019, the value of third-party mobile transactions in China totaled over 226 trillion-yuan renminbi. In contrast, in the United States, consumers only paid about $110 billion via proximity mobile payments. In nearly every metric, China has outpaced the rest of the world in mobile payments. In China, even street people accept handouts via QR codes; street musicians carry pictures of QR codes to allow passersby to provide tips with Alipay or WeChat Pay. The Chinese mobile payments market is nearly completely saturated.

Despite China's overwhelming adoption of proximity mobile payments, the country does not have a thriving marketplace of many companies jockeying (耍手段获取) for dominance; just as in the United States, a small number of tech titans have cornered (占据) most of the market. Founded in 1999 by Jack Ma and Peng Lei, Alibaba is China's largest e-commerce company, offering B2B e-commerce on its flagship Alibaba website, C2C e-commerce on its Taobao marketplace, and B2C e-commerce on its Tmall site.

Alipay offers financing for small and medium-sized companies. There are three types of loans: its Ant Micro Loan, which is intended for small businesses; its *JieBei* loans, for individual consumers with high credit scores, and its *Huabei* (or Ant Check Later) loan, which allows users to buy items on credit without paying interest.

In addition to reducing fraud, Alibaba's algorithmic approach also allows the company to process loan requests incredibly fast. Alibaba uses transaction data to analyze how a business is doing and how competitive it is in its market as well as the credit ratings of the companies it partners with. Alipay is also working on projects involving blockchain technology, AI, security, the Internet of Things, and many more.

Both WeChat and Alipay are also similar in the enormous trove (宝库) of data. Because Alibaba and WeChat are so central to Chinese consumers lives, both companies know a great deal about what their users buy, who their friends are, what their credit scores are, and much, much more.

Some analysts speculate that because privacy is simply not as significant a cultural value in China as it is in other countries, WeChat and Alipay are in a better position tomonetize (获利) their trove of user data than other companies might be.

While Alipay and WeChat Pay have been big winners in China's mobile payment market place over the last decade, American tech companies have been left to play catchup. Apple in particular has a small fraction of users using Apple Pay compared to both Alipay and WeChat Pay; WeChat also functions similarly on the iPhone and Android, making the two operating systems mostly indistinguishable to Chinese smartphone users. For that reason, Chinese consumers often prefer the lower-cost Android, at Apple's expense. Google has had its own problems with China over the years. It seems unlikely that Google Pay will make a dent in China's mobile payment marketplace without the ability to create a similar ecosystem of products and services to the ones that Alibaba and WeChat can offer.

Around the world, other payment systems are gaining traction (牵引力 ; 拉力). For example, in India, there are three major players: Google Pay, Walmart-backed PhonePe, and Alibaba-backed Paytm. In June 2020, Google Pay had 75 million transacting users and PhonePehad 60 million. Paytm[1], which previously had been the dominant player, has reportedly slipped into third place in terms of number of transacting users but remains in the lead in terms of reach with merchants. Just like WeChat and Alipay, Paytm allows users to make payments and send money to other users as well as book travel arrangements. In Malaysia, the popular ridesharing service Grab has continued to expand, opening its platform to third-party services to develop more functionality akin to WeChat as well as launching the GrabPay mobile wallet and GrabFood food delivery service. Boost is another popular payment service in Malaysia. In Singapore, DBS PayLah and Singtel DASH are in widespread use, as is GrabPay.

Another important battleground for mobile payment providers is China Hong Kong, which is unique in the region in its reliance on cash and credit cards. As a result, Westerntech companies are slightly more competitive with Alipay and WeChat in the region. On the other hand, Hong Kong citizens have widely adopted the Octopus stored value card, which is accepted by convenience stores, restaurants, and public transit. Launched in1997, there are more than 35 million Octopus cards in circulation, and it is used by more than 99% of the population, handling 14 million transactions a day. Mobile payment companies seeking to expand into Hong Kong and tap into its lucrative consumer base will require at least as competitive an option as Octopus.

Alipay and WeChat are well positioned going forward, with massive user bases in

---

[1] Alibaba announced its withdraw from India Paytm at the beginning of 2023.

China, profitable business models thanks to their vibrant ecosystems of services, and the backing of two of the biggest tech companies in the world in Alibaba and Tencent.

If Alipay and WeChat Pay are unsuccessful in growing into a particular region, they could simply opt to go the route of strategic acquisitions; Alipay and its parent Ant Financial have already begun doing this. However, both companies face challenges in their attempts to expand into Western markets, where credit cards are already in widespread use and are trusted by consumers. Without a sufficiently compelling reason, customers in Europe and the United States are unlikely to ditch their credit cards and switch not just to Alipay or WeChat Pay, but even to U.S. -based services like Apple Pay and Google Pay.

Critical Thinking and Questions:

1. What is proximity mobile payment?

2. What are the differences between Chinese consumer's payment method and that of the America and Europe?

3. What was China's situation of proximity mobile payment in 2019 and what were the differences from that of the United States?

4. What kind of technologies are used in third-party mobile payment?

5. What are the similarities and differences between Alipay and WeChat Pay?

More Resources:

1. 亚马逊收款方式有哪些?[①]

2. 一文读懂 BUSD 和 USDT 的区别.[②]

3. 稳定币是什么意思? 数字货币稳定币有哪些?[③]

4. Opinion: Silicon Valley Bank survived the dot-com crash and the Great Recession, but SVB met its match in Powell's hawkish Fed. [④]

Keys-5

①   https://www. cifnews. com/article/66410, 14-1-2023.

②   https://www. 120btc. com/baike/coin/158355261. html, 14-1-2023.

③   https://www. 528btc. com/zhuanti/531478. html. 14-1-2023.

④   https://www. marketwatch. com/story/silicon-valley-bank-survived-the-dot-com-crash-and-the-great-recession-but-svb-was-no-match-for-powells-hawkish-fed-1a53c25a, 24-3-2023.

Chapter 6

China's Cross-border Ecommerce Platforms
中国的跨境电商平台

Objectives

1. Master the classifications of China's cross-border ecommerce platforms

2. Know Ali's ecosystem in B2B and B2C cross-border ecommerce

3. Know China's representative cross-border ecommerce platforms and their features

4. Understand UGC representative platforms

5. Understand the link-and-sale rebate model and bonded-area platforms

Open Case: watch the video and answer the questions

Video: Alibaba. com introduction (2'52)

Questions:

1. Is Alibaba. com a B2B or a B2C business?

2. What are the two elements that enable users to find suppliers, get quotations and transact orders all in one place?

3. How could John find his products on Alibaba.com?

4. When alibaba.com covers an amount of trade assurance for its supplier, what is the assignment of amount based on?

视频资源链接

A cross-border ecommerce platform is a website that a business deploys to handle all their online commercial activities. These commercial activities include **product pages**, **reviews**, **transaction logs**, **order fulfillment and delivery**, **customer support** and **returns**, etc. Most of the platforms are currently offering easy, one-stop ecommerce store building and maintenance. For **online sellers**, the best ecommerce platform comes down to your unique business model and growth plan. For individual consumers, the best platform comes from your needs and preferences.

6.1   China's Cross-border Ecommerce 中国跨境电商

China benefited greatly by working as "the factory of the world" during the past 40 plus years since the reform and open-up policy. "Made in China" has been widely accepted by international society as a standardized and high-quality label which brings prosperity to the whole world. Chinese products, based on Chinese perfect supply chain and industrial chain, has been serving the world and securing the welfare of the world population.

6.1.1   Achievements of Chinese CBEC 中国跨境电商的成就

Cross-border ecommerce always adopts the latest new technology but with the same core of serving the world with increasingly abundant products and services. After years of development in both internet & information technology and manufacturing technology, China is qualified to present the world with more advanced and high-end products and services. At the same time, with a population of 1.4 billion, China opens its greatest consumer market to the world. We are consuming international brands and importing more brand products and an increase amount of high-end imported goods are put into the shopping cart of Chinese consumers, see Figure 6-1. The percentage of importing goes up slowly from 15% in 2014 to 23% in 2021.

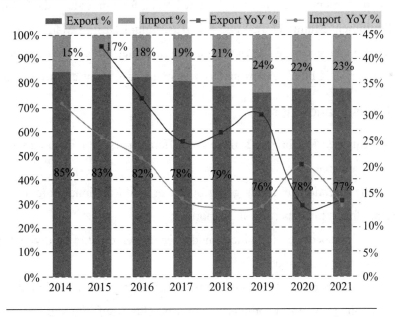

Figure 6-1   Percentage of Chinese CBEC import and export and their growth rate

A steadily rising number of Chinese cross-border ecommerce enterprises have been stepping into the world arena to do business globally. There is no other country in the world which embraces the world market as deep and open as China does. On the other hand, during the pandemic period, the external environment provides a rare opportunity for the development of cross-border ecommerce. According to customs statistics in 2021, see Table 6-1, China's cross-border ecommerce import and export volume reached 1.92 trillion Yuan, an increase of 18.6% year-on-year, and cross-border ecommerce entered a new foreign trade developmental *window* **period**. With the beginning of post pandemic period, traditional offline brick-and-mortar retailing is regaining market presence in Europe and North America, and cross-border ecommerce is facing new challenges.

Table 6-1　The volume of China's cross-border ecommerce (2019—2021)

year	Volume (unit: 100 million yuan)			Growth rate (YoY, %)			Rate of export/import
	gross	export	import	gross	export	import	
2019	12,903	7,981	4,922	22.2	30.5	10.8	1.6
2020	16,220	10,850	5,370	25.7	39.2	9.1	2.0
2021	19,237	13,918	5,319	18.6	28.3	-0.9	2.6

There are currently quite a few cross-border platforms for exporting because China has been an export-oriented country, which started doing foreign trade in the form of **OEM** (Original Equipment Manufacturer) and **ODM** (Original Design Manufacturer). Early platforms mainly engaged in B2B. Business, and B2B platforms have been undertaking roughly 4/5 volume of China's exporting business in the past few years, see Figure 6-1.

6. 1. 2　Classifications 分类

Just as mentioned in Chapter 2, there are different perspectives to classify China's cross-border ecommerce.

1. From the direction of goods going out of or into a national border, it could be classified as platforms for importing and exporting;

2. From the perspective of business model, ecommerce could be divided into B2B mode, B2C mode and C2C mode;

3. From the perspective of whether the platform itself gets involved in selling goods directly to customers or not, ecommerce could be classified into self-operating DTC platform and third-party platform (a platform for all other sellers and vendors to sell goods to consumers) or a combined model (doing self-operating business and at the same time,

providing a platform for other business).

4. Based on product **categories** the platform sells, platforms could be vertical platform and comprehensive platform. Vertical platform focuses on a certain nliché market and goods are confined to a certain field, such as platform for wedding gowns, platform for electronic products, platform for women's cosmetics, etc. While commodities on comprehensive platform are not so confined to a certain category. Their commodities are extensively displayed and sold.

5. With the development of social media websites and a surging number of mobile device users, new mixed forms appear. The most popular are social ecommerce platforms (mostly through apps, including social media live broadcasting model, for example, TikTok shop does business through live broadcasting) and mobile ecommerce platforms (apps). This chapter focuses on Chinese cross-border ecommerce platforms, see Table 6-2. We start from Alibaba.

Table 6-2　China's CBEC platform and model

	B2B	B2C	C2C
export	alibaba.com globalsources.com made-in-china.com diytrade.com dhgate.com	aliexpress.com; lazada.com lightinthebox.com dx.com; SheIn; Tiktok shop; Temu	Tiktok shop Temu (Pinduoduo)
import		tmall. hk; kaola.com jd. hk; vip.com; g. suning.com; ymatou.com; haituncun.com;55haitao.com; haitao.com kjt.com; kjb2c.com Xiaohongshu;	Xiaohongshu; WeChat applet WeChat public account

6. 2　Alibaba's Cross-border Ecommerce 阿里巴巴跨境电商

Alibaba is China's first and most successful cross-border ecommerce platform, so this part will focus on Ali's ecosystem and its cross-border ecommerce, see Figure 6-2.

6. 2. 1　The Ecosystem of Alibaba's Ecommerce 阿里电商生态系统

Alibaba has established its ecommerce ecosystem covering both domestic and cross-border ecommerce. They started their business, a B2B exporting business alibaba.com in

1999 and later introduced cross-border ecommerce platforms in B2C exporting (aliexpress.com, lazada.com) and importing (Tmall global), see Figure 6-2. Services of Alibaba group include B2B trade, online retail, shopping search engine, third-party payment and cloud computing services, etc. The group's subsidiaries include Alibaba.com, Taobao, Tmall, Yitao, Alibaba cloud computing, Alipay, Ant Financial, etc. It provides suppliers with many necessary tools to attract the global audience for their products and help buyers quickly and effectively find products and suppliers. Cross-border ecommerce of Alibaba covers exporting and importing business, including both B2B and B2C sections. Ali's exporting businesses are mainly performed through three platforms, alibaba.com, aliexpress.com and Southeast-Asia-based lazada.com. And there are 2 big importing platforms which adopt different business models: tmall.hk and kaolao.com. We would study them in the following parts.

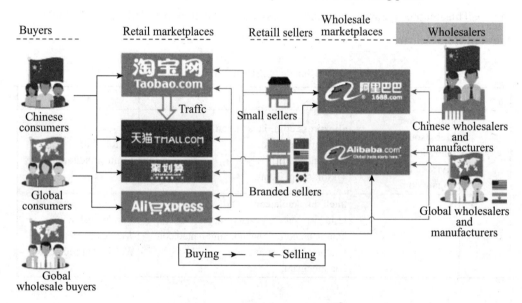

Figure 6-2　Alibaba's ecosystem[1]

6.2.2　Ali's Exporting Platforms 阿里出口平台

Exporting business was the first business of Aligroup. It conducted B2B business for Chinese small and medium-sized businesses.

6.2.2.1　B2B Exporting Platform: Alibaba.com　B2B 出口平台：阿里巴巴国际站

Alibaba.com, founded in 1999, also known as "*Alibaba international station*" in

---

① http://www.leshanvc.com/cygc/6276.html, 24-3-2023.

Chinese, is a pioneer B2B service platform in export marketing and promotion to help small and medium-sized enterprises expand international trade, see Figure 6-3. In Alibaba.com platform, buyers can search the company and product information published by the seller. Sellers can search the buyer's purchase information. The platform provides communication tools and account management tools for buyers and sellers. By displaying and promoting suppliers' enterprises and products to overseas buyers, alibaba. com is one of the preferred network platforms for Chinese and foreign export enterprises to expand international trade. It is a leading platform for global wholesale trade, serving millions of buyers and suppliers around the world.

The platform provides **customs clearance** services, and reconstructs cross-border trade in a digital way and eco-systematical way with the new development of AI, cloud computing, electronic payment, etc. In order to promote online products automatically, Alibaba robot (Ali Robot) was introduced as the first **automatic marketing** multi-function software in China. With the help of this software, marketers could conduct an intelligent mass release for their products by using multi-keyword all-round coverage, regular update of batch products, **keyword ranking**, **one-key query** and other functions. The result could be as good as that the number of product exposure could be doubled in 30 days and orders doubled in 6 months.

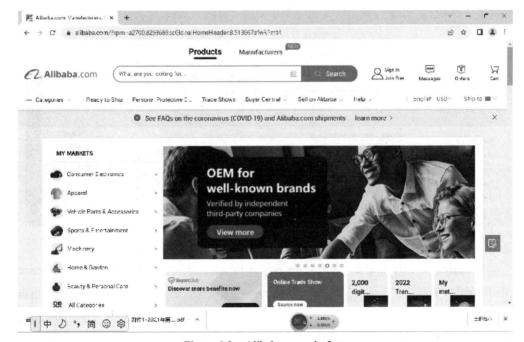

Figure 6-3   Alibaba.com platform

In addition, just like many third-party platforms, Alibaba. com offers some offline services:1. On-site service and one-to-one professional guidance. 2. Call center service hotline which distinguishes Alibaba from Amazon who doesn't offer this service. 3. Customer training which helps sellers become an ecommerce expert. 4. Global trade show promotion, which is oriented to buyers' procurement directly.

6. 2. 2. 2　B2C Exporting Platform: aliexpress.com　B2C 出口平台：全球速卖通

Aliexpress. com (also known as Global Express) is a cross-border B2C ecommerce platform created for international market, which is nicknamed "international Taobao" by Chinese sellers. Global Express is the third largest online shopping English website in the world. Headquartered in Hangzhou, China, Global Express aims at overseas buyers, conducts guarantee transactions through Alipay international accounts, and uses international logistics channels to transport and deliver goods. It has been performing especially well before the breakout of the Russia-Ukraine conflicts in these two areas, see Figure 6-4.

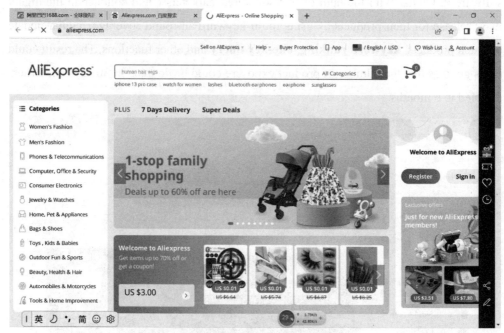

Figure 6-4　Aliexpress.com platform

Founded in 2010, aliexpress.com is the largest cross-border retail ecommerce platform of China. At present, it has opened websites in 18 languages, covering more than 200 countries and regions around the world. In March 2019, aliexpress. com launched online car sales services in Russia. Russian consumers can place an order directly on aliexpress.com, pay an **advance**, and pay the rest at the designated offline store to pick up the car. Unfortunately, with the breakout of the war between Russia and Ukraine on Feb 24, 2022, Alibaba group laid off about 40% of its Russian joint venture employees on May 14, 2022 because the continuous crisis in Ukraine affected its cross-border business.

Aliexpress. com covers 30 first-class industry categories, including **3C**, clothing, home furnishings, jewelry, etc. Among them, the dominant industries mainly include: clothing, mobile communication, shoes and bags, beauty and health, jewelry and watches, consumer electronics, computer networks, home furnishings, auto and motorcycle, accessories, lamps and lanterns, etc.

There are three types of logistics services on aliexpress.com, including postal packages, cooperative logistics and commercial express service. 90% of these transactions use postal services. **China Post (air parcel and air mail)** and Hongkong Post (air parcels) are characterized by low costs (for example, the approximate cost of sending a kilogram of goods to Russia is only 40 or 50 Yuan at a time), but the timeliness of postal parcels is relatively slow, and there is a certain **rate of packet loss**. Alibaba has a few cooperative expresses which are characterized by its low price, **performance-price ratio** and **adaptability**. It was launched in cooperation with Zhejiang post and China Post respectively. Alibaba also uses commercial express to do delivery. The four major commercial express is characterized by their speed, excellent service, professionalism and efficiency, but the price is high. It is suitable for small-size articles or transactions with high value and urgent requirements of buyers.

With the popularity of mobile devices, AliExpress seller mobile app offers almost complete **parity** to manage business online or on mobile device, with features for fulfilling orders, adding products, real-time sales and inventory updates, etc.

6. 2. 2. 3　B2C Exporting Platform: lazada.com　B2C 出口平台：莱赞达

Lazada, founded in 2012, is one of the largest online shopping websites in Southeast Asia. Supported by the German business **incubator** Rocket Internet, Lazada mainly targets users in Indonesia, Malaysia, the Philippines and Thailand. In 2016, it became the flagship ecommerce platform of Alibaba Group in Southeast Asia, see Figure 6-5. On Jan 2, 2023, RCEP[1] took effect in Indonesia, which means that Indonesia would grant China zero duty

---

① Regional Comprehensive Economic Partnership started in 2012. It has 15 memberships including China, Japan, Australia, South Korea and New Zealand, and 10 ASEAN countries (Singapore, Indonesia, Malaysia, Vietnam, etc.).

for importing more than 700 product categories, including car parts, motorcycle, TV set, apparel, shoes, plastics, bag and luggage, chemical products, etc. [①]

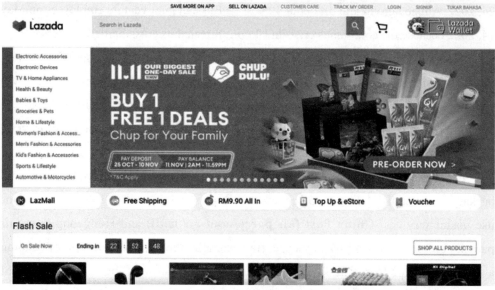

Figure 6-5　Lazada.com platform

Iprice (a large ecommerce website in Malaysia) 2018 annual report shows that Lazada ranks first in the online traffic of ecommerce in Southeast Asia with 27% of online visits. In 2019, Lazada was elected as the most popular shopping platform for the local millennial generation in Indonesia. On August 19, 2020, Lazada and Tmall jointly released the "new domestic goods cross borders plan", which set up a fast entry channel for Tmall brands settling in the brand mall LazMall.

Lazada's core pillars are logistics, technology and payment. On the part of logistics, Lazada built its own logistics network. LGS (Lazada Global Shipping solution, Lazada's own global shipping) solves the complex freight flow of the first mile and the last mile delivery, while significantly reducing the expensive freight generated by the backward infrastructure in some parts of Southeast Asia. At present, Lazada has more than 30 **storage centers** in 17 cities in Southeast Asia. It has established self-supporting warehouses, sorting centers and electronic technology facilities, cooperated with partner networks, and has cross-border and "last mile" logistics capabilities.

In particular, since 2018, Lazada has set up overseas warehouses in Malaysia, Indonesia, Thailand and the Philippines, integrating Hong Kong Central Warehouse and

---

① 　RCEP 正式对印度尼西亚生效, https://36kr. com/newsflashes/2071969957182600?f=rss, 12-1-2023.

Shenzhen Central Warehouse in China, covering three channels of delivery: direct mail, overseas warehouse, and domestic central warehouse. Working together with Cainiao logistics, Lazada has built a three-dimensional cross-border logistics network. On May 24, 2022, Lazada Singapore overseas warehouse officially opened, providing Singapore local warehousing and delivery services for cross-border businesses. It is expected to reduce logistics costs by 30%−90%, help comprehensively to improve logistics timeliness, and enable businesses to localize services to Southeast Asian consumers. On June 2,2022, Lazada Philippines cooperated with GrabExpress (an instant parcel delivery service in southeast Asia) to launch "the same-day delivery service". The delivery time of groceries, electronic accessories and other products was shortened from 3−5 days to a few hours.

The second core pillar of Lazada is about science and technology. With the help of technology, Lazada is committed to redefining retail experience. The application of real-time data enables Lazada to grasp the changes in consumer demand at the first time. With the synergy of Alibaba's leading technology, Lazada can develop and create large-scale and highly competitive products and technical solutions.

As to cross-border payment, E-payment in Southeast Asian countries is still in the infant stage. Lazada provides consumers with a set of diversified payment methods (such as cash on delivery) to meet current needs and guide consumers to use convenient and reliable e-payment methods. At the same time, platforms are cultivating consumers to use more advanced payments like mobile payment, etc.

6.2.3　Ali's Importing Platforms 阿里进口平台

Ali's importing cross-border ecommerce focuses mainly on B2C business.

6.2.3.1　B2C Importing Platform: Tmall.hk　B2C 进口平台：天猫国际

Tmall.hk, known as Tmall global, founded on February 2014, is an import retail platform under Alibaba's banner. It provides Chinese consumers with global imported goods and direct access to overseas lifestyles. At the same time, it is also the preferred platform to help overseas brands reach Chinese consumers, build brand awareness and cultivate consumer taste. With the goal of "importing the world with original packaging", Tmall directly supplies overseas imported goods with original packaging for domestic consumers, see Figure 6-6.

On May 2014, seven cross-border bonded warehouses were launched, and Tmall global began to establish a new cross-border bonded logistics model. On June 24, 2015, following the announcement of the launch of the first National flagship store — South Korea **flagship store** on May, it launched the beginning of the "global village" model. Eleven national flagship stores, including the United States, Britain, France, Spain, Switzerland, Australia, New Zealand, Singapore, Thailand, Malaysia and Turkey were unveiled at Tmall global. On the same day, Alibaba's *Juhuasuan*(a great bargain) platform announced the full launch of the cooperation process with the embassies of 20 countries.

In May 2016, Tmall global increased its **self-operating business**, performing the dual mode of third-party platform and self-operation. On July 21, 2020, Tmall global and Hangzhou **comprehensive bonded zone** officially launched the "bonded zone factory" project, a new national-level **"bonded import + retail processing"** importing model. Presently, a total of more than 29,000 overseas brands from 87 countries and regions have entered Tmall global, covering more than 5800 **sub-categories**, of which more than 80% have entered China for the first time.

The **merchants** who have settled in Tmall global are all foreign corporate entities outside Chinese Mainland and have overseas retail qualifications. All the goods sold are originated or sold overseas, and enter through the Chinese customs by international logistics. All Tmall Global's settled businesses will provide their stores with AliWangwang Chinese customer service and provide domestic after-sales services. Consumers can use Alipay to buy overseas imported goods just like shopping at Taobao. In terms of logistics, Tmall global requires merchants to complete the delivery within 120 hours and arrive within 14 working days, and ensure that the logistics information can be tracked throughout the process.

6.2.3.2　B2C Importing Platform: Kaola.com　B2C 进口平台：考拉海购

Kaola.com was founded in 2015. In 2019, Alibaba Group announced its $2 billion wholly-owned acquisition of kaola. com. It is a **membership** ecommerce model mainly engaged in cross-border import business under Alibaba, focusing on self-operating and global direct retail.

The characteristic of Koala.com is that it focuses on the concept of self-operating direct purchase from the world. It has branches or offices in the United States, Germany, Italy, Japan, South Korea, Australia, Hong Kong (China) and Taiwan (China). It goes deep into the origin of products to directly purchase high-quality goods, eliminates fake goods, and saves many intermediate links while ensuring the quality of goods. It is transported directly from the origin to China under the supervision of customs and national inspection, stored in bonded area warehouse. In addition, kaola.com launched an advanced system — Ant Blockchain Traceability System to control its product quality, see Figure 6-6.

Figure 6-6　Kaola.com platform

6.3　B2B Exporting Platforms　B2B 出口平台

6.3.1　Globalsources.com 环球资源

Globalsources.com is a professional B2B foreign trade platform with a deep industry background. Its mother company, Globalsources, started in 1970, is a professional exhibition organizer rooted in Hong Kong (China), facing south-eastern Asia and the world. It is also the preferred **procurement platform** and mainstream platform for global **high-end buyers**. Globalsources launches trade exhibitions in Hong Kong (China) in April and October every year, including the world's leading consumer electronics exhibition and mobile electronics exhibition, as well as lifestyle exhibition and fashion products exhibition, see Figure 6-7.

Figure 6-7　Globalsources.com platform

Globalsources.com took the lead in launching the world's first B2B online ecommerce cross-border trade website in 1995. The company once had more than 10 million registered buyers and users from all over the world, with 1.5 million sellers from around the world. Globalsources allows suppliers to register for free and publish up to 100 products. Most suppliers come from China, including Hong Kong and Taiwan. At the same time, suppliers use its export promotion services provided by global sources to enhance the company's image, obtain sales inquiries, and win purchasing orders and business opportunities from more than 240 countries and regions.

6.3.2　Made-in-China.com 中国制造网

Made-in-China.com is a B2B platform headquartered in Nanjing, China and was founded in 1998, see Figure 6-8. It serves small and medium-sized enterprises. The platform supports 11 languages and has more than 1 million suppliers, which can be registered free of charge. Made-in-China ranked among the top three in Chinese B2B ecommerce field, and has become an important channel for global buyers to purchase products made in China.

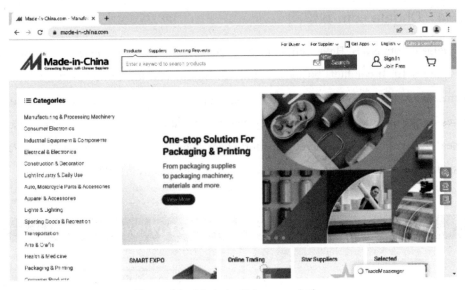

Figure 6-8   Made-in-China.com platform

6.3.3   Diytrade.com 自助贸易网

Diytrade.com is another online B2B platform for global suppliers and buyers launched firstly in 1998 in Hongkong, when foreign trade was surging at the time, creating opportunities for small and medium-sized enterprises and buyers. It is also an internationally influential ecommerce platform, and gradually becomes the preferred platform for global businessmen to purchase and promote goods, see Figure 6-9.

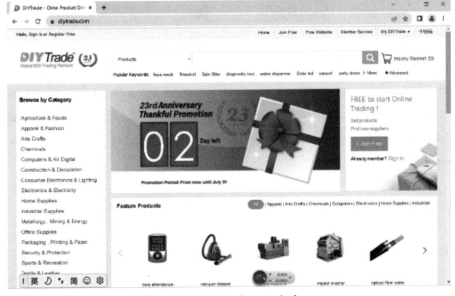

Figure 6-9   Diytrade.com platform

6.3.4　Dhgate.com 敦煌网

DHgate. com is a B2B platform founded in 2004 by a female entrepreneur Wang Shutong, see Figure 6-10. It conducts business mainly in Europe and the United States, adopting a commission system like other platforms. Though not as influential as alibaba.com, dhgate.com focuses on goods of low value and has its own niché market. At present, it also covers B2C business. According to PayPal trading platform data, dhgate. com ranks first in the Asia Pacific and sixth in the world in terms of online foreign trade transactions in 2011.

Figure 6-10　Dhgate.com platform

dhgate.com adopts EDM (email direct marketing) marketing mode to expand overseas market in a low-cost and efficient manner. Users can freely subscribe EDM commodity information in English and know the latest market supply at the first time. The group has also built a decentralized social ecommerce **SaaS platform** MyyShop in 2020 to help promote its business[①].

6.4　B2C Exporting Platforms　B2C 出口平台

B2C platforms offer retailing business to individual consumers. This is the most

① http://www. rmzxb. com. cn/c/2023-03-20/3316703. shtml, 24-3-2023.

popular business model which is appropriate for startups. Almost every country and region has its own local ecommerce platforms and there are many cross-border ecommerce B2C platforms conducting business across the world. Amazon is the largest B2C platform and has great market presence in North America, Europe and Australia.

6.4.1　Lightinthebox.com 兰亭集势

Lightinthebox, founded in 2007 and headquartered in Beijing, is a self-operating B2C platform that integrates supply chain services in China. Its main market is in Europe and North America, and it mainly sells clothing, electronic communication equipment, parts and accessories, home gardening and other products. The company has a series of suppliers, its own data warehouse and long-term logistics partners. At the beginning of 2010s, Lightinthebox was one of the leaders of China's B2C cross-border ecommerce platform, see Figure 6-11.

Lightinthebox is like an online retail supermarket. At first, it mainly made wedding dresses. The company has more than 500, 000 independent commodities, and its core categories include wedding dresses, men's and women's clothing, home life, outdoor sports, shoes, boots, bags, 3C electronics and various accessories. At the same time, the company supports more than 20 payment channels all over the world, such as PayPal, Visa, EBANX (a payment platform in Latin America, especially in Brazil), etc.

Figure 6-11　Lightinthebox.com platform

6.4.2 dx.com DX 跨境电商

In 2006, it was firstly launched as dealextreme.com, a comprehensive B2C website, and changed into dx.com in 2013, see Figure 6-12. Dx.com is a comprehensive B2C ecommerce website headquartered in Shenzhen. From 2008 to 2009, the financial crisis brought high growth to the small-article foreign trade market, and DX took advantage of the explosive growth, and became the largest foreign trade B2C and 3C electronic product provider. It communicates closely with users through blogs, forums, Facebook, YouTube, Google search and other channels. It conducts business in Europe, the United States, South American countries, South Asia, India, Australia, Africa, etc.

Figure 6-12　Dx.com platform

6.4.3 Mobile B2C Exporting APP: SheIn　移动 B2C 出口：希音

With the widespread of mobile phone, the number of mobile app users for online shopping is surging. A few platforms conduct their business through mobile apps. SheIn is one of the most successful.

SheIn is an international B2C fast fashion ecommerce company. The name comes from "She" + "In". Founded in 2008, headquartered in Nanjing, China, it mainly sold women's clothing at first. Now it also provides men's clothing, children's clothing, jewelry, shoes, bags and other fashion products. SheIn

grew exponentially during the epidemic. Its **"Small Order Quick Reaction"**
operating model distinguishes itself from the similar Zara and other fast fashion
counterparts. Its flexible supply chain and inventory management empower its
rapid growth. SheIn not only owns its own app, but also sells their products on
other platforms like Amazon, see Figure 6-13.

Figure 6-13　SheIn APP and the store on Amazon

SheIn has various ways to get traffic. Firstly, when opening a shop in Amazon,
the same product sold on the self-operating platform SheIn is cheaper than those sold
on Amazon. The purpose is to guide private traffic to its own platform. In addition
to the early diversion of internet traffic from Amazon[1], Internet marketing was done
very successfully by SheIn. From the beginning, it paid great attention to the operation
of overseas social media. The rise of mobile Internet and social platforms has made
it focus on Instagram, YouTube, Facebook, Pinterest, etc. , forming the first wave of
traffic accumulation through platform advertising and online popularity promotion.
SheIn is preparing to go public and expand its business to a wider category in 2023.
News says that it will change into a comprehensive platform to sell all categories
instead of focusing on fashion and clothes[2].

---

① Quite a few platforms have established their store at Amazon. com. For example, jd. com has its own
platform, and in order to get more traffic and marketing, it built a store in amazon.

② 做全品类平台，SHEIN 的野心开始暴露，https://baijiahao. baidu. com/s?id=1746352716691415488&wfr=
spider&for=pc. Jan-12-2023.

6.5　B2C Importing Platforms　B2C 进口平台

A huge amount of foreign products are welcome to Chinese consumers with the development of Chinese economy. A few platforms are actively dealing with online importing businesses including Tmall.hk, jd.hk and vip.com etc. And **China International Import Expo** has been held for 5 consecutive years since 2018.

6.5.1　jd.hk 京东国际

JD is a domestic online retailer characterized with a **fulfillment network** that reaches 99% of the Chinese population and has 471.9 million active customers. Founded in 1998 and headquartered in Beijing, JD is one of China's biggest Internet companies by revenue and largest online retailer. The company's fulfillment network maintains over 1,200 warehouses. Through its ecommerce platform, the company sells its customers everything from clothes, cosmetics, fresh food, household goods, furniture, appliances, and electronics. JD's net revenue for 2020 was $114.3 billion, a year-on-year increase of 29.3%. Annual active customer accounts grew by 30.3%, increasing from 362 million in 2019 to 471. 9 million in 2020.

As to cross-border importing, jd.hk (JD Worldwide) is a self-operating platform for imported goods under JD group. Formerly known as jd. com's "Haitun Global (a sea of overseas products in Chinese)" and "JD Global". In terms of **general trade import**, it has attracted nearly 20,000 brands and nearly 10 million **SKU**[①]s, covering product categories such as fashion, mother and baby, nutrition and health care, personal care and beauty care, 3C[②], household, imported food, automotive supplies, etc. , from more than 70 countries and regions such as the United States, Canada, South Korea, Japan, Australia, New Zealand, France, Germany, etc. , see Figure 6-14.

---

① Stock Keeping Unit (SKU) is a number assigned to a product by a retail store to identify the price, product options and manufacturer of the merchandise. A SKU is used to track inventory in a retail store. They are very valuable in helping to maintain a profitable retail business.

② Computer, Communication and Consumer Electronics.

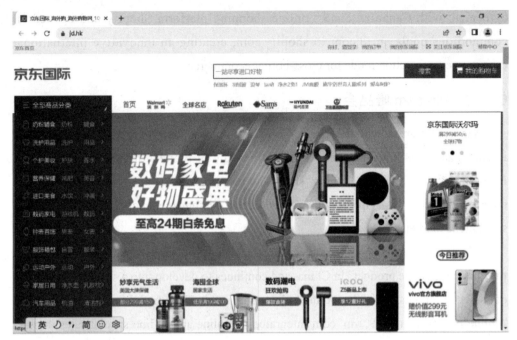

Figure 6-14   Jd.hk platform

In 2021, JD Worldwide cooperated with tax-free licensed enterprises such as Shenzhen duty-free group and Sanya maritime travel tax-free company, and launched online duty-free stores such as maritime travel tax-free and Shenzhen duty-free in JD Worldwide. It also cooperated with the world-famous duty-free operator Lagardère[1] to open offline stores in Sanya, and successively opened cross-border experience stores in Xi'an, Sanya and other places.

Jd.hk's marketing methods are entertainingly diversified and attractive. They have activities like building a live broadcast, short video, graphic and text marketing ecosystem inside and outside the station, and even introducing social ecommerce gameplay, with the help of *Jingxi* (a name overlapped with Jingdong in Chinese, meaning surprise), star stores and other forms, to enrich consumers' future intention of buying (*zhongcao* meaning planting grass literally). In 2021, "Black Friday" not only become a big promotion of the new round of "Super 10 billion subsidies", but also invited the main members of the famous talk shows like "**Roast**" and **"I can I BB"** to interact with consumers in the form of live broadcast on the night of "Black Friday". On Feb, 2022, it reached a cooperation

---

[1]   A French travel retail agency.

agreement with Canadian SaaS^① online shopping platform Shopify and opened all commodities pools on jd.com to shopify.com, creating an innovative international ecommerce cooperation mode for cross-border ecommerce.

6.5.2　Vip.com 唯品会

Vip. com, starting with the name of vipshop.com, was founded in 2008, headquartered in Guangzhou. Its main business is the online sale of branded discount goods on the Internet, covering branded clothing, shoes and bags, beauty, mother and baby, home and other major categories. Vip.com belongs to vertical ecommerce, and its products focus on some niché markets.

Vip.com has created an innovative ecommerce model of "famous brand discount + **flash purchase** + genuine product" in China, and continues to develop into a special sales model of "selected brands + big discounts + flash purchase". This model is vividly known as "online outlets". In 2019, vip. com integrated its online and offline special sales through the acquisition of Shanshan Outlet, creating an **omni-channel special sales** system, see Figure 6-15.

In 2012, vip.com **went listed** on the New York Stock Exchange (NYSE). As of June 30, 2021, vip.com has achieved profits for 35 consecutive quarters. In 2021, the number of active users was 51.1 million, an increase of 32% year-on-year. Deloitte's 2019 Global Retail Power Report showed that from 2012 to 2017, vip.com's compound growth rate was 73.8%, ranking second among the "top ten fastest-growing retailers in the world".

---

① SaaS Stands for "Software as a Service". It is software that is deployed over the Internet rather than installed on a computer. It is often used for enterprise applications that are distributed to multiple users. SaaS applications typically run within a Web browser, which means users only need a compatible browser in order to access the software. SaaS is considered part of cloud computing since the software is hosted on the Internet, or the "cloud". Because SaaS applications are accessed from a remote **server** rather than installed on individual machines, it is easy to maintain the software for multiple users. For example, when the remote software is updated, the client interface is also updated for all users. This eliminates **incompatibilities** between different software versions and allows vendors to make incremental updates without requiring software downloads. Additionally, users can save data to a central online location, which makes it easy to share files and collaborate on projects.

Figure 6-15　Vip.com platform

6.5.3　G.suning.com 苏宁国际

Founded at the end of 2014, g.suning.com is also known as Suning International. It is a cross-border ecommerce self-supporting platform under Suning Group. It is characterized by "buying quality goods, buying fashionable goods, buying fast, and buying economically". Its categories cover beauty, mother and baby, food, health care, 3C digital products, household daily use, clothing, luggage, etc. Suning overseas has established branches and purchase centers in the United States, Japan, South Korea, Hong Kong (China), Australia, New Zealand, Italy, Germany, Britain, France, Spain, Czech Republic and other places. It has established cooperation relations with overseas international brands. Suning International has successively built 8 overseas warehouses and 10 bonded warehouses to transport goods from places of origin to China and ensure the **timeliness of distribution**, see Figure 6-16.

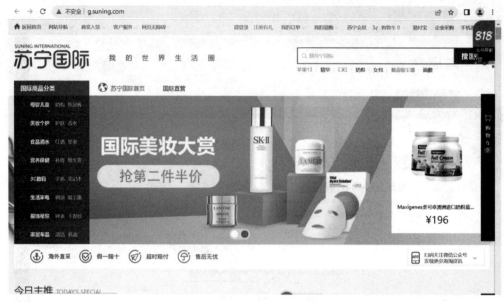

Figure 6-16　G.suning.com platform

6.5.4　Ymatou.com 洋码头

Founded in 2009, as a Chinese overseas shopping platform, ymatou.com was firstly a platform specially to purchase American goods. Sellers on the platform can be divided into two categories: one is the individual buyer, with the mode of C2C, and the other is manufacturer or agent, with the mode of B2C. The Buyer Mode (C2C mode) has increased the uniqueness of platform commodities. Relying on its own intrusive live broadcast system, it is attracting much attention of most of the female shoppers, see Figure 6-17.

Ymatou. com offers two specific services. On the one hand, its mobile app of "ymatou. com" offers the first "live broadcasting shopping" mode, which offers overseas products by the way of live broadcasting. On the other hand, its *Juyanghuo* program (means gathering foreign goods) provides group purchase projects.

It has built a cross-border logistics system. As the earliest ecommerce platform with its own logistics center in China, ymatou. com has overseas warehouses covering more than 20 countries and regions in the world, and has established 15 international logistics centers in the world. Ymatou. com has built a cross-border logistics system: Beihai international. Ten major international logistics and storage centers (New York, San Francisco, Los Angeles, Chicago, Melbourne, Frankfurt, Tokyo, London, Sydney and Paris) have been built overseas. In addition, it has cooperated with many international airlines to carry out international charter flight transportation. More than 40 global flights have entered the country every week.

Figure 6-17　Ymatou.com platform

After 2020, live ecommerce and cross-border ecommerce has been deeply integrated to provide comprehensive supply chain services. Ymatou. com started a special program for TikTok live broadcast. In addition, ymatou has launched a new retail strategy and opened 6 offline duty-free direct purchase stores, which are distributed in Shanghai, Chongqing. In 2021, the first offline flagship store was officially launched in Chongqing.

6. 5. 5　Haituncun.com 海豚村

There is a special business model in cross-border importing: **Link-and-sale & Rebate Mode** where a website or a platform offers links to a certain foreign goods platform or website and get commission by offering links. Haituncun. com, 55haitao.com and haitao.com are a few ones that were once successfully operated before 2019.

Haituncun.com provides cross-border import direct purchase and direct mail services for domestic users. Users can directly purchase overseas ecommerce products in Haituncun.com, and directly purchase direct mail throughout the whole process, so as to achieve transparency in goods source, price and logistics, see Figure 6-18.

Haituncun.com cooperates directly with overseas and local well-known ecommerce in the form of **exclusive commercial authorized agents**, minimizing intermediate links and transferring the **circulation costs** to consumers. Overseas ecommerce is directly mailed to domestic consumers through international logistics. There are no intermediate links such as buyers, purchasing agents and transshipment. One of the disadvantages of this mode is that most of the international logistics are done through air and the fees are high in transporting.

Figure 6-18　Haituncun.com platform

6. 5. 6　55haitao.com 55 海淘网

55haitao. com is **rebate website**. Founded in 2011 and headquartered in Shanghai, haitao.com is a platform that integrates global commodity discount information and provides consumers with consumption suggestions and shopping rebates. It creates Haitao community and provides a comprehensive strategy for hundreds of millions of consumers.

The unique value of 55 Haitao platform is not to sell goods, but to provide a way of life, see Figure 6-19. When consumers come to 55 Haitao, they are not only shopping, but also having a guide to broaden their horizons and harvest their lifestyles. By providing convenient shopping channels and abundant commodity supply, it makes global shopping a daily life and enables every ordinary person to enjoy a quality life that is convenient but not expensive.

Figure 6-19　55haitao.com platform

6.5.7　Haitao.com 海淘网

Founded in 2013, "Haitao" established a cooperation relationship with foreign B2C ecommerce websites, see Figure 6-20. Users benefit from zero agency purchase, direct overseas delivery, all genuine goods, direct mail, and the same price as abroad. It mainly recommends famous online stores and international brands from all over the world to consumers, and translates and displays commodity information to users, so that consumers can browse and buy commodities freely in the world. All commodities are directly mailed from overseas and payment could be made in RMB.

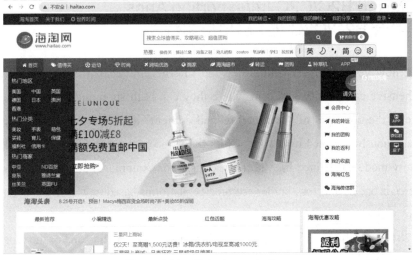

Figure 6-20　Haitao.com platform

6.5.8　Bonded Area Importing Model 保税区进口模式

Since the establishment of bonded area, business is conducted here. Just as what are mentioned in tmall.hk and jd.hk, bonded area is used widely in importing and exporting. Local governments build platforms to conduct cross-border importing ecommerce by making full use of the bonded areas. The following may be two of the earliest.

Kjt.com, started in 2013, is the official platform of Shanghai free trade zone and an overseas shopping mall for imported goods. It is also the first cross-border ecommerce platform in China established on the base of Chinese pilot free trade zones operation. On the platform, the cooperative merchants have been **filed by customs**, thus avoiding the risk of buying fake goods. The whole process of electronic management can guarantee the traceability of goods, so that consumers can obtain guaranteed service. On the other hand, each product on the platform will be marked with its own price, import tariff and logistics cost, so that consumers can clearly know the composition of their payment price at a glance, avoiding merchants from "clunking" the price, and consumers can also obtain corresponding tax payment **vouchers**. The shopping channel is more standardized and transparent, the price is more affordable than the domestic physical stores, and the source of goods is more secure and reliable.

kjb2c.com is one of the projects under Ningbo International Logistics Development Co., Ltd. and is licensed by the National Development and Reform Commission and the General Administration of Customs. It functions similarly as kjt.com.

6.6　Mixed B2C/C2C Im/exporting Apps
混合 B2C/C2C 进 / 出口应用程序

The new generation has integrated the Internet and real life, and tends to use a comprehensive community platform where they can both shop and express themselves. At present, the concepts of "commercialized content" and "content ecommerce" have been continuously accepted by market. Cross-border ecommerce in User Generated Content community mode has gained high user stickiness. For example, Xiaohongshu cross-border ecommerce is one of the cross-border ecommerce platforms based on the "UGC community + shopping" mode.

In 2013, "xiaohongshu" was established in Shanghai, which is one of the cross-border ecommerce importing platforms that started to adopt the "UGC community + shopping" mode in China, see Figure 6-21. At the beginning of its establishment, "xiaohongshu" was just an overseas travel shopping guide app. In 2014, "xiaohongshu" launched the community function of user generated content sharing and interaction, forming a clear UGC mode.

Figure 6-21　Xiaohongshu business

On March 2015, xiaohongshu successfully launched the ecommerce platform—"**welfare society**". Since then, it established and improved the cross-border logistics supply system of the platform, trying **a business loop** of "community + ecommerce" model. By January 2019, the number of xiaohongshu app users had exceeded 200 million, with an estimated value of more than US $3 billion. At present, xiaohongshu UGC community has become a life sharing platform, and its community model of "shopping list display+ sharing" has attracted many young female users[①]. According to iResearch consulting data, female users of xiaohongshu account for 80%. It is characterized by young female consumers who live in **the first and second-tier cities**, have a high economic& income level, and most of them have overseas studying and living experience.

Besides Xiaohongshu, TikTok Shop, Pinduoduo and WeChat etc. are also trying their own way of conducting cross-border ecommerce. TikTok Shop is exploring live

---

① https://www. 163. com/dy/article/H7QEBLD705118HJE. html, Jan-12-2023.

broadcasting in exporting in UK and Southeastern countries. Pinduoduo developed an app Temu in American market by reinventing its domestic share-buying model on Sep, 2022. WeChat has its **applets** and **subscription account** ready for importing foreign products.

In brief, more platforms are joining the army of cross-border ecommerce. ByteDance is trying its cross-border ecommerce platform Fanno and IfYooou after a few failures. Some platforms are coming and some others are going. It is from failure that Chinese enterprises learn to grow. The map of Chinese cross-border ecommerce players is in constant change.

📖 Words and Phrases 词汇和短语

product pages 产品页

reviews（用户）评论；（宝贝）评价

transaction logs 交易记录

order fulfillment and delivery 订单配送

customer support 客户服务

returns 退货

businesses 公司；卖家

window period 窗口期

OEM (Original Equipment Manufacturer) 原始设备生产商

ODM (Original Design Manufacturer) 原始设计生产商

category（产品）大类

customs clearance 海关清关

automatic marketing 自动化营销

keyword ranking 关键词排名

one-key query 一键式查询

advance 预付款

3C　3C产品；计算机、通信、消费类电子产品

rate of packet loss 丢包率

performance-price ratio 性价比

adaptability 合用性

parity 对等

incubator 孵化器

storage centers 存储中心

flagship store 旗舰店

self-operating business 自营模式

comprehensive bonded zone 综合保税区

bonded import + retail processing 保税进口；零售加工

sub-categories 子品类；小类目

merchants 卖家；商户

membership 会员制

procurement platform 采购平台

high-end buyers 高端用户

SaaS platform 软件即服务平台

"Small Order Quick Reaction" operating model 小单快反运营模式

China International Import Expo 中国进口博览会

fulfillment network 配送网络

general trade import 一般贸易进口

SKU 最小存储单位

Roast 吐槽大会（娱乐节目）

I can I BB 奇葩说（娱乐节目）

server 服务器

incompatibilities 不兼容

flash purchase 秒杀

omni-channel special sales 全渠道促销

go listed 上市

timeliness of distribution 配送及时性

link-and-sale & rebate model 链接销售—返利模式

exclusive commercial authorized agents 独家商业授权代理；独家代理

circulation costs 流通费用

rebate website 返利网站

filed by customs 海关备案

vouchers 凭证

welfare society 福利社

a business loop 商业闭环

the first and second-tier cities 一、二线城市

applets 小程序

subscription account 订阅号

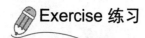

Exercise 练习

I. Reflections and Critical Thinking Questions.

1. What are the classifications of cross-border ecommerce in China?

2. Could you describe Alibaba's cross-border ecommerce ecosystem?

3. There are quite a few B2B platforms working well in China. Please introduce the platform that you think is promising and tell the reasons.

4. Some B2C platforms are booming. Which one do you think is the most promising one? Why?

5. What do you think of the trend of Chinese cross-border ecommerce? Please give your illustrations.

II. True or False

1. Thanks to the complete industrial chain and supply chain, China has developed successful foreign trade in the past 40 years. (   )

2. China's cross-border ecommerce business dominates China's foreign trade. (   )

3. In Alibaba's cross-border ecommerce ecosystem, it not only covers B2B exporting, but also covers B2C importing and exporting. (   )

4. Alibaba.com conducts both exporting and importing ebusiness. (   )

5. Every cross-border ecommerce platform has its overseas warehouse. (   )

6. Logistics is the hurting point for cross-border ecommerce. (   )

7. With the popularity of mobile devices, most of the cross-border ecommerce platforms, like AliExpress, conduct online business both on website and app. (   )

8. E-payment is popular in south-eastern countries. (   )

9. Tmall.hk makes good use of Chinese bonded area and all the sellers on the platform are foreign entities. (   )

10. Dhgate is a B2B comprehensive platform focusing customers in south east Asia. (   )

11. Lightinthebox. com is a self-operating B2C platform focusing on selling wedding dresses. (   )

12. JD.hk is a self-operating comprehensive platform with its own fulfillment network. (   )

13. Being successful in mobile ecommerce, SheIn excels at its efficiency in fast fashion new product and logistics. (   )

14. Xiaohongshu, being good at UGC ecommerce, focuses on female customers of big cities. (　　)

15. Most of the importing and exporting cross-border ecommerce platforms would take advantage of Chinese bonded areas or free trade zones to improve their efficiency in logistics. (　　)

III. Nouns Explanation

1. alibaba.com; aliexpress.com; lazada.com; tmall. hk; kaola.com

2. globalsources.com; made-in-china.com; diytrade.com; dhgate.com

3. lightinthebox.com; dx.com

4. jd.hk; vip.com; g. suning.com; ymatou.com; haituncun.com

5. SheIn; Xiaohongshu; TikTok shop

6. mobile ecommerce; UGC cross-border ecommerce; rebate model; bonded area cross-border ecommerce importing

IV. Reading and Critical Thinking

Case 1

Baby Goods Marketplace Mia.com to Suspend Operation[①]

Beijing, July 8 (TMTPOST) 2022– Chinese baby goods online marketplace Mia.com announced that it will suspend the operation of its mobile application on September 10 and remove the application from application stores. Mia.com is a Sequoia-backed mother and baby product ecommerce platform once valued at over 10 billion yuan (US$1.5 billion).

The ecommerce platform said in the announcement that orders on its platforms made before the suspension of mia.com's mobile application will continue to be processed and will be completed. After Mia.com suspends the operation of its mobile application, it will delete user accounts and user information. The platform will also stop collecting information and data on consumers and vendors on its platform.

Mia.com's mobile application is no longer

---

① https://baijiahao. baidu. com/s?id=1737799543571330748&wfr=spider&for=pc, 1-1-2023.

accessible on Apple's App Store now. Users could still find the mobile application on some Android app stores. However, none of them are available for download.

The company decided to shut down the mobile application because of "changes in users' shopping habits, " according to a statement. However, Mia.com's mini-app on the Chinese social media application WeChat will remain active, the company said.

Mia.com was established by Liu Nan in 2011. It started as a vendor on the Chinese ecommerce platform Taobao and became popular for its bestselling diapers. It took Mia.com only two years to become a major vendor on Taobao. In February 2014, Mia.com created its own website and left Taobao, officially transitioning itself to an ecommerce marketplace.

Between 2014 and 2016, Mia.com received five rounds of financing, raising around two billion yuan in total. Investors include ZhenFund, Sequoia Capital China, K2VC and Baidu, etc. In 2015, Mia.com completed its series D round financing at US$150 million, raising money from H Capital, Sequoia Capital China and Baidu. However, Mia.com has not been able to raise fund in the past few years. The company completed its Series E round financing in October 2016 and has not disclosed any further financing information since then.

Case 2

On July 12, 2022, Eachnet.com（易趣全球集市）announced to stop its business on August 12, 2022.

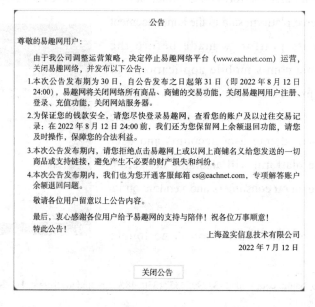

Case 3

Though a wealth of opportunities in cross-border ecommerce, there are fierce competitions and challenges facing the management of companies. Lightinthebox, once an influential marketer in the arena, is now facing decreasing business. International big companies like eBay, Amazon all shrank their business and did the layoffs globally at the end of 2022.

Critical Thinking and Questions:

1. What are the key elements in building and maintaining a global ecommerce business?

2. What are the challenges in this field?

More Resources:

1. Chinese billionaire Jack Ma made an on-stage appearance at the World Economic Forum in Davos in 2017 (24:43)[①]

2. An interview on the world economic forum 2017 (30:37)[②]

Keys-6

---

① https://www. bilibili. com/video/BV1KT4y127a1, Jan-1-2023.

② https://www. bilibili. com/video/BV1rb411A7F8/?spm_id_from=autoNext, Jan-1-2023.

Chapter 7

Policy, Practice and Innovation of China's Cross-border Ecommerce
中国跨境电商政策、实践和创新

Objectives

1. Understand international rules and regulations in developing CBEC

2. Know the framework of China's CBEC from policy to practice

3. Master the functions of free trade zone and CBEC comprehensive pilot area

4. Master the innovations of China's CBEC practice

5. Master the significance, technology, challenge of overseas warehouse

Open Case: watch the video and answer the questions

Video: Jack Ma at Viva Tech 2019 (50:52, focus on the 8-10th and the 40-43th minutes)

Questions:

1. What does Jake Ma think of the rules and regulations to cross-border ecommerce?

2. What is the difference in making rules between China and Europe?

3. Do you agree with him? Please state your reason.

视频资源链接

With the rapid development of foreign trade in economic globalization, China's cross-border ecommerce is developing in a particularly rapid speed. Cross-border ecommerce is a new form of foreign trade with a big growth rate, the greatest potential in the past 5 years since 2017. It has become a new driving force for China's foreign trade development, a new channel for economic transformation and upgrading, and a new economic growth point for high-quality development.

According to statistics from Chinese customs, China's cross-border ecommerce total revenue increased by nearly 10 times in the past five years from 2017 to 2022. In 2021, the import and export volume reached 19. 2 trillion Yuan, an increase of 18.6% (refer to table 6-1). There are about 33,900 cross-border ecommerce firms currently[①]. The number of cross-border ecommerce enterprises has been increasing year by year since 2017. In 2020, 6,313 new enterprises started their e-business, with a year-on-year increase of 58.42%. In 2021, there were 10,900 new enterprises, with a year-on-year increase of 72.2%. In 2022, with the downturn of global economy, quite a lot of enterprises are facing pressure and challenges[②]. It seems that cross-border ecommerce is entering a stage of readjustment in 2023.

Since the establishment of Hangzhou comprehensive pilot zone for cross-border ecommerce in 2015, after several rounds of expansion, China has set up 165 comprehensive pilot zones in 31 provinces by Nov. 24, 2022. The expansion would provide more powerful support for the innovation and development of cross-border ecommerce.

Modern information and communication technology (ICT) empowers the development of ecommerce, and various countries extend their hands to welcome ecommerce. Local or International organizations have been actively participating in international rules and regulations for global ecommerce. For instance, in the early development of ecommerce, the U. S. government released "*A Framework for Global Electronic Commerce*[③]" in 1997. WTO issued the *Declaration on Global Electronic Commerce*[④] in 1998, OECD published *A Global Action Plan for Electronic Commerce*[⑤] in 1998 and the United Nations published *Draft Uniform Rule on Electronic Signature*[⑥] in 1999, etc.

On the other hand, global agreements on ecommerce face a lot of challenges due to various political, cultural and economic **discrepancies**. Regional economic cooperation agreements like **RCEP** (Regional Comprehensive Economic Partnership), **CPTPP** (Comprehensive and Progressive Agreement for Trans-Pacific Partnership), **USMCA**

---

① https://new. qq. com/rain/a/20220303A02PHI00, 1-3-2023.

② https://baijiahao. baidu. com/s?id=1752621614945340911&wfr=spider&for=pc, https://baijiahao. baidu. com/s?id=1752726167746853948&wfr=spider&for=pc, 1-3-2023.

③ 《全球电子商务框架》, https://www. docin. com/p-9777469. html, 12-1-2023.

④ 《全球电子商务宣言》。

⑤ 《全球电子商务行动计划》, https://www. oecd-ilibrary. org/science-and-technology/a-global-action-plan-for-electronic-commerce_236544834564, 12-1-2023.

⑥ 《电子签名统一规则（草案）》http://www. 110. com/falv/dianzishangwufa/dianzishangwufagui/2010/0719/137503. html, 12-1-2023.

(United States-Mexico-Canada Agreement) are performing in a more active way than global economic organizations like WTO. Most countries especially developed ones have made their own legal system to regulate the conduct of ecommerce including data transfer, privacy, **collection and exemption of duties**, etc. This chapter will focus on China's practice on cross-border ecommerce in recent decade.

7.1　Policy in China 中国的政策

As an important breakthrough to promote the transformation and upgrading of foreign trade and create a **new economic growth point**, cross-border ecommerce has been supported continuously by favorable policies.

7.1.1　Scope of Policy Support 政策支持的范围

There are as many as hundreds of guidelines and policies regulating and guiding the development of Chinese cross-border ecommerce. It is under the government's **policy bonus** that China's cross-border ecommerce is developed prosperously especially since the year of 2015 when the State Council approved the first establishment of China (Hangzhou) **Cross-border Ecommerce Comprehensive Pilot Area** and started building 165 pilot areas across China in 8 years.

The scope of cross-border ecommerce legislation (including laws, policies, guidelines, etc.) usually revolves around the following aspects: to promote the development of cross-border ecommerce including decisions of establishing comprehensive pilot area; to regulate and standardize cross-border ecommerce trade; to guarantee commodity quality and consumer rights protection and transportation; to protect intellectual property; and to supervise cross-border ecommerce business conducts, etc. To be specific, there are many regulations and guidelines on tax and tariff issues, electronic payment, **delivery and logistics**, overseas warehouse, Intellectual Property protection, **security and confidentiality** (personal privacy), telecommunications infrastructure, technical standards, **universal services**, labour issues, **electronic signature**, etc.

A few guiding laws are functioning and directing the development of CBEC. Among them, *The Electronic Commerce Law of the People's Republic of China*[①] is the most

---

① 《中华人民共和国电子商务法》。

influential ecommerce law guiding Chinese ecommerce conduct. As to the field of cross-border ecommerce, there are as many as a hundred guidelines, rules, announcements from the central government at the national level, and correspondingly, numerous provincial and municipal proposals, decisions guiding the practice of cross-border ecommerce. Every province and province-level municipality has correspondent orders, circulars and guidelines that are in line with local economic specialty and economic level. Take Zhejiang Province and Canton Province for instances, there are dozens of local rules and practices guiding the conduct of the 2 provinces' cross-border ecommerce ranging from seaport, comprehensive pilot area, logistics, payment, platforms, overseas warehouse, courier service, offline industrial park, exhibition activities, China Railway Express, postal service etc. , see appendix 1.

Besides, China's cross-border ecommerce is closely related to China's macro-economic development planning and strategies, like **the Belt and Road Initiative (BRI)**, **Yangzi River Economic Belt**, **Beijing-Tianjin-Hebei Integration Initiative**, **Made in China 2025 Program,** RCEP, Internet Plus Program, etc.

7. 1. 2　Policies in 2021 and 2022　2021 年和 2022 年的政策

On July 9, 2021, *the Guidelines of the General Office of the State Council on Accelerating the Development of New Forms and Models of Foreign Trade*[①]were published, which proposed to apply the B2B direct export of cross-border ecommerce and the overseas warehouse supervision mode of cross-border ecommerce export across the country, facilitate the management of cross-border ecommerce import and export commodity return and exchange, optimize the list of cross-border ecommerce retail imported goods, expand the pilot cities and areas of cross-border ecommerce comprehensive pilot zone. By 2025, the goal is to cultivate about 100 excellent overseas warehouse enterprises and establish a new foreign trade logistics network covering the world and developing in a coordinative manner by relying on overseas warehouses.

In May 2022, the General Office of the State Council issued the ***Circular on Promoting a Steady and High-quality Growth of Foreign Trade***[②], which proposed that firms in cross-border ecommerce declare themselves high-tech enterprises, which is the extension of the State's supporting policies for high-tech enterprises to enter the cross-

---

① 《国务院办公厅关于加快发展外贸新业态新模式的意见》。
② 《关于推动外贸保稳提质的意见》。

border ecommerce field and to promote the innovation and development of China's cross-border ecommerce. China will encourage cross-border ecommerce and other new business forms and models to grow even quicker to foster new driving force of foreign trade.

7. 1. 3 Importing Policy 进口政策

China's cross-border ecommerce is not only focused on exporting, but also on importing.

On January 17, 2020, the Ministry of Commerce, the Development and Reform Commission and other 4 Ministries and Commissions[①] jointly issued a notice on expanding the pilot areas of cross-border ecommerce retail import, which incorporated 50 cities (regions) including Shijiazhuang (in Hebei Province) and the whole island of Hainan into the scope of cross-border ecommerce retail import pilot. On March 18, 2021, the Ministry of Commerce and other Ministries and Commissions jointly issued another circular on expanding the cross-border ecommerce retail import pilot and strictly implementing the regulatory requirements, which clearly expanded the scope of the cross-border ecommerce retail import pilot to all cities (and regions) where **free trade pilot zone**, cross-border ecommerce comprehensive pilot zone, comprehensive bonded zone, import trade promotion & innovation & exhibition zone and **bonded logistics center (type B)** are located. All pilot cities should assume the main responsibility, implement the regulatory requirements, and investigate and deal with the illegal behaviors such as "online purchase from bonded area + offline self-picking"[②] and second-hand sales outside the special supervision area of customs, and to ensure the progress of the pilot areas and promote healthy and sustainable development of foreign trade industry.

7. 2 China's CBEC Practice 中国跨境电商的实践

China has set aside special areas and zones for the development of cross-border ecommerce business, and formed a complete multi-level framework starting from demonstration base to free trade zone and foreign economic cooperation area.

---

① The General Administration of Customs, the Ministry of Finance, the State Administration of Taxation, the State Administration for Market Regulation.

② 线上购买，线下自提。

7.2.1   National Ecommerce Demonstration Base 国家电子商务示范基地

Though not cross-border oriented, **national ecommerce demonstration base** has been working as a trial for cross-border ecommerce. It is based on the accumulated experiences from ecommerce base that cross-border business could be developed further in a rapid and successful way.

In 2012, in order to promote a healthy, rapid and coordinated development of ecommerce in the 12th Five Year Plan (2011-2015), the Ministry of Commerce decided to launch the establishment of the national ecommerce demonstration base. Since then, the ecommerce demonstration base has become a central place for local ecommerce service enterprises and innovation platforms. 155 demonstration bases have been established by the year of 2022 in 4 batches. It promotes the rapid and standardized development of ecommerce, incurs the formation of large-scale, standardized and industrialized development of ecommerce service industry, and is conducive to the development of the cross-border ecommerce. The policy environment, infrastructure construction environment, personnel training have been established since then. At the same time, a complete ecommerce transaction service system has been formed: including the third-party online payment, mobile payment, security certification, credit evaluation, data deposit, **logistics distribution**, **operation outsourcing**, and technical support, which has promoted the organic integration of the offline physical market and the online virtual market, improved the modern supply chain and **duel circulation** system, and thus laid a solid foundation for the development of cross-border ecommerce.

7.2.2   Cross-border Ecommerce Comprehensive Pilot Area
跨境电商综试区

7.2.2.1   Establishment and Significance 建立和意义

As a great trial, China established its first cross-border ecommerce comprehensive pilot zone — a special economic area aimed at boosting foreign trade and cultivating new competitive edges globally — as early as 2015 in Hangzhou. For now, there have been a total of 165 such zones[①], covering 31 provinces, autonomous regions and municipalities, see Figure 7-1. While the first two batches of 13 zones were located in larger cities in the

---

① https://www. xiaohongshu. com/explore/6385b83b000000001b017856, 25-3-2023.

eastern coastal areas, the latter batches extended to the vast central and western regions, with all the prefecture-level cities of Jiangsu, Zhejiang, and Guangdong provinces included.

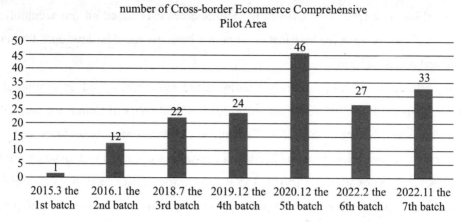

Figure 7-1　165 comprehensive pilot zones for cross-border ecommerce

Despite the unprecedented challenges brought by the COVID-19 pandemic, cross-border ecommerce, with its specific advantages, has boomed in China in the past few years.[①] China has seen the establishment of more than 30, 000 enterprises related to cross-border ecommerce, with the Gross Merchandize Volume climbing every year.

The establishment of cross-border ecommerce comprehensive pilot area is an initiative to deepen the reform of the foreign trade system and cultivate new advantages in foreign trade competition. Over the past years, China's cross-border ecommerce comprehensive pilot area has achieved positive results, forming a set of policy systems to adapt to cross-border ecommerce development, accumulating empirical practices that can be replicated across the country, and building a few leading global cross-border platforms and enterprises. The cross-border ecommerce **industry agglomeration effect** is promoting the transformation and upgrading of foreign trade, and supporting national development strategies.

7. 2. 2. 2　Functions 功能

According to the State Council, these pilot areas will work to settle deep problems in cross-border ecommerce, build complete industrial chains and offer experience that can be borrowed by the foreign trade sector across the country.

---

① https://investinchina. chinadaily. com. cn/s/202202/21/WS621342a8498e6a12c121f903/chinas-cross-border-ecommerce-pilot-zones-at-a-glance. html. Jan-12-2023.

In these pilot zones, both the central and local government provide a series of preferential policies in the field of customs clearance, tax, exchange settlement, commodity inspection, logistics, and financial service to facilitate businesses. For instance, the pilot zone in Hangzhou took the lead in the national **integration** of customs clearances. Enterprises could make customs declarations in Hangzhou and export from any port they want, e.g. Shanghai, Ningbo, Xiamen or Tianjin. The measure, which was later spread across China, reduces the customs declaration time from an average of 4 hours to just 1 minute.

In addition, these pilot zones have extensive warehouse storage facilities at home and abroad. Ecommerce enterprises are allowed to import unsold goods from overseas and store them in advance in bonded warehouses. Once consumers place an order, customs clearance starts immediately and the products can be delivered in merely two or three days. And it is cheap as there is no **international first leg transportation**.

In 2021, cross-border ecommerce B2B export supervision pilot was officially approved and expanded to other national-level customs, according to the General Administration of Customs. Meanwhile, China Railway Express has gradually supported the cross-border ecommerce, as China launched regular operation of freight train services since 2011.

7. 2. 3   China Free Trade (Pilot) Zones 中国自贸（实验）区

China free trade zone refers to a multi-functional special economic zone set up inside and outside the customs, with **preferential tariff** and special customs supervision policies as the main features and **trade liberalization and facilitation** as the main purpose. The State Council officially approved the establishment of China free trade zone on August 22, 2013. China's free trade zone is a "focus" of building an "upgraded version" of China's economy. Just as China's accession to the World Trade Organization has further stimulated the vitality of China's economy, the construction of the pilot free trade zone also promotes the great development of market economy, including the service industry. The innovative financial services, business services, culture, entertainment, education, medicine and medical care industries that were previously subjected to strict control have greater opportunities than before.

China free trade (pilot) zones work as important areas for cross-border ecommerce and often closely connected with the cross-border ecommerce comprehensive pilot areas. The 21 free trade zones cover even larger areas and are positively supportive to cross-border e-business, see Table 7-1.

Table 7-1　Free Trade (pilot) Zone in China

	China free trade pilot zone	
year	Batch(no)	place
2013	1st (1)	Shanghai
2014	2nd (3)	Guangdong, Fujian, Tianjin
2016	3rd (7)	Liaoning, Henan, Zhejiang, Hebei, Chongqing, Sichuan, Shaanxi
2018		Hainan Free Trade Port
2019		Lingang (Shanghai)
2019	4th (6)	Shandong, Jiangsu, Guangxi, Hebei, Yunnan, Heilongjiang
2020	5th (3)	Beijing, Hunan, Anhui

On September 27,2013, the State Council approved the establishment of China (Shanghai) pilot free trade zone. On April 20, 2015, it was expanded to a larger area. On April 20,2015, the State Council approved the establishment of three free trade pilot zones: Guangdong, Tianjin and Fujian. On March 31, 2017, 7 more were added: Liaoning, Zhejiang, Henan, Hubei, Chongqing, Sichuan and Shaanxi. On October 16,2018, the State Council approved Hainan free trade pilot zone. On August 2,2019, Shandong, Jiangsu, Guangxi, Hebei, Yunnan and Heilongjiang were added to the pilot zone family. On June 1,2020, the CPC Central Committee and the State Council issued the plan for the construction of Hainan free trade port. On September 21,2020, the 6th batch added Beijing, Hunan, Anhui and expanded Zhejiang pilot free trade zone to a larger area. All the 23 pilot free zones are functioning in a coordinative way for cross-border ecommerce and other businesses.

7. 2. 4　Service Trade Comprehensive Pilot Area 服务贸易全面深化试点

Foreign trade includes both physical goods and invisible service. China has been developing well in visible goods during the past 40 years in the time of globalization. The invisible trade, which is also called service trade, is a sensitive area where progress is often slow in many countries. Developed countries like the UK and the United States have a strong performance in service trade like finance and technology transfer, insurance, transportation, travel, intellectual property and digital products, construction project consulting and legal service, etc.

Starting from the year of 2016, Chinese have been reforming service trade including

offshore financing business, payment, travel, professional personnel flow, etc. The first and second pilots cover a 2-year span. In August 2020, the Ministry of Commerce launched a 3-year pilot program[①] improving China's international service trade by establishing 28 pilot cities and regions in major big cities across China.[②]

Through the comprehensive and deepening exploration of the pilot project, its purpose is to promote the in-depth reform of service trade, optimize the business environment, and increase the market vitality. The program is to promote a high-level opening-up in an orderly manner, accelerate the internationalization of the service industry, and practice a full opening-up and competitive business environment. It encourages an all-round innovations, integrates industry clusters, and enhances the innovation ability of market players. The service trade pilot program is to promote the optimization of China's foreign trade structure and high-quality economic development.

According to the data of the Ministry of Commerce, in 2021, China achieved rapid growth in service industry, with the total service trade reaching US $821.2 billion, up 16% year on year.[③] In the first half of 2022, China's import and export of services totaled 2891.09 billion yuan, up 21.6% year on year.[④]

7.2.5　Overseas Economic and Trade Cooperation Zone 海外经贸合作区

China's cross-border ecommerce is multilevel and multidimensional, not only including pilot areas at home, but also developing economic cooperation area globally. The establishment of RCEP is a great trial for that purpose. Besides, China has established dozens of overseas economic and trade cooperation zones along **the Silk Road Economic Belt** and some provinces[⑤] have encouraged their enterprises to establish economic area with foreign government, involving industries such as resource exploitation and processing, manufacturing processing, agricultural processing, trade logistics and scientific

---

① 　A plan to deepen pilot projects for the innovative development of the service trade, China Daily, 12-8-2020.

② 　https://m. thepaper. cn/newsDetail_forward_2185964, 3-3-2023.

③ 　服务业已成为全球经济支柱性产业 , 中国服务贸易规模连续八年居世界第二 , https://m. thepaper. cn/baijiahao_19756351. 12-1-2023.

④ 　上半年中国服务贸易交出亮眼成绩单 , http://www. scio. gov. cn/31773/35507/35513/35521/Document/1729753/1729753. htm. 12-1-2023.

⑤ 　《境外经贸合作区产能合作白皮书》, 中国电子信息产业发展研究院 ; 帮助合肥本土企业 "抱团出海" 2022 年市级境外经济贸易合作区认定工作正式启动 , http://www. myzaker. com/article/630c024c1bc8e04742000009/. Jan-12-2023.

and technological research and development, etc.

Chinese government supports big enterprises to carry out various forms of mutually beneficial cooperation overseas to promote mutual development with the host country. By 2022, there were more than 100 overseas cooperation zones[①]along the silk road economic belt and African countries with approvals from the Ministry of Commerce. For example, China-Egypt Economic Cooperation Zone is one of them in middle-east and there are 2 economic cooperation areas in the United Arab Emirates.[②]

7.3　China's Cross-border Ecommerce Innovation 中国跨境电商的创新

In the process of promoting cross-border ecommerce, China has developed a few unique foreign trade forms and modes which have been proved to be successful.

7.3.1　Market Procurement Trade Mode 市场采购贸易方式 [③]

As this trade model originated from China, there are a few English equivalence on internet news and newspapers, such as market purchasing trade unit, market purchase trade model, market procurement trade model, market purchasing trade mode, or market procurement trade method, etc.

7.3.1.1　Definition and Situation 定义和现状

Market procurement trade mode is an innovative trade mode, in which qualified operators purchase goods with a value of less than US$150,000 (including US$ 150,000) in a single customs declaration form in one **market agglomeration area** recognized by the Ministry of Commerce, and handle the **customs clearance formalities** for export goods at the place of purchase. This trade mode is created for the foreign trade transactions of "various categories, multi batches and small quantity[④]" in professional market. It's characterized by fast customs clearance, and **exemption from value-added tax**.

---

① https://www. investgo. cn/channel/v3_0/hzq/hzqList. shtml, 3-3-2023. 唐拥军等,"一带一路"背景下境外工业园区商业模式动态更新路径:基于中国－印度尼西亚经贸合作区的案例研究 [J]. 世界经济研究, 2021(11): 120-134+137.
② 崔政涛,中东地区境外经贸合作区的发展现状、机遇与挑战 [J]. 对外经贸实务, 2021(9) 40-45.
③ 市场采购贸易联网信息平台,义乌国际贸易综合信息服务平台, http://trade. yw. gov. cn/, 1-3-2023.
④ 多品类,多批次,小批量。

This mode is designed for bitty commodity. **Bitty commodity** includes articles regularly sold in local department stores, such as hardware, some daily necessities, stationery, gifts, etc. These articles are often produced in large quantities with a variety of patterns, rapid consumption turnover rate and with relatively low price.

The first procurement market was piloted in Yiwu, Zhejiang Province on April 18, 2013. By 2022, there have been 31 pilot areas of national market procurement trade mode approved in 5 batches, see Figure 7-2.

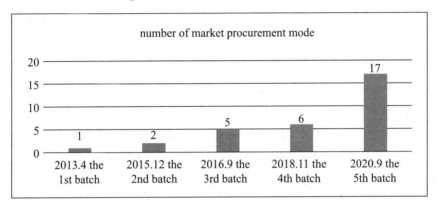

Figure 7-2   Number of market procurement mode[①]

According to the Announcement No.54 of the General Administration of Customs in 2014 and the Announcement No.4 of Hangzhou Customs in 2014, the customs added the market procurement supervision code (1039) to supervise the conduct of this mode.

7. 3. 1. 2   Features 特色

1. Small commodities exporting. The quality management of small commodity export has long restricted China's bitty commodity export. The emergence of market procurement trade mode has standardized this trade of small quantity, multi batch, and scattered products, which helps to establish a quality traceability system and implement effective management, stimulate market vitality and promote trade development.

2. Convenient customs clearance. For commodities exported through market procurement trade, if there are more than 10 commodities in each customs declaration form, simplified declaration can be implemented, and the customs can enjoy 24-hour electronic customs clearance, simplified declaration, and smart card clearance, so as to improve the convenience of customs clearance of export commodities.

---

① See the places at https://baijiahao. baidu. com/s?id=1730048412486716215&wfr=spider&for=pc, 26-3-2023.

3. VAT exemption. Commodities exported through market procurement trade are directly exempted from value-added tax. Goods that have not obtained or cannot obtain value-added tax invoices can be exported through market procurement trade. In terms of foreign exchange collection, the foreign exchange can be collected and settled by the pilot market procurement operators, or by the individual market operators who act as their agents for export, which greatly improves the efficiency of enterprise payment collection.

4. Reduce foreign trade risks. Through the market procurement of trade exports, the goods can be directly handled with the export customs clearance procedures at the place of purchase, without the need to be transported to the port customs, thus reducing the logistics cost. Since the customs clearance procedures have been handled in advance, the uncertainty is reduced, and the foreign trade risks are effectively avoided.

5. Improved information exchange and sharing. A shared trading platform for the large number of small, medium-sized and micro enterprises offers a convenient channel to the international market, opens the door to the internationalization of bitty commodities, and helps enterprises participate in international competition.

7.3.1.3　Challenges 挑战

In the process of operation, there appear a few challenges:

1. Low market participation rate. Taking Yiwu as an example, as of April 2019, 525 commodity groups had been registered and filed on the integrated service platform, with a declared business volume of 270,000 **declaration forms**. This number is almost insignificant compared with the 500,000 business households in the whole Yiwu market. In particular, registered enterprises are mainly logistics companies or customs brokers who have obtained government trade subsidies, and few real trade economic entities do the registration.

2. Single service function. Although the comprehensive service platform tries to expand scope of customs clearance, commodity certification and traceability, intellectual property and other services, the popular service is **foreign exchange settlement**. As of April 2019, more than 20,000 people have promoted the settlement of foreign exchange, 310,000 transactions have been settled, and the amount of foreign exchange settlement is US $10 billion, accounting for about 50% of the transaction scale of Yiwu market.

3. Un-authentic trade data. In practice, customs declaration is mainly made through brokers and logistics companies, and it is difficult to avoid misreporting, over-reporting,

and underreporting. Therefore, the authenticity of data cannot be guaranteed, and it is difficult for financial institutions to provide supply chain financial services based on these data.

7. 3. 2　China Railway Express 中欧班列

China Railway Express (CRexpress) is an express freight train running between China and Europe on fixed train, fixed line, and fixed schedule. It is safe, low-cost and efficient to transport goods between China and European continent, see Figure 7-3. It serves as an important channel and starting point for economic and trade cooperation. China Railway Express made an outstanding performance during the 2019 pandemic. When the pandemic in 2020 has incurred global traffic restrictions and transportation was restricted at harbors and airports, China freight trains carried supplies such as masks, protective suits and ventilators to many countries. In the year of 2022, more than 10,000 trains have transported various goods to European countries.

Figure 7-3　China Railway Express

7. 3. 2. 1　History of CR Express 中欧班列的历史

The primary reason for running the China Railway Express is to solve the logistics and transportation problems of the Chongqing production base of China Hewlett Packard Co. , Ltd (HP). HP's laptops used to be transported to Europe by sea-rail **multimodal transportation**. Because of the low labor price in Chongqing, HP built a factory there. In August 2009, HP signed an agreement with Chongqing municipal government on the annual output of 20 million laptops for export. Since then, 60% to 70% of the products produced by HP in China were transported to Europe by sea and then by rail to different countries, and the rest have been transported by air. However, it took more than 30 days to reach Europe by sea, which extended the delivery time. After arriving in Europe, the market price of the products sometimes dropped significantly. HP was eager to find a solution. HP headquarters set up a special team to study the Eurasian Continental Bridge. Previously, HP tried to transport through the south line, the north line and the Eurasian Continental Bridge, but failed. In order to break the bottleneck of transportation, Chongqing municipal government submitted a request to the General Administration of Customs, the former Ministry of Railways and other departments for the operation of the five scheduled trains on Chongqing Europe railway corridor. On March 19, 2011, the first China Railway Express "YUXIN' OU" (from Chongqing to Duisburg) was successfully launched.

Previously, the trade between China and Europe mainly relied on seaways, and the most important route was Chinese Mainland - Taiwan Strait - South China Sea - Malacca Strait (Makassar and Sunda Strait in Indonesia) - Indian Ocean - Mandela Strait - Red Sea - Suez Canal - Mediterranean (reaching the countries along the Mediterranean) - Gibraltar Strait - Europe. The transportation time was long and full of uncertainty.

Since then, Wuhan (Hubei Province), Zhengzhou (Henan Province), Chengdu (Sichuan Province), Suzhou (Zhejiang Province), Changsha (Hunan Province), Yiwu (Zhejiang Province) and other cities have successively opened railway container trains to Europe. In particular, after the formation of "the Belt and Road" Initiative, China Railway Express was regarded by many cities as a great channel to promote local development.

7. 3. 2. 2   Present Situation 现状

At present, the direct railway transportation between China and Europe usually takes 12-16 days, which saves at least 10 days compared with the traditional sea transportation. This will divert the goods originally transported by sea to land transport to a large extent, and increase an optional mode of logistics.

China Europe Express serves the country's westward strategy, breaking the restrictions on the development of inland cities caused by transportation problems, and thus promoting the economic development of inland cities. At present, CR Express has become an important part of the Silk Road Economic Belt. As a high-speed railway freight from China to European countries, the Express is conducive to promoting the economic development of China's mainland and maintaining close ties with the international market.

At present, the CR Express has three lines: the west, the middle and the east. The western channel passes through the central and western regions of China and exits through Alashankou and Horgos ports. The central channel passes through North China and exits through Erenhot port. The eastern channel passes through the coastal areas of Southeast China and exits through Manzhouli and Suifenhe ports. On June 8, 2016, China Railway officially launched the unified brand and logo of China Railway Express.

The Express is known as the *"land silk road of the new era"* . After years of operation, its characteristics of low freight, high speed and top security have become increasingly prominent. The significance of the operation has already risen to the national strategic level, and it has played a positive role in promoting economic exchanges and regional cultural exchanges. During the pandemic of 2020–2022, the Express operated safely, and continued to play the role of "artery" in all major economic channels.

In the first half year of 2022, a total of 10, 000 trips have been operated, and a total of 972,000 TEUs of goods have been sent, an increase of 5% year-on-year, and the ratio of loaded container reached 98. 4%. At present, the Express has 82 operating lines, reaching 200 cities in 24 countries in Europe. The transport service network covers the whole of Europe. Goods transported cover 53 categories, including clothing, shoes and hats, automobiles and accessories, grain and wood, etc.

7. 3. 2. 3   Challenges 挑战

Though CR express has been in operation for more than 10 years, challenges remain:

1. Insufficient supply and needs, and vicious competition

Due to shortage of goods variety, some provinces allocated goods from other places and fought for resources. There appeared the chaos of price competition.

2. Backward national supporting infrastructure

Many of countries along the line have poor infrastructure construction, low level of informatization, and low efficiency in multimodal transport and distribution which affects the storage and transfer of goods. What's more, the size of China's rail is different from the size of Russia and other countries. When CR express arrives at the agreed place, the train must be transferred to local trains and goes to destination.

3. Complex and unmature customs procedures

Each country has different procedures, resulting in time and cost waste in quarantine and customs clearance. For example, when goods arrive at a country, the customs code of that country will have to be changed again. In addition to the high cost of changing the code, enterprises also have to bear the cost of **goods detention**.

7.4　Overseas Warehouse 海外仓

Overseas warehouse is critical in promoting cross-border ecommerce in better logistics and fulfillment services. It is expected to solve the pain point of logistics and offers good customer experience. Chinese government encourages the layout of overseas warehouse by stipulating a set of policies. Overseas warehouse is not only the product of cross-border ecommerce and cross-border logistics, but also the general trend of logistics industry in the era of cross-border ecommerce. What's more, improving the overseas warehouse service system can effectively reduce the overall operating cost of the global supply chain of China's foreign trade enterprises.

7.4.1　Definition and Situation 定义和现状

"Overseas warehouse" refers to the storage facilities established overseas. In this mode, cross-border ecommerce enterprises export goods to overseas warehouses in bulk in the terms of general trade mode, and then deliver the goods to overseas consumers after the ecommerce platform completes the sales. Ecommerce platforms or export enterprises may lay out overseas logistics systems by building or renting "overseas warehouses". It enables export enterprises to send goods to overseas warehouses in batches, so as to realize local sales and local distribution in the country. It is an optimization and integration of existing cross-border logistics and transportation schemes. After customers place orders, export enterprises could deliver goods locally through overseas warehouse, reducing the delivery time and customs clearance barriers.

Data from the Ministry of Commerce showed that Chinese businesses now operate more than 1,900 overseas warehouses[1], covering a total floor area of 13.5 million square meters. Almost 90 percent of those facilities are in North America, Europe Mainland and Asia. The need of developing overseas warehouses has been high on the government's agenda in recent years. It is seen as an infrastructure to inject fresh momentum into China's foreign trade and ensure the stability of **industry chain** and supply chain.

7.4.2　Government Support and Goal 政府支持和目标

Chinese government encourages the development of overseas warehouse by providing supportive policies and guiding enterprises and finance to establish overseas warehouses

---

[1] https://baijiahao. baidu. com/s?id=1709778490691549741&wfr=spider&for=pc, 25-3-2023.

(see Figure 7-4) in alignment with the operation of cross-border ecommerce. China learned from the model of FBA (Fulfillment by Amazon) and established different overseas warehouses along the silk road economic belt, in well-developed ecommerce business regions like Europe and North America.

By 2025, the goal is to cultivate about 100 high-caliber overseas warehousing businesses that will stand out in fields such as information technology, intelligent development, diversified services and local operations, according to a guideline issued by the General Office of the State Council on July 9, 2021.

Figure 7-4　Overseas warehouse

7.4.3　Functions 功能

The purpose of the existence of overseas warehouses is to facilitate the storage of goods by cross-border ecommerce export enterprises and to realize shorter distance and more efficient distribution. Therefore, storage is the core function, and the level of storage management is critical. An overseas warehouse often covers tens of thousands of square meters, more than 100,000 items, millions of pieces of inventory, huge freight yard and massive inventory.

In addition to that, such facilities can enable quicker customs clearance and faster delivery, with some offering one- or two-day delivery services in destination countries. It has accurate overseas inventory management, flexible sales strategy and decision support system. When goods are delivered from overseas warehouses to customers in 1-3 days, logistics cost becomes low. For cross-border ecommerce customers, customer experience would thus be enhanced.

At present, overseas warehouses have become a popular logistics mode in the industry, such as eBay's introduction of Winit's US warehouse, UK warehouse and German warehouse as the focus of publicity and promotion. JD invests heavily on overseas logistics and warehouses. Logistics service providers such as Chukou1 and 4PX have also made great efforts to build overseas storage systems and continuously launch new products.

7.4.4   Challenges 挑战

Although overseas warehouse can solve the problems of low efficiency in cross-border logistics, it also faces challenges.

(1) High requirements for information technology

The core problem in the operation of overseas warehouses is the high requirements for information technology. Vendors would prepare their goods in advance in overseas warehouse. When the overseas customer places the order, it needs to issue the operation instructions remotely. At the same time, it also needs to monitor the inventory situation, which requires high information technology.

(2) Right and high-quality goods

When sellers store goods in batches in overseas warehouses in advance, there are inventory risks. It is hard to know whether the prepared goods are **hot-cake products** with a high turnover rate or not, otherwise it may lead to a **stock explosion** which would increase cost for storing and warehousing.

(3) Localization and Multicultural management

Overseas warehouse is regarded as a local company rather than an affiliated "warehouse", which needs to pay taxes. Localization management of overseas warehouses also requires local operators, local employees, and people who are consistent with local consumers in terms of language, culture and belief to participate in the marketing, management and operation of the entire enterprise.

In brief, China is now experiencing trials and errors in cross-border ecommerce both in policies and practices. Some of these experiences would prove to be successful in some areas and not so acceptable in other places. Trial-and-error is the mother of success for China's cross-border ecommerce.

Appendix 1   Chinese policies of cross-border ecommerce[①] (2017—2022)

2022 年中国跨境电商相关政策汇总一览		
发布日期	政策名称	主要内容
2022.1	《"十四五"现代流通体系建设规划》	规划提出发展外贸新业态，促进跨境贸易多元化发展，鼓励跨境电商平台完善功能，引导企业优化海外仓布局，提高商品跨境流通效率。
2021.11	《"十四五"对外贸易高质量发展规划》	明确"十四五"期间对外贸易发展指导思想、主要目标和工作重点，引导市场主体行为，积极扩大进口、优化出口，推动对外贸易高质量发展，服务构建新发展格局，开拓合作共赢新局面。支持加快发展贸易新业态，包括促进跨境电商持续健康发展、推进市场采购贸易方式发展、发挥外贸综合服务企业带动作用、加快海外仓发展、推动保税维修发展、支持离岸贸易发展等。
2021.9	《国企电子商务创新发展行动计划》	推动跨境电商协同发展。
2021.9	《"十四五"电子商务发展规划》	倡导开放共赢，支持跨境电商和海外仓发展。
2021.7	《"十四五"商务发展规划》	推动外贸创新发展，开展跨境电商"十百千万"专项行动、规则和标准建设专项行动、海外仓高质量发展专项行动等，到 2025 年，使跨境电商等新业态的外贸占比提升至 10%。
2021.7	《国务院办公厅关于加快发展外贸新业态新模式的意见》	在全国适用跨境电商 B2B 直接出口、跨境电商出口海外仓监管模式，便利跨境电商进出口退换货管理，优化跨境电商零售进口商品清单，扩大跨境电商综试区试点范围；到 2025 年每年培育 100 家优秀海外仓企业，并依托海外仓建立覆盖全球、协同发展的新型外贸物流网络。
2021.3	《中华人民共和国国民经济和社会发展第十四个五年规划和 2035 年远景目标纲要》	加快发展跨境电商，鼓励建设海外仓，保障外贸产业供应链运转。
2020.1	《区域全面经济伙伴关系协定》	RCEP 协定的第十二章，详细列出了"电子商务"的具体条款。在第十二章电子商务部分中，第四节促进跨境电子商务。这里包括：计算设施的位置和通过电子方式跨境传输信息。在通过电子方式跨境传输信息上，一是缔约方认识到每一缔约方对于通过电子方式传输信息可能有各自的监管要求。二是一缔约方不得阻止相关人员为进行商业行为而通过电子方式跨境传输信息等。
2020.1	关于印发全国深化"放管服"改革优化营商环境电视电话会议重点任务分工方案的通知	推进跨境电商综合试验区建设。
2020.1	关于推进对外贸易创新发展的实施意见	促进跨境电商等新业态发展。

[①]   2022 年中国跨境电商行业最新政策汇总一览 | 外贸 | 物流 | 跨境电商 _ 手机网易网 (163.com), 31-7-2023.

续表

2022 年中国跨境电商相关政策汇总一览		
发布日期	政策名称	主要内容
2020.8	关于进一步做好稳外贸稳外资工作的意见	支持跨境电商平台，跨境物流发展和海外仓建设。
2020.7	关于做好自由贸易试验区第六批改革试点经验复制推广工作的通知	在全国范围内复制推广跨境电商零售进口退货中心仓模式。
2020.6	关于落实《政府工作报告》重点工作部门分工的意见	加快跨境电商等新业态发展,提升国际货运能力。
2020.6	《关于开展跨境电子商务企业对企业出口监管试点的公告》	自 2020 年 7 月 1 日起，跨境电商 B2B 出口货物适用全国通关一体化，也可采用"跨境电商"模式进行转关。首先在北京、天津、南京、杭州、宁波、厦门、郑州、广州、深圳、黄埔海关开展跨境电商 B2B 出口监管试点，根据试点情况及时在全国海关复制推广，有利于推动外贸企业扩大出口，促进外贸发展。
2020.5	《关于支持贸易新业态发展的通知》	从事跨境电子商务的企业可将出口货物在境外发生的仓储、物资、税收等费用与出口货款轧差结算。跨境电子商务企业出口至海外仓销售的货物，汇回的实际销售收入可与相应货物的出口报关金额不一致。跨境电子商务企业按现行货物贸易外汇管理规定报送外汇业务报告。
2020.5	《关于同意在雄安新区等 46 个城市和地区设立跨境电子商务综合试验区的批复》	同意在雄安新区、大同市、满洲里市、营口市、盘锦市、吉林市、黑河市、常州市、连云港市等 46 个城市地区设立跨境电子商务综合试验区。
2020.4	国务院常务会议	推出增设跨境电子商务综合试验区、支持加工贸易、广交会网上举办等系列举措，积极应对疫情影响努力稳住外贸外资基本盘；决定延续实施普惠金融和小额贷款公司部分税收支持政策。
2020.3	《海关部署关于跨境电子商务零售进口商品退货有关监管事宜公告》	跨境电子商务出口企业、特殊区域内跨境电子商务相关企业或其委托的报关企业可向海关申请开展跨境电子商务零售出口、跨境电子商务特殊区域出口、跨境电子商务出口海外仓商品的退货业务。
2020.1	《关于扩大跨境电商零售进口试点的通知》	将进一步扩大跨境电商零售进口试点范围，本次扩大试点后，跨境电商零售进口试点范围将从 37 个城市扩大至海南全岛和其他 86 个城市（地区），覆盖 31 个省、自治区、直辖市。
2019.3	2019 年全国两全	将改革完善跨境电商等新业态扶持政策。推动服务贸易创新发展，引导加工贸易转型升级、向中西部转移，发挥好综合保税区作用。优化进口结构，积极扩大进口。办好第二届中国国际进口博览会。加快提升通关便利化水平。

发布日期	政策名称	主要内容
	2022 年中国跨境电商相关政策汇总一览	
2018.12	《关于跨境电子商务零售进出口商品有关监管事宜的公告》	该公告进一步全面规定了跨境电子商务企业管理、零售进出口商品通关管理等事项。为跨境电子商务零售进出口监管工作提供了详细的法律依据，促进跨境电子商务的健康有序发展。
2018.12	《关于做好电子商务经营者登记工作的意见》	要求电子商务经营者申请登记为个体工商户的，允许将网络经营场所作为经营场所进行登记，允许将经常居住地登记为住所，但不得开展线下经营活动。
2018.11	《关于实时获取跨境电子商务平台企业支付相关原始数据有关事宜的公告》	该公告要求参与跨境电子商务零售进口业务的跨境电商平台企业应当向海关开放支付相关原始数据，供海关验核。
2018.11	《关于完善跨境电子商务零售进口税收政策的通知》	通知对税收进行三个方面的调整：一是将年度交易限值由每人每年 2 万元调整至 2.6 万元，将单次交易限值由每人每次 2000 元调整至 5000 元；二是明确完税价格超过单次交易限值但低于年度交易值且订单下仅一件商品时，可以通过跨境电商零售渠道进口。按照货物税率全额征收关税和进口环节增值税、消费税，交易额计入年度交易总额；三是明确已经购买的电商进口商品不得进入国内市场再次销售。
2018.9	《关于跨境电子商务综合试验区零售出口货物税收政策的通知》	自 2018 年 10 月 1 日起，对综试区电子商务出口企业出口未取得有效进货凭证的货物，同时符合下列条件的，试行增值税、消费税免税政策。
2018.8	《关于深化电子商务领域知识产权保护专项整治工作的通知》	加大重点区域整治力度，加大重点案件打击和曝光力度，加大线下源头追溯和打击力度。
2018.7	《关于同意在北京等 22 个城市设立跨境电子商务综合试验区的批复》	明确了新设一批综试区，逐步完善促进其发展的监管制度、服务体系和政策框架，推动跨境电商在更大范围发展。
2018.4	《关于规范跨境电子商务支付企业登记管理》	进一步规范海关跨境电子商务监管工作。
2018.3	《关于做好电子商务统计工作的通知》	强化电子商务统计制度执行，建立企业联系机制；优化样本结构，抓好重点企业；提高数据质量，确保工作时效。
2017.11	《关于复制推广跨境电子商务综合试验区探索形成的成熟经验做法的函》	将跨境电商线上综合服务和线下产业园区"两平台"及信息共享、金融服务、智能物流、风险防控等监管和服务"六体系"等成熟做法面向全国复制推广。现将上述成熟做法的说明和具体举措印发，供各地借鉴参考。另请各地结合实际，深化"放管服"改革，加强制度、管理和服务创新、积极探索新经验，推动跨境电商健康快速发展，为制定跨境电商国际标准发挥更大作用。

📖 Words and Phrases 词汇和短语

discrepancy 差异，不一致

RCEP《区域全面经济伙伴关系协定》

CPTPP《全面与进步跨太平洋伙伴关系协定》

USMCA《美墨加三国协议》

collection and exemption of duties 税收征收和减免

new economic growth point 新经济增长点

policy bonus 政策红利

cross-border ecommerce comprehensive pilot zone 跨境电商综试区

delivery and logistics 配送和物流

security and confidentiality 安全和机密

telecommunications infrastructure 通信基础设施

technical standards 技术标准

universal services 统一服务

electronic signature 电子签名

the Belt and Road Initiative (BRI) "一带一路"倡议

Yangzi River Economic Belt 长江经济带

Beijing-Tianjin-Hebei Integration Initiative 北京—天津—河北综合发展计划

Made in China 2025　2025 中国制造计划

circular(法律、政策等的) 意见

free trade pilot zone 自贸试验区

bonded logistics center (type B) B 型保税物流中心

national ecommerce demonstration base 国家电子商务示范基地

logistics distribution 物流配送

operation outsourcing 运营外包

duel circulation 双循环

industry agglomeration effect 产业集聚效应

integration 整合

international first leg transportation 国际头程运输

preferential tariff 优惠税

trade liberalization and facilitation 贸易自由化、便利化

offshore financing business 离岸融资服务

the Silk Road Economic Belt 丝绸之路经济带

market procurement trade mode 市场采购贸易方式

market agglomeration area 市场聚集区

customs clearance formalities 海关清关手续

exemption from value-added tax 增值税免除

bitty commodity 小商品

declaration forms 报关单

foreign exchange settlement 外汇结算

multimodal transportation 多式联运运输

goods detention 货物滞留

industry chain 产业链

hot-cake products 爆品

stock explosion 爆仓

 Exercise 练习

I.　Reflections and Critical Thinking Questions.

1. What are the areas for cross-border ecommerce policies to cover?

2. What are the functions and advantages in building 165 cross-border ecommerce comprehensive pilot areas?

3. What are China's cross-border ecommerce innovations and what are their features?

4. A news on Dec. 23, 2022 said goods of over 43, 085 containers in Belgium EQ2 warehouse were detained by Belgium customs and were fined € 1394487.12 to pay for value-added taxes and other charges.[①]

What do you think of the challenges in international logistics and rules and regulation compliance in customs clearance?

5. What are the strengths and challenges of building overseas warehouse for Chinese companies?

II. True or False

1. One country's domestic rules prioritize over international laws in cross-border ecommerce. (　　)

---

① 　https://baijiahao. baidu. com/s?id=1753258088346430067&wfr=spider&for=pc, and https://zhuanlan. zhihu. com/p/594402746, 12-1-2023.

2. The Electronic Commerce Law of the People's Republic of China is the guiding law for Chinse cross-border ecommerce . (   )

3. Though Chinese exporting ecommerce dominates the marketplace, importing ecommerce grows at a faster speed. (   )

4. Cross-border ecommerce comprehensive pilot area is selected and built on the consideration of industry agglomeration effect. (   )

5. China's free trade pilot zones implement more open policies and practices than Cross-border Ecommerce Comprehensive Pilot Area. (   )

6. China's overseas economic cooperation areas mainly run along the silk and belt initiative and undertake multitask functions including economic cooperation and political cooperation. (   )

7. Market procurement trade mode is especially good for bitty commodity like gifts, hardware, daily necessities, accessories, stationery, etc. (   )

8. CR Express shortens the time of transportation and improves efficiency of logistics between China and European Countries. (   )

9. Overseas warehouse would reduce the cost of transportation and reduce the cost of logistics, so it is good for all commodities. (   )

10. Good political and economical environment is the premise to conduct cross-border commerce. (   )

III. Noun Explanation

1. Cross-border ecommerce comprehensive pilot area

2. China free trade (pilot) zones

3. overseas economic and trade cooperation zone

4. market procurement trade mode

5. China Railway Express

6. overseas warehouse

IV. Watching and Critical Thinking

Video: Jack Ma on the China Opportunity at Gateway (57:16)[1]

---

[1] https://www. bilibili. com/video/av11540455/, 14-03-2023.

Critical Thinking and Questions:

1. What are the qualities an entrepreneur represents in the video?

2. What conditions are good for the development of ecommerce?

3. What is the future of cross-border ecommerce according to the speaker? Do you agree with him? Why?

More Resources:

1. 美国电子商务发展的政策框架及我国的应对措施 [1]

2. 跨境电商相关税收政策国际比较研究 [2]

3. 美国数字贸易政策三十年及启示 [3]

4. 陈寰琦 . 国际数字贸易规则博弈背景下的融合趋向——基于中国、美国和欧盟的视角 [J]. 国际商务研究 , 2022

5. A case of YLT overseas warehouse. [4]

Keys-7

---

[1]　https://max. book118. com/html/2021/1203/7143122150004055. shtm, 26-3-2023.

[2]　https://new. qq. com/rain/a/20220805A066ME00, 26-3-2023.

[3]　https://www. fx361. com/page/2021/0723/8606465. shtml, 26-3-2023.

[4]　http://www. ylt-global. com/en/h-col-126. html, 26-3-2023.

Chapter 8

Supervision and Future of Cross-border Ecommerce
跨境电商监管和未来

Objectives

1. Master the connotation of different supervision code

2. Know the achievement of cross-border ecommerce in the past decade

3. Understand the future of cross-border ecommerce

4. Understand the challenges, concerns and opportunities facing cross-border ecommerce

Open Case: read the following news and answer the questions

1. Tax evasion of Wish, SheIn in Brazil

2. Intellectual property violation checked by Chinese customers

3. 400,000 infringement of shaving razor blade was detected by customs

Questions:

1. Why are there so many misconducts in cross-border ecommerce?

2. What should the international society, government, customs, enterprises and individuals do in order to curb illegal acts?

视频资源链接

International **supervision** on cross-border ecommerce is developed within the framework of international organizations or regional trade agreements. However, a few regional agreements have achieved some progress in the aspect of supervision and regulation. A one-suit-for-all supervision agreement is practically unachievable due to complex factors such as various national power and influence, economic level and stringent requirement on political safety etc. Each country also stipulates its own unique mode of supervision. Supervision is usually performed by customs which makes a comprehensive management system based on import and export. Its purpose is mainly for customs' taxation, statistics and management. To be specific, supervision means to supervise customs' declaration form of imported and exported goods.

In China, supervision of cross-border ecommerce is mainly undertaken by the General Administration of Customs (GAC), which stipulates rules and policies and adds new codes contingently for the sake of supervision and statistics.

Customs sets requirements for supervision, taxation and statistics by employing different supervision modes. In order to improve management and service, the supervision code in **the customs declaration automation system** adopts a **four-digit structure**, in which the first two digits are codes for classification, and the last two digits are codes for statistics. For example, codes 9710 and 9810 belong to different types: 97 and 98, and they share the same "10" for the convenience of statistics. While codes 1210 and 1239 belong to the same supervision mode but under different **statistics parameter,** see Table 8-1.

Table 8-1　China's supervision code in cross-border ecommerce

	mode	sub-type	scope	time
supervision code	cross-border B2B	B2B exporting	9710 (direct B2B export)	July 2020
			9810 (B2B export to overseas warehouse)	July 2020
		others	0110 (general trade)	-
			1039 (market procurement mode)	July 2014
	cross-border B2C	retail importing/ exporting	9610 (direct mail)	Feb 2014
			1210 (bonded area ecommerce)	July 2014
			1239 (bonded area ecommerce model A)	Dec 2016

8.1　Modes of Supervision in CBEC 跨境电商监管模式

For a foreign-trade-oriented country like China, we have created a few Chinese-style exporting and importing supervision modes in cross-border ecommerce, thus being represented by different codes stipulated by the General Administration of Customs, namely 9710, 9810, 9610, 1210, 1039, 1239, etc. It is with the development of cross-border ecommerce that new modes of supervision come into being. Besides, supervision code 0110 for general trade is still widely in use. ·

8. 1. 1 General Trade Supervision Code: 0110 一般贸易监管码 0110

The supervision code of general trade supervision is "0110" which suits traditional importing or exporting.

Before 2014, goods were mainly imported through the mode of either general trade or personal postal items. General trade is more applicable to business to business (B2B) importing. Under this situation, domestic enterprises in China purchase goods overseas in a whole batch and sell them in China. **Personal postal articles** (including EMS) were originally applicable only to the import of gifts or other personal articles (C2C) between relatives and friends through postal service. Because the customs did not have special **provisions** for cross-border ecommerce import and export, goods sent directly to Chinese consumers from abroad were also imported through post channel. With the development of cross-border ecommerce, post service cannot meet the new situation and new modes emerged accordingly. New supervision modes were needed.

8. 1. 2 B2C Importing Supervision Code: 9610 and 1210
B2C 进口监管码：9610 和 1210

On February 2014, **the General Administration of Customs (GAC)** officially published the customs supervision mode code "9610" in its No.12 **Announcement** of 2014. The full name of this mode was "cross-border trade ecommerce" abbreviated as "ecommerce". On July 2014, GAC added "1210" in its No.57 Announcement of 2014, which was fully named "bonded cross-border trade ecommerce" abbreviated as "bonded ecommerce". With the two announcements, cross-border B2C ecommerce has its own separate customs supervision code, see table 8-1.

On March 2016, the Ministry of Finance, the General Administration of Customs and the State Administration of Taxation jointly issued *The Notice on Tax Policies for Cross-border Ecommerce Retail Import* (CGS [2016] No. 18), which stipulated that **customs duties, import value-added tax** and **consumption tax** shall be levied on cross-border ecommerce retail import goods. It also stipulated a single transaction value limit of cross-border ecommerce retail imported goods (no more than 5,000 Chinese yuan/year since 2021) and the annual transaction limit of individuals (no more than 26,000 yuan/year since 2021). At the same time, imported goods are required to provide the customs with electronic information of "**three orders**" of transaction, payment and logistics. This notice enables cross-border ecommerce imports to subject to special supervision and **preferential**

tariff policies that are different from other trade modes.

On December 2018, the Announcement No. 194 of the General Administration of Customs made systematic provisions on enterprise management, customs clearance management, tax collection and management, **on-the-site management, quarantine, inspection,** logistics management and **return management** in retail import and export cross-border ecommerce, and clarified the respective responsibilities of all participants.

In code "9610", "96" is the code of classification, and "10" is the code for customs statistics. It could be used for both B2C exporting and importing. When used for exporting, it is not used in cross-border ecommerce comprehensive pilot areas but used in other places and cities, and the supervision is almost the same as that in general trade[1]. But for importing, it is called "9610 direct import purchase". Under the "9610 direct import purchase" mode, once consumers (orderers) purchase goods on the cross-border ecommerce platform, ecommerce enterprises or platform enterprises, payment enterprises and logistics enterprises transmit "three orders" information (commodity transaction orders, payment documents and logistics transportation documents) to the customs respectively. After the goods arrive at the customs' supervised workplace (site), ecommerce enterprises or their agents go through declaration and tax payment procedures with the customs. It is mostly adopted by cross-border ecommerce platforms and overseas ecommerce enterprises operating in a wide range of categories. Customs clearance procedure is handled in the mode of "verification and release of good goes by individual list, declaration of customs clearance goes in a whole batch[2]".

Comparatively, "1210" means "bonded cross-border trade ecommerce" (abbreviated to "bonded ecommerce"). "12" stands for bonded area. The "1210" supervision mode is only applicable to **customs special supervision areas** and bonded logistics centers (type B[3]) approved to carry out cross-border ecommerce import pilot.

---

① https://page. om. qq. com/page/OOZCnnFrDwSKj7i20UKxUNHQ0?source=cp_1009, 14-1-2023.

② 清单验放 , 汇总申报。

③ There are 2 types of(pioneer) bonded logistics center in China at present. Bonded logistics center (type B) refers to the place supervised by the customs, run by one legal representative of anenterprise within Chinese territory and participated by multiple enterprises to engage in bonded warehousing and logistics business. While Type A bonded logistics center is a place run by one legal representative and participated by one enterprise in the business of warehousing and logistics business.

8. 1. 3　B2B Exporting Supervision Code: 9710 and 9810
　　　　B2B 出口监管码：9710 和 9810

The two modes are used for B2B exporting only. In 2020, the General Administration of Customs issued Announcement No.75 on *the Pilot Export Supervision of Cross-border Ecommerce Enterprises to Enterprises*[①], adding two B2B foreign trade customs supervision mode codes "9710" and "9810". The announcement was officially implemented on July 1, 2020, and was piloted at a few customs in China. Later, it issued Announcement No. 47 in 2021, officially "replicating and promoting cross-border ecommerce B2B export supervision pilot across the national customs".

Code "9710" is "cross-border ecommerce enterprise to enterprise direct export", abbreviated as "CBEC B2B direct export", which is applicable to goods directly exported to foreign business. Similarly, code "9810" is "cross-border ecommerce export to overseas warehouse", and the abbreviation is "CBEC export overseas warehouse", which is applicable to goods exported to overseas warehouse.

8. 1. 4　Bonded Area B2C Importing Supervision Code: 1239
　　　　保税区 B2C 进口监管码：1239

1239 is applicable only to importing. Due to China's great gap between importing and exporting, and in order to enhance importing, a series of new policies have been stipulated to simplify importing process and supervision.

According to No. 75 Announcement of the General Administration of Customs [2016], it adds code 1239 implemented on 1st Dec. 2016. The full name is "bonded area cross-border trade ecommerce", referred to as "bonded ecommerce A". It is applicable to cross-border ecommerce retail import commodities imported by domestic ecommerce enterprises through special customs supervision area or bonded logistics center (type B). And, noticeably, the 1239 is not applicable to the cross-border ecommerce retail import business in 10 cities, including Tianjin, Shanghai, Hangzhou, Ningbo, Fuzhou, Pingtan, Zhengzhou, Guangzhou, Shenzhen and Chongqing.

After the new cross-border ecommerce policy (after 2020), domestic bonded imports are divided into two groups: one is for the above 10 cities with bonded area approved before the new policy; the other type is for other cities that started their bonded import

---

① 《关于开展跨境电子商务企业对企业出口监管试点的公告》。

business after the new policy, such as Xi'an and Taiyuan, etc. Since the new policy allows the **suspension and extension measures**, and the suspension and extension measures are allowed only for the previous 10 cities, the customs have to distinguish the two when do supervising: for the 10 cities that are exempt from customs clearance, the code 1210 will continue to be used; for other cities that need to provide customs clearance, the new code 1239 is adopted.

8. 1. 5   Market procurement Trade Supervision Code: 1039
市场采购监管码：1039

In July 2014, the General Administration of Customs issued Announcement No. 54 of 2014 (*Announcement on the Measures for the Supervision of Market Procurement Trade and Related Matters of its Supervision Mode*[①]), adding the customs supervision mode code "1039", which is fully called "market procurement trade mode".

Customs supervision code 1039 refers to the trade mode of "market procurement". It is a trade mode in which eligible operators purchase goods with a single customs declaration form of less than US $150,000 (including US $150,000) in the market agglomeration area approved by the Ministry of Commerce, and handle customs clearance procedures for export at the place of purchase.

Goods purchased under 1039 mode can be quickly cleared through customs procedure. If tax exemption policy allows, there is no need to issue an invoice for export and no need to apply for export tax rebate. For goods exported in the form of market procurement trade, the **foreign currency revenue** can be transferred through legal channels, avoiding the risk of **bank account closure**. Goods could be classified for easy customs clearance and customs formalities are reviewed every second, which can greatly save time in customs clearance.

1039 is a trade mode tailored for small and medium-sized export enterprises selling toys, daily necessities, furniture, hardware and clothing etc. This trade mode began with the export in Yiwu market cluster, Zhejiang Province. By the end of 2020, the number of national market procurement trade pilot marketplaces had reached 31. It is an innovative foreign trade style for China to export goods to European countries through China Railway Express.

---

① 《关于修订市场采购贸易监管办法及其监管方式有关事宜的公告》。

8.2　Achievements of China's CBEC 中国跨境电商的成就

In the past decade, cross-border ecommerce is embracing businesses and consumers from more than 200 countries and regions around the world, with huge market potential. With the strong support of the Chinese government and globalization, a clear and complete industrial chain has been formed from marketing to payment, from logistics to financial services.

8.2.1　Great Trade Volume and Growth Rate 规模大、增速快

Foreign trade has always been a driving force for the development of China's economy, and China's cross-border ecommerce has been rising for more than 10 consecutive years, contributing greatly to the national economic growth. In 2020, among the whole cake of ecommerce, the percentage of cross-border ecommerce reached 33.6%. Cross-border ecommerce possibly prevails with the widespread of mobile ecommerce and with the increasingly supportive policies.

In addition, according to data from Chinese customs, in 2020, the number of online orders (import and export) checked and released through the customs cross-border ecommerce management platform reached 2.45 billion, with a year-on-year growth of 63.3%, and the import and export volume reached 1.7 trillion Yuan, with a year-on-year growth of 31.1%, 10 times higher than that in 2015. According to the Ministry of Commerce, China has more than 1,500 comprehensive foreign trade service enterprises and more than 1,900 overseas warehouses (90% of which are in North America, Europe and Asia).

8.2.2　Dominating B2B Mode B2B 模式主导

From the perspective of business model, in 2019, about 80% of the cross-border trade under customs supervision is B2B transactions, and about 20% is B2C transactions. The eastern coastal areas are in the leading position, in which Guangdong Province rate much larger than other provinces and municipalities.

In the B2B export ecommerce, platform-based ecommerce is in the leading position. In 2021, the proportion of GMV (gross merchandise volume) of comprehensive ecommerce platforms exceeded 80%. B2C retail platforms are active. Big sellers such as Anker Innovation and Aukey Technology develop their offline entities and ecommerce platforms. While fast fashion seller SheIn reached its prime stage. In addition, in recent years, live broadcasting ecommerce has shown a strong growth momentum, with GMV accounting for 14% of total ecommerce.

8.2.3   Fierce Competition 竞争激烈

Due to the rapid development of information technology, China's telecommunication and internet infrastructure has been established, the penetration rate of smart phones has been high and the number of online shoppers is steady. By December 2021, the number of online shopping users in China has reached 840 million, an increase of 7.67% over December 2020. On the whole, export cross-border ecommerce has entered into a stable phase. **DTC platforms**, third-party platforms, mobile ecommerce, community ecommerce are in full bloom. Participants of cross-border ecommerce are in fierce competition, and a considerable part of them will inevitably be eliminated in the process of competition. Starting from 2022, ecommerce platforms began to lay off employees in order to survive in fierce competition. Ali and JD are optimizing their management and personal structure, and Amazon announced to lay off 18,000 and another 9,000 workers at the end of 2022 and the beginning of 2023.

8.2.4   Policy Dividends 政策红利

Since 2004, the government has continuously introduced favorable policies to promote the development of cross-border ecommerce. Especially since 2013, China has significantly enhanced its support for cross-border ecommerce, which has become an important catalyst for the development of the industry. For example, on June 2015, *the Guiding Opinions of the General Office of the State Council on Promoting the Healthy and Rapid Development of Cross border Ecommerce*[①] has been put into practice. It combined cross-border ecommerce with national strategies such as the "Belt and Road Initiative", and created a good industrial development environment for cross-border ecommerce enterprises in terms of financial support, comprehensive services, etc. Since 2015, 165 comprehensive pilot zones for cross-border ecommerce have been established in 7 batches to provide layout and guidance for the development of cross-border ecommerce. In July 2021, the General Office of the State Council issued *the Opinions on Accelerating the Development of New Business Types and Models of Foreign Trade*[②], clearly proposing to

①   《关于促进跨境电子商务健康快速发展的指导意见》。
②   《国务院办公厅关于加快发展外贸新业态新模式的意见》。

improve the support policies for cross-border ecommerce development, solidly promote the construction of cross-border ecommerce comprehensive pilot areas.

On May 26,2022, the General Office of the State Council issued *the Opinions on Promoting the Stability and Quality Improvement of Foreign Trade*[①]. It helps foreign trade enterprises to cope with challenges, facilitates the return and exchange of goods for cross-border ecommerce exports, supports the development of overseas warehouses, and formulates guidelines for the protection of intellectual property rights in cross-border ecommerce.

8.3　Trends of Cross-border Ecommerce 跨境电商的未来

With increasingly conducive and supportive industrial policies and accumulatively complete supply chain development, the status of cross-border ecommerce will become increasingly significant and become a driving force for economic development.

8.3.1　Globalization and Localization 全球化和本地化

Though cross-border ecommerce is a global business, more comprehensive platforms like alibaba.com and Lazanda.com and DTC APPs like SheIn are booming and developing greatly in different areas or regions. Though globally operated, most business are done locally and designed to attract local consumers. **Localization** is the secret of cross-border ecommerce: employ local people, speak local language and do local things. The operation mode of cross-border ecommerce is to use "local language" to tell brand stories and "local people" to sell brand products. **Globalization** is the best scenario for "local users-driven growth".

8.3.2　Products & Categories 货品多元化

Categories of commodity in cross-border ecommerce transactions have gone through an upgrading process: from simple to complex, from online music, video and other zero logistics-cost digital products, to clothing, computers and accessories, jewelry, cosmetics, consumer electronics and other convenient transportation products, to fresh food, home appliances, EV cars and other products with higher logistics requirements. With the continuous emergence of diversified cross-border **logistics solutions**, commodity categories continue to expand. Furthermore, for some advanced markets, with the

---

① 《国务院办公厅关于推动外贸保稳提质的意见》。

popularity of **VR (virtual reality)** technology, virtual shopping is to offer more diversified commodities online.

8. 3. 3　Niche Markets 市场细分化

The growth of cross-border ecommerce in the future would mainly come from the diversified growth of niche market. Compared with the continuous growth of mature markets such as Europe and the United States, emerging markets such as Brazil and Southeastern Asia are rising rapidly. In Southeast Asian countries, Indonesia, Malaysia, the Philippines, Thailand and other countries are seriously differentiated in terms of economic development stage and language. These emerging markets have accumulated a large amount of consumer demand due to their unreasonable local industrial structure, especially the underdeveloped consumer goods industry. Singapore, in particular, as a developed country with a per capita GDP of almost US $ 80,000 in Southeastern Asia, has a much higher penetration rate of cross-border ecommerce than other countries.

EU appears to be a big market, but each member country is different in terms of language, culture and consumption habits. UK, France, Germany, Italy, etc. have formed their own niche markets. Few countries could form as perfect market as China and the United States, for both have the largest and most unified markets.

8. 3. 4　Service and Customer Experience 服务和顾客体验

With the development of cross-border ecommerce, the information-based cross-border ecommerce platform that relies on commission and advertising is facing a bottleneck, while the comprehensive service-based platform prospers in meeting the satisfaction of both trading parties by providing **one-stop service**. Platforms with good services often have a high conversion rate. Some comprehensive cross-border ecommerce platforms are forming their own industry ecosystems to better integrate the connection of the entire industrial chain and greatly improve logistics efficiency.

8. 3. 5　Mobile Ecommerce and Social Ecommerce 移动电商和社交电商

With the continuous development of mobile technology and the rapid popularization of social media, cross-border ecommerce in the future will enter a mobile and social media era. Mobile ecommerce allows consumers to shop at any time, and anywhere, allowing suppliers to do business without time and space constraints. Emerging countries that directly enter into the mobile market are bringing huge **incremental markets**. The development of China's mobile terminal is rapid, and the penetration rate of China's mobile Internet users is high. In 2021, the number of cross-border online shoppers in China reached 155 million, fee Figure 8-1.

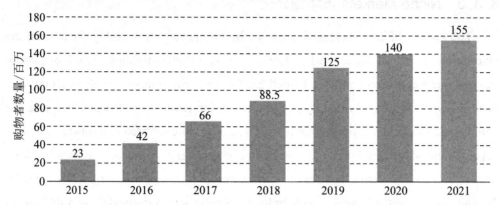

描述：2021年，中国约有1.55亿人使用跨境电子商务，高于上一年的1.4亿人。
当年，中国跨境进口电子商务市场规模达到约0.2万亿元。
注：中国；2015年至2021年。
来源：100eC.cn*

Figure 8-1   Population of cross-border ecommerce in China (2015–2021) (Unit: million)

8. 3. 6   Information and Telecommunication Technology 信息和通信技术

Not only China but also the whole world considers the development of cross-border ecommerce a historical opportunity on the basis of modern information technology, internet and website, etc. Information Technologies including big data, 5G, AI, cloud computing, Internet of Things (IOT), blockchain technology, etc. provide fundamental premises for the booming of cross-border ecommerce.

8. 3. 7   The Largest Market 最大的市场

Thanks to a stable economic and political environment, a complete industrial chain system, and a fast-responding supply chain, China is providing a wide range of high quality goods, which has won the favor of overseas consumers. According to statistics of PayPal, China has become the world's largest B2C cross-border ecommerce market. About 26% of global payment transactions occur in Chinese Mainland, and the United States accounts for 21%, ranking second, followed by Britain, Germany and Japan. A survey (5005 questionnaires from the United States, the United Kingdom, Germany, Spain and France) showed that clothing, footwear and socks were the categories with the highest frequency of cross-border procurement, and also the preferred categories for consumers to experience online shopping for the first time[①].

8.4 Challenges in CBEC 跨境电商的挑战

Though facing a great opportunity, there are still some challenges around the world which go against the force of economic integration and cooperation. Considering the theory of cross-border ecosystem in chapter 1, challenges may be macro and micro factors.

8.4.1 Anti-globalization Wave 反全球化浪潮

In recent years, developed countries and regions like the United States and EU have witnessed a massive **anti-globalization** wave: which are shown by the **Brexit referendum** of the United Kingdom, the establishment of a series of alliances after President Biden of the United States came to power, and the European **populist** parties coming into power and having introduced a series of anti-globalization measures. They have evolved from supporters into opponents of globalization, and the once **neoliberalism-based globalization**, which has made great progress all the way, has encountered unprecedented difficulties.

Global trade under the guidance of classic free trade theory has partly led to **income distribution effects** among different industries and countries. Unequal gains among countries in the process of economic globalization have led to the rise of conservatism, while **populism** has emerged from the polarization of social wealth in some countries, and the two forces have jointly promoted anti-globalization.

In 2004, Paul Samuelson, the western economic magnate, put forward **Samuelson's Concern**. He proposed that free trade and globalization could sometimes turn technological progress into benefits for both sides, but the increase in productivity of one country will not only bring benefits for itself, but also hurt another country by reducing the potential trade benefits between the two countries. He pointed out that free trade was very beneficial to China. It has swept away the happiness that the United States has gained in free trade in the past. In the future, other countries would not have new inventions and would repeatedly reduce the absolute per capita income of the United States in free trade and globalization.

---

① http://www. woseller. com/post/43165. html, 26-3-2023.

8.4.2　Sino-US Trade War 中美贸易战

It is under the background of the anti-globalization and de-Sinicization that the Sino-US trade disputes started when Donald Trump came into power in 2018. Sino-US trade frictions mainly occur in two aspects: first, export areas in which China enjoys absolute advantages; Second, high-tech areas in which China has relative advantages.

The United States believes that it has suffered losses in Sino-US trade. On March 2018, Trump exclaimed "China has stolen millions of American jobs" and started a trade war with China. Since then, he has imposed high tariffs on China's goods of about 360 billion dollars for three rounds. As soon as Biden administration came to power in 2022, it defined China as the "most severe competitor" and "most severe long-term challenge". On trade issues, Biden has always claimed that he "will never give up the tariff weapon", and has kept forging alliances in high-tech fields such as information technology, artificial intelligence and quantum computing to "**precisely decouple**" China.

For example, on September 2021, the United States announced that it would open the "232 Investigation" on whether Nd-Fe-B Permanent Magnetic Materials would damage the national security of the United States. In fact, the problem of US trade deficit has a long history and is closely related to its unbalanced **industrial structure**. As the world's largest economy, the United States has a strong service industry and high-tech industry, but many products rely on imports.

8.4.3　The Pandemic 疫情

The COVID-19 pandemic brings great damages to business for many companies and the world has thus entered into a long period of recession. International trade suffered a lot during to the spread of the virus. Life was being endangered and factories and companies suffered great loss because of the pandemic. The long-lasting effects of pandemic is beyond calculation and the world trade conflicts and disputes are increasing.

8.4.4　Carbon Neutrality 碳中和

In order to achieve **carbon neutrality** goals set by the Paris Agreement, most countries are implementing more sever environment-friendly measures in importing and exporting. Many countries are implementing more strict importing policies on the basis of green and low CO_2 emission and set new and strict environment standard, which is unfavorable for traditional goods exporting. For example, in the afternoon of June 22,

$2022^{①}$, the European Commission voted to construct the first regulation on the Carbon Boundary Adjustment Mechanism (CBAM) in the worldwide range. Regulation on **carbon tariffs** is around the corner and the European Parliament has made preparations to negotiate with member states. Once passed by individual countries, the implementation of carbon tariff would increase import and export cost for international trade. The involved industry includes electricity, iron and steel, cement, aluminum, fertilizers, organic chemical, plastic, hydrogen, ammonia, on which China has a great market share.

On the other hand, Chinese government are implementing low-carbon policies domestically which would increase the manufacturing cost of export goods. Among the five major tasks outlined by Chinese government (including creating a green, low-carbon and recyclable economy, improving energy efficiency, increasing the share of non-fossil energy consumption, lowering CO_2 emissions and boosting the carbon sink capacity of ecosystems), enterprise would follow more strict standards in carbon-related trade barriers (like carbon tariff, carbon labelling, carbon emission reduction certificate) by increasing their green energy efficiency and paying more taxes for carbon-emission.

In September 2020, China clearly proposed the goals of "carbon peaking" by 2030 and "carbon neutrality" by 2060. In a narrow sense, dual carbon targets refer to the equilibrium between the emission and absorption of carbon dioxide, while broadly speaking, dual carbon goals refer to the equilibrium between the emission and absorption of all greenhouse gases. The main approach is to reduce carbon dioxide emissions by adjusting energy structure, improving resource utilization efficiency, and increasing carbon dioxide absorption through technologies such as CCUS (carbon capture, utilization, and storage), bioenergy, and afforestation/reforestation.

8.4.5   Regional Economic Organizations 区域性经济组织

Under the background of anti-globalization, regional economic organizations emerged one after another. China-initiated-RCEP came into force in January 2022 and accordingly, the US-dominated international organizations are trying to enclose China and establishing their own economic circle. USMCA (the U. S. -Mexico-Canada Agreement) is one of the most successful one coming into force at the end of 2018.

In addition, CPTPP (the Comprehensive and Progressive Trans-Pacific Partnership),

---

① A Further Step to the EU Carbon Tariff, https://www. cirs-group. com/en/chemicals/a-further-step-to-the-eu-carbon-tariff, 20-9-2022.

a 11-country free-trade deal coming into force on Dec. 30,2018, is a "21st-century trade agreement" with high standards for workers' rights and ecommerce rules. It is run mainly by Japan after the withdraw of the United States in the year of 2017. The13-country **IPEF** (Indo-Pacific Economic Framework) is also "a 21st-century economic arrangement" formed on June, 2022[①]. The members accounts for nearly 40% of global GDP. Most crucially, China is still excluded. The IPEF, like the CPTPP, is an attempt to build a trading structure in Asia that enshrines both America's economic principles and its economic power——welcomed by many in the region as a counter balance to China's heft. The pact runs on four pillars: to promote trade, to make supply chains more resilient, to promote infrastructure investment and clean energy, and to form new rules on taxation and anti-corruption.

8.4.6　Logistics and Overseas Warehouse 物流和海外仓

Cross border logistics is an important support for the development of cross-border ecommerce, and also a key factor to improve the consumer experience. According to the relevant report jointly released by Ipsos[②] and PayPal, nearly 1/4 of global online shoppers believe that the delivery speed is a key factor in their choice of platform. In addition, ecommerce enterprises will choose logistics providers that meet their own needs based on comprehensive consideration of logistics costs, warehousing speed, **distribution efficiency**, **complaints handling capacity**, etc. Building a high-level overseas warehouse is an effective way to improve the quality of logistics services.

8.4.7　Rule Compliance 合规

The capacity to comply to international rules should be improved quickly. Cross-border ecommerce should follow not only domestic laws but also the target-country/area's regulations and practices. Many developed countries like the United States and EU have stipulated many relevant laws and rules to regulate, supervise the conduct of ebusiness. Accordingly, *Chinese Ecommerce Law* has been implemented since 2019. The National Ecommerce Quality Management Standardization Committee has reviewed and approved five national standards, including the guidelines for the exchange of cross-border ecommerce product quality evaluation results, the guidelines for the sharing of product

---

① 经济学人外刊精读：亚洲的新协定, 16-6-2023。

② Ipsos, established in Paris, France in 1975, is a Global leader in market research. It delivers reliable information and true understanding of Society, Markets and People, see www. ipsos. com/.

traceability information, the specifications for online dispute resolution documents, the specifications for the description of export commodity information etc. The introduction of a series of cross-border ecommerce laws and regulations has made clear provisions on commodity security, taxation, logistics, after-sales and other aspects, and strengthened standardized information communication between sellers, logistics enterprises and customs in customs clearance, tax refund, foreign exchange settlement and other aspects. The application of blockchain technology will also help the traceability of product sources and accountability, so that enterprises have rules to follow, while strengthening the protection of consumers' rights and interests, and promoting the standardized development of cross-border ecommerce industry.

For example, in an economic and trade agreement signed between China and the United States in 2020, corresponding provisions have been made on the infringement of intellectual property rights involved in ecommerce. The agreement requires both parties to take effective actions (including effective notification and off shelf system) against major ecommerce platforms with IPR (intellectual property rights) infringement issues, and also makes detailed provisions on the production, export, destruction of **pirated (counterfeit) products**. In the future, driven by both domestic and international forces, the standardization process of China's cross-border ecommerce market will accelerate significantly.

All in all, we are still in the primary stage of cross-border ecommerce. Innovation, creation, further accumulation in investment and experiment would help the development of cross-border ecommerce. In the ecosystem of cross-border ecommerce, political, economic, social, technological, environmental and legal factors play distinctive roles in the process of development.

📖 Words and Phrases 词汇和短语

supervision 监管
the customs declaration automation system 海关申报自动化系统
four-digit structure 4 位数结构
statistics parameter 统计参数
personal postal articles 个人行邮物品
provisions 规定条款

the General Administration of Customs (GAC) 税务总局

announcement 公告

customs duties 关税

import value-added tax 进口附加税

consumption tax 消费税

three orders 三单

preferential tariff 优惠税

on-the-site management 现场管理

quarantine 检疫

inspection 检验

return management 退货管理

customs special supervision areas 海关特殊监管区

suspension and extension measures 暂停和延期措施

foreign currency revenue 外汇收入

bank account closure 银行账号关闭

DTC platforms 独立站平台

localization 本地化

logistics solutions 物流方案

VR (virtual reality) 虚拟现实

one-stop service 一站式服务

incremental markets 增量市场

anti-globalization 反全球化

Brexit referendum 脱欧公投

populist 民粹主义者

neoliberalism-based globalization 新自由主义全球化

income distribution effects 收入分配效应

populism 民粹主义

Samuelson's Concern 萨缪尔森陷阱

precisely decouple 精准脱钩

industrial structure 产业结构

carbon neutrality 碳中和

carbon tariff 碳税

IPEF 印太经济框架

distribution efficiency 配送效率

complaints handling capacity 问题处理能力

pirated (counterfeit) products 盗版（假冒）产品

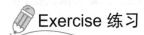 **Exercise 练习**

I. Reflections and Critical Thinking Questions

1. Why did CBEC supervision start from B2C importing in China?

2. What's the meaning of 9610 and 1210?

3. What are the achievements of China's CBEC?

4. Some people hold the following opinion, see Figure 8-2: Ecommerce growth around the world in 2023 has decelerated precipitously (突然地) since the pandemic-driven boom of 2020. In 2022, digital shopping lost ground to brick-and-mortar in

> ## Global Retail Ecommerce Forecast 2023
> **Welcome to the Slower-Growth New Normal**
> Report by Ethan Cramer-Flood | Feb 21, 2023
>
> Report   Deck   Charts   One-Pager   NEW
>
> ### Executive Summary
> Ecommerce growth around the world has decelerated precipitously since the pandemic-driven boom of 2020. Last year, digital shopping lost ground to brick-and-mortar in several major markets. This year will be slightly better for digital retailers, but the boom times of the 2010s are not coming back.
>
> **Key Question:** Following years of volatility, how will ecommerce fare globally and country by country over the next few years?

Figure 8-2   Global retail ecommerce forest 2023

several major markets. The year of 2023 will be slightly better for digital retailers, but the boom times of the 2010s are not coming back. It seems that there would be a slower-growth new normal in the years of 2023 and since. Following the years of volatility (变化、波折), how will ecommerce fare globally over the next few years? Please illustrate your reasons.

II. True and False

1. Supervision codes 9710 and 9810 share the same category in Chinese customs declaration automation system. (   )

2. General trade is still widely used in cross-border ecommerce importing and exporting. (   )

3. China's cross-border ecommerce supervision code starts from B2C importing business. (   )

4. Supervision code 1239 is designed to supervise market procurement mode in 2014. (   )

5. China has the largest B2C cross-border ecommerce market. (　　)

6. Domestic rules and regulations prioritize over international rules and regulations in cross-border ecommerce. (　　)

7. Political and economic factors are important factors that should be considered in cross-border ecommerce. (　　)

8. Regional economic organizations are placing a more important role in the present global economy. (　　)

9. Wealthy countries benefit the most from international trade according to Samuelson's Concern. (　　)

10. The construction of overseas warehouse is mainly for enhancing customer experience and improve fulfillment efficiency. (　　)

III. Nouns Explanation

1. Supervision code: 0110, 9610, 1210, 9710, 9810, 1239, 1039

2. RCEP, CPTPP, USMCA, IPEF

3. Samuelson's Concern

IV. Reading and Critical Thinking

A Further Step to the EU Carbon Tariff [①]

July 19, 2022 from *CIRS*

On the afternoon of June 22, the European Commission voted to construct the first regulation on the Carbon Boundary Adjustment Mechanism (CBAM, 碳边境调节机制) in the worldwide range. This event marks that the European Commission (欧盟委员会) (on July 15,2021), the Council of the European Union (欧盟理事会) (on March 15,2022), and the European Parliament (欧盟议会) (on June 22,2022) have released their own versions of the CBAM regulations.

The construction of official regulation on carbon tariffs is around the corner and the European Parliament has made preparations to negotiate with member states. After the agreement is reached through the negotiation of the European Commission, the Council of the European Union and the European Parliament, the legislation of carbon tariffs will be completed.

1. Updates to the EU Carbon Tariff

As to the collection of carbon tariffs, the European Parliament has made subtle

---

① https://www. cirs-group. com/en/chemicals/a-further-step-to-the-eu-carbon-tariff, 14-03-2023.

adjustments to the collection industry, time, scope, and EU-ETS[①] free allowances(补贴). Here are the main differences of three versions of the CBAM regulations:

Main contents comparisons

Contents	CBAM (EC)	CBAM (ENVI)	CBAM (EP)
Involved Industry	Electricity, iron and steel, cement, aluminum, fertilizers	Electricity, iron and steel, cement, aluminum, fertilizers, oil refinery, hydrogen production, organic chemical, polymer	Electricity, iron and steel, cement, aluminum, fertilizers, organic chemical, plastic, hydrogen, ammonia
Time	2026	2025	2027
Scope	Direct emission	Direct and indirect emission	Direct and indirect emission
Free allowances for EU-ETS	Phasing out by 2035	Phasing out by 2030	Phasing out by 2032

It is evident that the European Parliament has modified the radical proposal by the Environment, Public Health and Food Safety (ENVI) in terms of the transitional period, which postpones its implementation time, retards the progress of phasing out free allowances granted to EU industries under the EU-ETS and releases an official proposal on phasing out the free allowances. According to the official proposal, the free allowances will be gradually reduced in the following steps: 100% in 2023-2026; 93% in 2027; 84% in 2028; 69% in 2029; 50% in 2030; 25% in 2031; and phasing out in 2032. The CBAM will be adopted to provide services to all sectors in EU-ETS at that time.

2. Status of China-EU Trade

According to the report published by the Eurostat on the 23rd EU-China summit hold on April 1, 2022, China remains the largest partner for EU imports of goods. In 2021, the volume of EU imports from China reached € 472 billion with a year-to-year growth of 37%, accounting for about 22% of the total imports of the EU. The exports are concentrated in mechanical and electrical products (机电产品) (56% of the EU imports in this category), other manufactured goods (35%) and chemicals (7%).

Between 2011 and 2021, EU imports and exports to China are on an upward trend and the trade deficit with China also keeps increasing.

3. The Impact of CBAM on China Export to the EU

According to the statistics released by the Central Administration of Customs of the

①　European Union Emissions Trading System, 欧盟排放贸易体系 , 欧盟碳交易机制。

PRC, the export volume of China to the EU reached 3,348. 3 billion CNY, accounting for 15.41% of the total export in 2021. Among all international trade commodities arranged in 99 chapters and 22 categories, commodities that have a large proportion rank in subsequent: mechanical and electrical products (accounting for 43.00%); raw materials and products of textile (9.06%); miscellaneous (混杂的) products (7.87%); base metal (steel and aluminum) and their products (7.86%); products in the chemical industry and relevant industries (6.35%); vehicles, aircraft, ships and transportation equipment (5.17%); plastics, rubbers and their products (4.82%). Although the top three are not included in the drafted range of carbon tariffs, products under key supervision of CBAM are included such as steel, aluminum, organic chemicals, fertilizers, ceramics, glass, paper, plastics, etc.

The Exclusive Report on CBAM and Its Impact on Energy-intensive Commodities in China made by the CITIC Futures (中信期货) suggested that CBAM has a relatively limited influence on China Export to the EU. The volume of four major energy-intensive industries, including iron and steel, aluminum, fertilizer, and cement industries, only accounts for 1.33% of the total volume of China's exports to the EU in 2020. However, the export volumes of these four industries to the EU accounted for 11.25%, 5.55%, 1.02%, and 0.07% respectively of the export volume of this industry. A conclusion can be made from these figures that iron and steel, and aluminum industries have been greatly affected.

The CITIC Futures also unveiled that the carbon tariffs (碳税) of these four industries respectively account for 17%, 20%, 17%, 31% of their export volumes with a carbon price of € 80/ton, which could cause fierce competitiveness to carbon-intensive industries (碳密集型企业).

Critical Thinking and Questions:

1. What are the difference among the 3 bodies (EC, ENVI, EP) according to the table?

2. What are the main categories of China-EU foreign trade in the paper?

3. In the last 2 paragraphs, the report suggested that CBAM has a relatively limited influence on China's export to EU. Do you agree with the opinion? Why or why not?

4. How could China cope with the issue facing carbon tariffs and other strict policies in EU?

More Resources:

1. THE FUTURE OF ECOMMERCE: HOW ECOMMERCE WILL CHANGE IN 2023 by Adeel Qayum, 14 Dec, 2022.[1]

2. 2023 年跨境电商行业面临的机遇和挑战有哪些?[2]

3. Joe Bidden: confrontation, competition, international rules, reestablish alliance.[3]

Keys-8

---

[1] https://www. oberlo. com/blog/future-of-ecommerce, 26-3-2023.

[2] https://www. 163. com/dy/article/HU6SMV120553X6V0. html, 26-3-2023.

[3] https://haokan. baidu. com/v?vid=12393914532094721201&pd=bjh&fr=bjhauthor&type=video, 28-3-2023.

References

[1] Asha K.S. Nair & Som Sekhar Bhattacharyya, Is sustainability a motive to buy? An exploratory study in the context of mobile applications channel among young Indian consumers [J]. *Foresight*, 2019, 21 (2): 177-199.

[2] Charles W. L. Hill, International Business: competing in the global market place [M]. US: McGraw-Hill, 2009.

[3] Kenneth C. Laudon & Carol Guercio Traver. E-commerce 2021–2022: business. technology. Society (17th edition) [M]. UK: Pearson Education Limited, 2022.

[4] Manners-Bell J & Lyon K. The logistics and supply chain innovation handbook: disruptive technologies and new business models [M]. UK: Kogan Page Limited, 2019.

[5] Maria Giuffrida, Riccardo Mangiaracina, Alessandro Perego & Angela Tumino, Cross-border B2C e-commerce to Greater China and the role of logistics: a literature review [J]. International Journal of Physical Distribution & Logistics Management, 2017, 47(9): 772-795.

[6] 阿里巴巴(中国)网络技术有限公司, 从0开始跨境电商实训教程[M]. 北京: 电子工业出版社, 2016.

[7] 2021年度中国跨境电商市场数据报告[R].

[8] 崔政涛. 中东地区境外经贸合作区的发展现状、机遇与挑战[J]. 对外经贸实务, 2021 (9): 40-45.

[9] 杜志平. 跨境物流联盟运作机制与决策优化[M]. 北京: 首都经济贸易大学出版社, 2020.

[10] eMarketer, 2022, 2022年全球电商市场预测报告[R].

[11] 李鹏博. 揭秘跨境电商[M]. 北京: 电子工业出版社, 2015.

[12] 马丁·克里斯托弗(著). 何明珂等(译). 物流与供应链管理[M]. 北京: 电子工业出版社, 2019.

[13] 36氪研究院. 2021年中国电商SaaS行业研究报告[R]. 2021-7-26.

[14] 速卖通大学. 跨境电商物流——阿里巴巴速卖通宝典[M]. 北京: 电子工业出版社, 2016.

[15] 苏杭.跨境电商物流管理[M]. 北京: 对外经济贸易大学出版社, 2017.

[16] 唐亮、许再宏、郑晨光. 出口跨境电商供应链管理[M]. 北京: 中国财政经济出版社, 2018.

[17] 王淑翠. 跨境电商出口零售实务[M]. 北京: 人民邮电出版社, 2020.

[18] 肖旭. 跨境电商实务[M]. 北京: 中国人民大学出版社, 2015.

[19] 张夏恒. 跨境电商类型与运作模式[J]. 中国流通经济, 2017, 31(1): 76-83.

[20] 中国跨境电商行业"十四五"发展趋势与投资机会研究报告[R].

[21] 朱秋城. 跨境电商3.0时代[M]. 北京: 中国海关出版社, 2016.

[22] 纵雨果. 亚马逊跨境电商运营从入门到精通[M]. 北京: 中国工信出版集团、电子工业出版社, 2018.

公众号：

亿邦动力；36氪出海；罗杰把酒看航运；粤知东西；跨通社；跨境必读；圣地亚哥young；跨境电商长期主义；跨境电商。

网站：

雨果跨境；环球网；哔哩哔哩；知乎；搜狐网等。

教师服务

感谢您选用清华大学出版社的教材！为了更好地服务教学，我们为授课教师提供本书的教学辅助资源，以及本学科重点教材信息。请您扫码获取。

>> **教辅获取**

本书教辅资源，授课教师扫码获取

>> **样书赠送**

国际经济与贸易类重点教材，教师扫码获取样书

 清华大学出版社

E-mail: tupfuwu@163.com
电话：010-83470332 / 83470142
地址：北京市海淀区双清路学研大厦 B 座 509

网址：https://www.tup.com.cn/
传真：8610-83470107
邮编：100084